Agriculture, Trade, and the WTO

Creating a Trading Environment for Development

DIRECTIONS IN DEVELOPMENT

Agriculture, Trade, and the WTO

Creating a Trading Environment for Development

Merlinda D. Ingco, Editor

THE WORLD BANK
Washington, D.C.

Table of Contents

Foreword ix
Kevin Cleaver

Abstract xii

Acknowledgments xiii

Contributors xiv

Glossary of Abbreviations and Acronyms xvi

1. Introduction and Overview 1
   Merlinda D. Ingco

2. The New Trade Debate and Options for Developing Countries . . . 12
   Ian Johnson

Part I. Lessons from the Implementation of the Uruguay Round

3. The Uruguay Round Agreement on Agriculture in Practice:
   How Open Are OECD Markets? 21
   Dimitris Diakosavvas

4. Lessons from Implementation of the Uruguay Round Agreement
   on Agriculture: A Cairns Group Perspective 60
   Simon Tucker

5. Agriculture and Other Items on the World Trade Organization
   Agenda 65
   Hugh Corbet

Part II. Evaluating the Benefits of Liberalization to Date for Developing Countries

6. The Role of the World Trade Organization Accession in Economic Reform: A Three-Dimensional View 85
   Craig VanGrasstek

7. Small Developing Economies in the World Trade Organization . . 108
   Richard L. Bernal

8. Evaluating Benefits of Liberalization to Date for Developing Countries 123
   Usha Jeetah

9. Leveraging Trade and Global Market Integration for Poverty Reduction 129
   Krisda Piampongsant

Part III. The World Trade Organization, the New Trade Round, Development, and Poverty Reduction

10. Options for Agricultural Policy Reform in the World Trade Organization Negotiations. 135
    Mary E. Burfisher

11. Policies for Price Risk under Trade Liberalization. 145
    Bruce L. Gardner

Part IV. New Trade Issues and Challenges: The Way Forward

12. Time for Coherence among the World Trade Organization Escape Clauses 155
    Gary Horlick

13. Multifunctionality and Optimal Environmental Policies for Agriculture in an Open Economy 165
    Jeffrey M. Peterson, Richard N. Boisvert, and Harry de Gorter

14. Genetically Modified Foods, Trade, and Developing Countries . . 193
    Chantal Pohl Nielsen, Karen Thierfelder, and Sherman Robinson

15. Trade Liberalization, the World Trade Organization, and Food Security 225
    Eugenio Díaz-Bonilla and Marcelle Thomas

Index 247

Figures

3.1   World Export Performance, 1989–99 26
3.2   Tariff Quota Fill Rates in OECD Countries
      (Simple Average), 1995–99 39
3.3   Composition of Domestic Support, 1995–98 44
3.4   Notified Subsidized Exports in OECD Countries, 1995–98 46
6.1   The Three Dimensions of the GATT/WTO System 88
6.2   The Key Dimension of Height in Early GATT History 89
6.3   The Key Dimension of Depth in Recent GATT/WTO History . . 93
6.4   The Three Dimensions in Current WTO Relations:
      Both Depth and Width Are Expanding 97
6.5   Relative Size of Countries by WTO Status:
      Countries' Shares of Global Exports, 1999 97
10.1 Many Countries Would Share Consumer Purchasing
      Power Gains from Elimination of Agricultural Tariffs
      and Subsidies. 136
11.1 Corn and Soybean Prices Received by Farmers,
      Monthly, September 1973 to May 2001 147
14.1 Endogenous Choice between GM and Non-GM Foods 202
14.2 Consumer Preferences Modeled as Different
      Degrees of Price Sensitivity 204
14.3 Consumer Preferences Modeled as a Structural Change 205
14.4 Base Case Experiment: Price Wedges between Non-GM
      and GM Products in Developing Countries 207
14.5 Price Sensitivity Case: Price Wedges between Non-GM
      and GM Products in Developing Countries 209
14.6 Structural Change Case: Price Wedges between Non-GM
      and GM Products in Developing Countries 211
14.7 Production Effects in the United States 215
14.8 Production Effects in Low-Income Asia. 216
14.9 Production Effects in South America 217
14.10 Production Effects in Sub-Saharan Africa 218
14.11 Changes in Total Absorption 219
15.1 Conceptual Framework for Food Security 226
15.2 Consumption Measured by Calories per Capita per Day 228
15.3 Consumption Measured by Protein per Capita per Day 228
15.4 Ratio of Food Imports to Total Exports 229
15.5 Agriculture Production, 1961–98 231

Tables

3.1   Relative Comparisons of Trade Performance Indicators
      in OECD Countries. 27
3.2   Relative Comparisons of Support Indicators
      in OECD Countries. 30
3.3   Import Penetration Model 34
3.4   Export Performance Model. 35

3.5   Agricultural Tariffs 40
3.6   Ranges of Notified Current Total AMS Levels in
      OECD Countries, 1995–99 42
A.1   OECD: Producer Subsidy Equivalent by Commodity 49
A.2   Composition of Producer Subsidy Equivalent 52
A.3   Who Has Tariff-Rate Quotas? 54
A.4   Tariff-Rate Quotas by OECD Member 55
A.5   Evolution of Aggregate Measurement of Support and
      Producer Subsidy Equivalent 56
A.6   Who Can Subsidize Exports? 57
10.1 Effects of Alternative Tariff Reduction Formulas
      on Average and Dispersion of Tariffs 140
10.2 Reduction Commitments if Uruguay Round Base
      Is Lowered an Additional 20 Percent 141
10.3 Commodity-Specific AMS: Reduction Needed to Keep
      Commodity-Specific AMS Less than 30 Percent 142
11.1 Some Evidence for Corn and Soybeans 148
13.1 Parameter Values 181
13.2 Base Data and Simulation Results 182
14.1 Trade Dependence: Agricultural and Food Products, 1995 ... 197
14.2 Composition of World Trade, 1995 198
14.3 Pattern of Exports from Low-Income Asia, 1995 200
14.4 Pattern of Exports from South America, 1995 200
14.5 Pattern of Exports from Sub-Saharan Africa, 1995 201
14.6 Selected Trade Results of Base Experiment,
      Percentage Changes 208
14.7 Selected Trade Results of Price Sensitivity Experiment,
      Percentage Changes 213
14.8 Selected Trade Results of Structural Shift Experiment,
      Percentage Changes 214
15.1 Coefficient of Price Variability in Agriculture:
      Constant Value 230
15.2 Top 20 Food Products Exporters, Importers, and
      Net Exporters Average in Value, 1995–99 233
15.3 Classification of Countries in 12 Clusters: Mean
      Values of the Food Security Variables 235
15.4 Country Profile Summary 236

Foreword

The successful integration into the world economy of countries that are home to 3 billion people has meant that developing countries have increased their share in global trade, from less than a quarter of all trade in 1970 to more than a third now. Most of those gains have come from increased exports of manufactured products. Integration in agriculture is lagging behind. Whereas prior to 1970 agriculture was the more important export for developing countries, there have been numerous impediments to the rapid growth of agricultural exports. Manufacturing exports from developing countries, however, have risen from around US$20 billion in 1970 to more than US$1.3 trillion now. It is really only the middle-income countries among the developing countries that have participated in this massive expansion of manufactured trade. Their share of world trade has increased by around 6 percent in the 1990s, whereas the share of low-income countries stagnated and that of the least-developed countries actually declined. One reason for this failure is that poor countries have a comparative advantage in agriculture and in labor-intensive products. These are precisely the categories of products that face the highest levels of protection. In fact, the goods produced by the poor (who are defined as earning less than $2 a day) face tariffs that are twice as high as the tariffs on goods produced by those who are not poor.

Subsidies and other support to agriculture in the high-income countries are particularly pernicious and are now running at roughly US$1 billion a day, more than six times all development assistance. In contrast to the rising farm subsidies, official development assistance has been declining since the late 1980s and now accounts for barely 0.2 percent of the rich countries' gross domestic product (GDP).

Reshaping the world's trade system and reducing barriers to trade could accelerate medium-term growth and reduce global poverty. Expanding trade could well increase annual GDP growth by an additional 0.5 percent over the long run, and by 2015 lift an additional 300 million people out of poverty. Developing countries stand to gain an estimated US$1.5 trillion of additional income in the 10 years after liberalization has begun. Meanwhile, the rich countries could see their incomes rise by some US$1.3 trillion.

To make this happen, industrial countries have to be willing to reduce their protection of agriculture. For most developing countries, including those that are net food importers, agriculture is the key sector for poverty reduction. The poor are predominantly rural. More than 70 percent of the populations of developing countries live in rural areas, and 97 percent of their rural populations are engaged in agriculture. For many developing countries, incomes generated from agricultural exports are the largest source of employment, revenue, and foreign exchange.

Much of any extra income that is generated by increased sales or prices remains within the local economy, boosting incomes of other, usually poor, households. Increased opportunities for agriculture hence tend to benefit the whole of the rural economy, and not just farmers. In Asia, for instance, the increases in agricultural productivity brought about by the green revolution in the 1970s were effective in reducing poverty, and it was found that an extra dollar of agricultural income was typically associated with an additional 80 cents of nonagricultural income for local enterprises. For Africa it was thought, until recently, that such linkages were of less importance, but extensive evidence suggests that household spending out of the extra income generated by increased exports could stimulate further rural incomes increases on a scale that even surpasses the experiences in Asia.

In spite of the differences among them, developing countries as a group have an enormous stake in the global trade talks taking place at present. Several aspects of these talks are of interest to developing countries:

- Potential gains exist from the strengthening of a "rules-based" global trading system. Developing countries are the weaker players in the present system, and thus would benefit the most when the dominant trading countries play by a common and more liberal set of rules.
- Multilateral agreements and trade negotiations should help developing countries to undertake and lock in their own trade and domestic policy reforms needed to advance development objectives. In many cases, their own tariffs on imports are very high. Ideally, developing countries should implement trade and other policy reforms unilaterally because it is to their benefit. However, in practice, most countries do not operate so efficiently, and historically, various sectors collide when protectionism and other trade reforms, both foreign and domestic, are on the table. Simply put, reciprocal trade agreements in the World Trade Organization (WTO) and among regional partners are an important part of the political economy of policy reform in developing countries.

- Agricultural trade liberalization in the countries of the Organisation for Economic Co-operation and Development should be advanced by the new round of trade negotiations, particularly further cuts in export and domestic subsidies and reductions in high tariffs, that would be difficult to achieve outside the context of global trade talks.
- Developing countries would benefit from reforms in antidumping rules, which fail to constrain the use of these measures in an increasing number of countries. Small economies would especially benefit from the expansion of beneficial provisions for developing country exporters.

Given the importance of the new WTO trade round for developing countries, the World Bank organized a conference on "Leveraging Trade, Global Market Integration, and the New WTO Negotiations for Development," which was held in Washington, D.C., July 23–24, 2001. The conference was designed to examine key issues, prospects, and strategies faced by developing countries when considering more open agricultural trade and policy reforms, and to identify how developing countries can best advance their interests in the new WTO negotiations. The new trade round in the new century promises to be at least as dramatic as the past trade rounds and for the world trading system, with which their fortunes are now so closely linked.

This volume contains several of the region-specific studies presented at that conference. The studies have been revised and updated to reflect comments and peer reviews received following the meetings. It is hoped that policymakers, analysts, and other stakeholders from both industrial and developing countries will benefit from the valuable perspectives, insights, and interests of the different regions and countries presented in these studies.

Kevin Cleaver
Director
Rural Development Department
The World Bank

Abstract

World trade and production in agriculture is highly distorted by a variety of policy interventions applied in industrial and developing countries. Autonomous reforms in these countries and reforms through the new multilateral trade negotiations under the auspices of the World Trade Organization (WTO) will further help to correct these distortions by bringing the sector more fully under the disciplines of the multilateral trading system. However, this process needs to be carried forward in the new WTO round of multilateral negotiations on agriculture, currently in progress and scheduled to be completed by January 1, 2005. Issues to be addressed will include market access, domestic supports, and export subsidies as well as state trading, sanitary and phytosanitary rules, and environmental considerations.

This volume contains studies designed to provide answers to the following questions: First, what were the lessons to be learned from the Uruguay Round of negotiations and implementation of the rules, and how can these lessons be applied to the next round? Second, what benefits were there, if any, to date for developing countries in liberalizing their trade? Third, what is the relationship between trade liberalization and rural poverty? Fourth, what are the new trade issues, and what is the best means to move forward? The book concludes with a discussion of the necessary role of the international development community in fostering a trading system that will result in development.

Acknowledgments

This book of selected papers is based on the conference titled "Leveraging Trade, Global Market Integration, and the New WTO Negotiations for Development," which was held July 23–24, 2001, at the World Bank, Washington, D.C. It would not have been possible without the work and contributions of a large number of friends and colleagues. We would like to thank the speakers and authors, who gave their time and energy to prepare their papers: Richard Bernal, Richard N. Boisvert, Mary Burfisher, Hugh Corbet, Harry de Gorter, Alan Deardorf (University of Michigan), Dimitris Diakosavvas, Eugenio Díaz-Bonilla, Bruce Gardner, Kayode Garrick (Embassy of Nigeria, Washington, D.C.), Ashok Gulati (International Food Policy Research Institute), Alberto Herrou-Aragon (Universidad Siglo 21), Gary Horlick, Merlinda Ingco, Usha Jeetah, Ian Johnson, Rolf Moehler (European Commission), Chantal Pohl Nielsen, Jeffrey M. Peterson, Krisda Piampongsant, Charles Riemenschneider (Food and Agriculture Organization of the United Nations), Sherman Robinson, Christopher Schepis (International Fund for Agricultural Development), Karen Thierfelder, Marcelle Thomas, Simon Tucker, Craig VanGrasstek, and Kevin Walker (American Institute for Co-operation in Agriculture).

Next, we would like to thank the moderators: Robert L. Thompson, John Nash, and Merlinda Ingco of the World Bank's Rural Development Sector; the discussants: Claude Barfield (American Enterprise Institute), Kevin Cleaver (World Bank), Luis De Azcarate (World Bank), Carlos Jaramillo (Embassy of Colombia, Washington, D.C.), Odin Knudsen (World Bank), Patricia Sheikh (U. S. Department of Agriculture [USDA]), David Skully (USDA), Marcelle Thomas, and Carol Wilson (U.S. Agency for International Development); and the more than 100 participants whose lively engagement prompted challenging discussions. Finally, we would like to thank Jason Yauney, Tonia Kandeiro, Cicely Spooner, and Moni Toppin of the World Bank's Rural Development Sector, who helped to organize the conference.

Contributors

Richard L. Bernal
Embassy of Jamaica, Washington, D.C.

Richard N. Boisvert
Cornell University

Mary E. Burfisher
U.S. Department of Agriculture

Hugh Corbet
Cordell Hull Institute

Harry de Gorter
Cornell University

Dimitris Diakosavvas
Organisation for Economic Co-operation and Development

Eugenio Díaz-Bonilla
International Food Policy Research Institute

Bruce L. Gardner
University of Maryland

Gary Horlick
O'Melveny & Myers LLP

Merlinda D. Ingco
World Bank

Usha Jeetah
Embassy of Mauritius, Washington, D.C.

Ian Johnson
World Bank

Chantal Pohl Nielsen
Danish Research Institute of Agricultural and Fisheries Economics

Jeffrey M. Peterson
Kansas State University

Krisda Piampongsant
Embassy of Thailand, Washington, D.C.

Sherman Robinson
International Food Policy Research Institute

Karen Thierfelder
U.S. Naval Academy

Marcelle Thomas
International Food Policy Research Institute

Simon Tucker
Embassy of New Zealand, Washington, D.C.

Craig VanGrasstek
Harvard University

Glossary of Abbreviations and Acronyms

ADA	Antidumping Agreement
AFTA	ASEAN Free Trade Area
AGOA	African Growth and Opportunity Act
AMS	Aggregate measurement of support
AoA	Agreement on Agriculture (UR)
AOSIS	Alliance of Small Island States
ASCM	Agreement on Subsidies and Countervailing Measures
ASEAN	Association of Southeast Asian Nations
ATC	Agreement on Textiles and Clothing
Cairns Group	Eighteen agricultural exporting countries
CAP	Common agricultural policy
CARICOM	Caribbean Common Market
CEPT	Common effective preferential tariff
CES	Constant elasticity of substitution
CGE	Computable general equilibrium
CGIAR	Consultative Group on International Agricultural Research
CNPCs	Consumer nominal protection coefficients
CRS	Constant returns to scale
EIT	Economies in transition
FAIR	Federal Agriculture Improvement and Reform Act of 1996
FAO	Food and Agriculture Organization
FAOSTAT	FAO Statistical Database
FTAA	Free Trade Area of the Americas
GATS	General Agreement on Trade in Services
GATT	General Agreement on Tariffs and Trade
GDP	Gross domestic product
GM	Genetically modified
GMOs	Genetically modified organisms
GSP	Generalized System of Preferences

GTAP	Global Trade Analysis Project
IAI	Initiative for ASEAN Integration
ILO	International Labour Organisation
IMF	International Monetary Fund
IPR	Import penetration ratio
MFN	Most-favored nation
MNCs	Multinational corporations
NAC	Nominal assistance coefficient
NGOs	Nongovernmental organizations
NPC	Nominal protection coefficient
NTC	Nontrade concerns
NAFTA	North American Free Trade Agreement
OECD	Organisation for Economic Co-operation and Development
%CSE	Percentage consumer support estimate
%PSE	Percentage producer support estimate
PNPCs	Producer nominal protection coefficients
PSEs	Producer subsidy equivalents
S&D	Special and Differential (Treatment)
SMP	Skimmed milk powder
TRI	Trade Restrictiveness Index
TRIPs	Trade-Related Aspects of Intellectual Property
TRQs	Tariff-rate quotas
UNCTAD	United Nations Conference on Trade and Development
UR	Uruguay Round
USDA-ERS	U.S. Department of Agriculture Economic Research Service
VERs	"Voluntary" export restraints
WMP	Whole milk powder
WMW	Wilcox-Mann-Whitney
WTO	World Trade Organization
XP	Export performance

1

Introduction and Overview

Merlinda D. Ingco

In the seven previous multilateral trade negotiations under the General Agreement on Tariffs and Trade (GATT) before the landmark Uruguay Round (UR) of 1986–94, the agricultural sector did not have the rules-based discipline that trade in industrial products had. Because of this lack of discipline, there were significant distortions in world agricultural markets. The UR Agreement on Agriculture (AoA) marked a start in bringing more rules-based GATT discipline to agricultural trade and trade-related domestic policies. Even though the AoA was path breaking, much remains to be done before international agricultural trade is as fully disciplined or as liberalized as trade in manufactures. Further improvements in the rules and in their actual implementation are needed if the objectives of real liberalization are to be achieved. After seven years of implementation of the AoA (1995–2001), import protection for major export products from developing countries remains prohibitively high in the industrial countries and in many developing countries. Applied protection in some products has even increased when compared with applied rates before the agreement.

The current agricultural trade negotiations in the World Trade Organization (WTO) are taking place at a time when protection and support for agriculture are the highest ever estimated. World agricultural markets continue to be distorted by government action in Europe, North America, and several developing countries. In 2001, protection and subsidies for agriculture in the Organisation for Economic Co-operation and Development (OECD) countries amounted to US$311 billion, compared to US$302 billion in 1986–88. The losers from these arrangements are widespread. Consumers in countries that provide market-distorting support are denied the benefits from competitively produced food and agricultural products while taxpayers are forced to subsidize high cost and often environmentally damaging production. Such market-insulating policies depress and destabilize world market prices, disadvantaging producers in economies that either cannot afford, or are unwilling to provide, protection. Efficient farmers are thwarted in their efforts in realizing their economic potential because their access to foreign markets is restricted by extensive import barriers that are far higher, on average, for agricultural products than for manufactures.

Developing countries have much to gain from further progress in trade and domestic policy reform and in a further opening of global markets for their exports. Advancing this process during the current WTO negotiations will be important both to realize the gains made possible by previous efforts and to make future progress easier. The international development community has an interest in aiding the process with the aim of keeping the negotiations responsive to the needs of developing countries.

Why is it important to continue the process of trade and agricultural policy reform, and why should developing countries participate? First, for many countries agriculture is still a significant sector of the economy. Developing countries provide more than 60 percent of the world's value-added in agriculture. In most low- and middle-income developing countries in Sub-Saharan Africa, East Asia, the Pacific, and South Asia, a large proportion (64–70 percent) of the labor force remains dependent on agriculture. As trade patterns diversify, developing countries will make even more use of agricultural markets, both as exporters and importers. Thus, the future world trading system for agriculture will be a lifeline to development for many of the poorer parts of the world. At present, however, world agricultural markets remain significantly distorted by a range of domestic policies and border protection that impede the export performance of developing countries and reduce the world market price of certain commodities.

Developing countries have much to gain from a multilateral trading system based on strong rules, both to protect them against pressures from more powerful countries and to help them improve their own trade and domestic policies. Developing countries in recent trade negotiations have gained more secure access to developed markets (through reductions in the scope of restrictions on imports into these markets) in exchange for providing better access to their own expanding markets (through lower tariffs on imports from the industrial countries). Trade liberalization will facilitate food security for many developing countries by providing access to world market supplies as well as agricultural raw materials that will encourage light manufacturing in rural areas. Many developing countries have a stake in building an efficient food system and maintaining market stability. For all these reasons, developing countries will gain by participating fully in WTO agricultural discussions aimed at progressive trade liberalization.

Second, the multilateral trading system can provide a framework to improve developing countries' trade and domestic policy regimes in agriculture and in the rural sector. Continuing reform of the global trading system, by making it easier to adopt agricultural policies that will reduce or eliminate trade distortions and to allocate scarce resources in these countries more efficiently, can provide significant gains both in terms of consumer welfare and incomes. In fact, previous World Bank research indicates that the gains to developing countries from the UR were much larger, relative to their GDP, than the gains made by industrial countries. Plus, two-thirds of the estimated welfare gains to developing countries resulted from their own trade policy liberalization.

Third, supply response to trade and agricultural policy reform depends upon the credibility of reforms. Establishing the credibility of policy measures is at least as important as choosing the efficient policy solution. Experience in many countries indicates that the private sector does not invest if the sustainability of reforms is in doubt. Unfortunately, reform programs have frequently been reversed or halted. Moreover, government policy has frequently been unpredictable. Establishing the credibility of policy measures can be achieved through a framework of multilateral rules that are equipped with built-in instruments that prevent policy reversals and backsliding and through which member governments are encouraged to lock in unilateral trade reforms.

Perspectives in the Agricultural Trade Negotiations

The present agricultural negotiations in the WTO were formally started in March 2000, in accordance with the provisions of Article 20 of the AoA. This article provides that negotiations should start one year before the end of the implementation period of the UR agreement. These negotiations will seek to continue the reform process of long-term substantial progressive reduction in agricultural support and protection. The work was carried forward in the WTO's standing Committee on Agriculture, meeting in special session. During the first phase of the negotiations, which lasted until March 2001, more than 40 initial proposals were put forward by 121 member countries and were then reviewed. In a second phase, which lasted until February 2002, these and a smaller number of further proposals were examined in greater depth to assess their implications and support. However, the context of the agricultural negotiations was significantly altered by the outcome of the fourth Ministerial Conference of the WTO, held in Doha, Qatar, in November 2001, that put in place a wider framework for multilateral trade negotiations. The Ministerial Conference agreements that were adopted by all WTO member governments extended further trade liberalization for industrial products and services as well as a wide range of other trade-related issues. The Doha Declaration defines the round as a single undertaking and sets a series of deadlines and a concluding date of "not later than 1 January 2005." The declaration also emphasizes that the negotiations as a whole should stress development. For agriculture specifically, the declaration reconfirms the commitment of members to the reform program, and also puts a bit more bite into Article 20 of the AoA by committing members (though "without prejudging the outcome of the negotiations") to comprehensive negotiations aimed at "substantial improvements in market access; reductions of, with a view to phasing out, all forms of export subsidies; and substantial reductions in trade-distorting domestic support."

The prospects for a successful outcome of the new agriculture negotiations are difficult to predict. The change in their context, as a result of the Doha decisions, will almost certainly be helpful for several reasons: countries that are asked to make painful concessions may obtain compensatory gains in areas outside agriculture, goals are now stated somewhat more precisely than in the very general terms of Article 20, the introduction of target dates should keep the negotiations moving along, and the increased political attention given to a broader negotiating round should help to get results.

Nevertheless, the changing political context and new developments since the UR, combined with the different perspectives and new dimensions on trade reform, have produced a highly contentious agenda, and the atmosphere in which the talks are taking place has also changed considerably. Historically, developing countries have played a passive or reactive role in multilateral trade negotiations. Richer countries—mainly the United States, Japan, and those in the European Union—historically have set the agenda and then agreed on terms, and the smaller and developing countries went along. However, as was made apparent by the unsuccessful WTO Ministerial meeting in Seattle in 1999 and in the successful meeting in Doha in 2001, that is no longer the way the system works. The rise of developing countries as major players in the WTO has changed the dynamics of trade negotiations.

Proposals submitted before the 1999 Seattle meeting, and since March 2000 in the context of the agriculture negotiations, reflect profound differences in approach, policies, and attitudes and include differences in member countries' specific objectives in trade in agricultural products, as well as more general issues about the scope and nature of the agriculture reform process. While proposals and statements preach and recognize the need to move toward liberalization, the reality of policies, in both the industrial and developing countries, indicates a revival of protectionist influences.

Changes in recent years (for instance, the Asian financial crisis and its aftermath) have cast doubts on the wisdom of further liberalization and have fuelled new protectionist tendencies. In least-developed countries, which are still only marginally integrated into the multilateral trading system, the policies and attitudes reflected in the proposals are clouded with uncertainty. The Asian financial crisis has heightened concerns about the adverse impact of globalization and integration on fragile economies with pervasive poverty.

Many developing countries have also expressed serious concerns about whether relevant areas of the UR agreements have been implemented with the intent and the expectations they had at the time of the agreements. Indeed, several governments, responding to the pressures of domestic forces, are rethinking their policies and slowing their process of liberalization. The failure in Seattle illustrates that both industrial and developing countries were politically unready at that time to launch a broader new round of negotiations, with the result that negotiations on agriculture and on services mandated by the UR agreements had to be started in isolation, with apparently limited prospects of success. However, the Doha decisions have made prospects considerably brighter, but agriculture remains highly controversial, with widely differing concerns and objectives among both industrial and developing countries.

Presently (mid-2002) the bulk of the proposals on the table are those that were submitted to the Committee on Agriculture Special Sessions and ones that were discussed as of February 2002. These proposals will certainly be revised, supplemented, and developed as the negotiations progress. Nevertheless, the proposals provide what is likely to prove a fairly complete insight into the issues and underlying concerns that will be predominant throughout the negotiations.

The proposals illustrate at least two different perspectives: One vision reflects the ultimate goal of the Cairns Group;[1] that is, fully integrating agriculture into the structure of GATT/WTO disciplines that already applies to other goods. In other words, world agricultural trade should be subject to multilateral rules and disciplines to eliminate restrictions and distortions. The Cairns proposal is supported by the United States but strongly rejected by the European Union and some other WTO members, including Japan, Switzerland, the Republic of Korea, and Norway. It is also opposed by a few developing countries, such as the net food importers, that are uncertain about the impact of full integration of agriculture into the GATT/WTO system. The concept of "multifunctionality" of agriculture has been advanced to oppose moves toward liberalization and total integration.

These developments are taking place against the backdrop of globalization—that is, the linking of countries at different levels of development by technology, information, and knowledge. Globalization of the food and agricultural trade system has brought a new set of issues beyond the so-called "built-in agenda" bequeathed to the WTO by the UR agreements, and to some extent even beyond the agenda explicitly set out in the Doha Declaration. These new issues include intellectual property, food safety, harmonization of standards, and competition policy. Further, globalization has engaged a new set of interest groups—the nongovernmental organizations (NGOs)—among which many see trade liberalization as inimical to their social and environmental objectives.

Basic Lessons from the Implementation of the Uruguay Round Agreements

This is not the place for a detailed examination of lessons learned from the experience of the eight-year-long UR negotiations and their aftermath. However, some broad conclusions, most of which are widely supported, can be stated briefly here:

- Negotiations on rules were more complex than market access talks; gains were less "automatic."
- Significant policy distortions remain.
- Agreements emerged that were not beneficial to many countries, especially least-developed economies.
- Effective participation of many developing countries in WTO negotiations remains in doubt.
- Implementation issues remain on several UR agreements, including the AoA.
- Information often does not exist, and even when information does exist, there is a lack of transparency.
- Rules and commitments are not linked to development.
- Development priorities have been neglected.
- Implementation timetables were unrealistic.
- Technical and financial assistance was insufficient and not always properly targeted; that is, commitments were not binding so that assistance was often not forthcoming.

Overview

This book covers some of the key issues in the present WTO agriculture negotiations, as initiated in 2000 in accordance with the requirements of Article 20 of the AoA and more recently redefined and supplemented by the Doha Declaration. These issues include the continuation of the reform process involving the "three pillars" of market access, domestic support, and export competition; special and differential treatment of developing countries; and the new issues such as food security (particularly relevant to the fuller participation of developing countries in agricultural negotiations), food safety and standards, rural development, and intellectual property. This book will draw on key findings of a World Bank major research program on the new WTO round of trade negotiations, and in particular on the program's analyses of implementation and experiences of both industrial and developing countries.

The book has four main objectives: First, to ask, in the light of new developments, how effective are the existing WTO agreements in agriculture, and what new rules and options would improve the outcomes of the present negotiations. Would market-opening measures be enough to trigger other needed reforms? Second, to identify the trade issues crucial to developing countries' agriculture and to assess the impact of the implementation of the UR and of domestic actions. Third, to discuss some of the themes for broader negotiations covering traditional trade barriers as well as new issues beyond border policies (for example, input subsidies and regulatory and safety trade barriers). Fourth, to provide a framework for evaluating the varying interests, and for identifying options and strategies for both industrial and developing countries. The success of some developing countries suggests that the same economics are good for both industrial and developing countries, and that all would benefit from being part of one open trading system.

Finally, this book, it is hoped, will instigate an examination of the economics underlying the options on trade and domestic policies coherent with bringing agricultural trade more fully under the GATT/WTO disciplines. Getting the underlying economics right and complete will assist national governments and private economic interests in regaining confidence in the relevance of the GATT/WTO and in its facility in achieving food security and development goals. Both industrial and developing countries will benefit from an open discussion, and this will result, it is hoped, in a rekindling of the international resolve to extend and defend the global trading system.

The GATT/WTO Meetings Highlighted

An impression of the 45 formal proposals submitted on behalf of a total of 121 countries during Phase 1 of the work of the Committee on Agriculture Special Sessions—that is, during the period March 2000 to March 2001, when WTO members were setting out the goals they sought to achieve in the agricultural negotiations—indicates a comprehensive coverage of issues embraced by the AoA.[2] More than half the proposals were made by developing countries, with several further proposals supported by both groups of developing and industrial countries. A review of the proposals illustrates substantial divergences in interests among members, but also some common interests.

There is a general call to simplify trade conditions and restrictions by cutting tariffs and by addressing the remaining problems of tariff peaks, tariff escalation, and the complexities of the tariff regimes implemented after the UR. Notably the system of tariff-rate quotas (TRQs) and their administration are discussed. Specific proposals about how to approach the tariff cuts are discussed. Different tariff-cutting approaches and formulas, such as "across the board," "zero for zero," and the "Swiss formula," have been proposed in negotiations. On the issue of special safeguards, since comparatively few countries reserved the right at the end of the UR to use the special safeguards mechanism established for agriculture, some members have proposed to make its use available more widely.

There is a general call to eliminate or substantially reduce export subsidies. This is complemented by proposals aiming to avoid circumvention of commitments by including disciplines on export credits, food aid, and operations of state trading agencies engaged as single exporters. This book provides an analysis of the different forms of export competition to establish which forms are the most trade distorting and to suggest alternative rules and options. Some developing countries, such as net food importers, are concerned about the potential impact that elimination of export subsidies might have on food prices. Some countries have argued that elimination of subsidies could actually benefit net food importers if the higher prices led to an increase in prices received by their farmers, thus triggering a supply response, and increased food production.

On domestic support, most liberalization proposals are oriented toward reducing and simplifying trade-distorting measures. A review of domestic support levels in the industrial countries indicates that total transfers to agriculture in OECD countries have risen in the last five years, even though most countries utilized less than half of the support allowed under the commitments on the aggregate measurement of support (AMS) imposed under the AoA. Thus, countries have the potential to increase support levels even further, contrary to the objectives of the UR. Developing countries are also asking for more flexibility in allocating resources to their agricultural sector and in expanding the "green box" provisions that exempt specified forms of support from reduction commitments.

Two other dominant issues emerge in the proposals: Special and Differential (S&D) Treatment and "nontrade concerns" (NTC). S&D and NTC are linked to domestic support and market access regimes. The purpose of S&D is to help and encourage developing countries in being more integrated, and in participating more fully, in the WTO to share the benefits from trade. NTC, and a related concept of the "multifunctionality" of agriculture, is an umbrella concept that embraces a number of considerations, such as environmental interests and food security, which are cited as arguments to be used against those for agricultural trade liberalization.

Many developing countries have repeatedly asked that the current negotiations be aimed at leveling the playing field to reduce the disparity between themselves and the richer countries in the use of domestic support and protection and improving market access conditions. These developing countries have focused on how new rules might be introduced to enhance their own internal protection and domestic support. In practice, however, governments in developing countries have effectively "taxed" their agricultural sector, and their domestic farm prices are below world prices. Total domestic support or subsidies in agriculture are a very small proportion of their GDP, and in certain countries are actually negative. Some proposals have questioned whether developing countries, given their limited resources, can afford to provide domestic support and subsidies and have suggested that concessions at a multilateral level to permit developing countries to raise domestic support would be meaningless or, at best, a cheap concession for industrial countries.

It was clearly evident during the UR that, by and large, the developing countries were on the margin of the negotiations, even though analysis showed that, on a relative basis, the outcome of the UR would have a greater impact on developing countries than on industrial countries. Given the overall relative importance in developing countries of agriculture, and the rural economy more generally, it is crucial that developing countries not only understand the implications of changes in the global agricultural trading regime but also actively participate in rendering the system more transparent and beneficial to a broader range of participants. Trade issues are also becoming significantly more complex. As tariffs have been reduced in successive trade rounds (both unilateral and multilateral), the trade agenda is more heavily weighed toward nontariff trade measures that are inherently more complex to understand, measure, and analyze. Developing countries, given their limited resources, need assistance in evaluating their interests and options and in developing strategies to capture the benefits from the negotiations.

Interests, options, and objectives in a new trade round diverge greatly across countries. Developing countries are widely heterogeneous. Interests, options, objectives, and strategies differ according to a country's size, export orientation, indebtedness, prosperity, trade composition, and trade links. There is no such thing as a typical developing country. Developing countries also differ in their susceptibility to external shocks. Depending on resource endowments and production patterns, interests even diverge within countries (for example, the interests of sugar producers in Brazil are unlikely to be the same as those of wheat farmers). Countries are also divided between net food importers and net food exporters with, again, a likely divergence in interests. A further example is the costs and benefits to developing countries of export subsidies. A number of countries benefit from these subsidies, either indirectly by lower world commodity prices or directly through food aid programs. Heterogeneity of interests is also evident in the aftermath of the Asian financial crisis: clearly, the agricultural interests of Thailand and Indonesia are quite different from the interests of Korea, for which agricultural exports are not very important. Thus, a relevant concept is whether agricultural policies have had countercyclical effects (for instance, through achieving a better export performance than the manufacturing sector or by ability to absorb surplus labor)

Certain developing countries have a definite comparative advantage in a variety of agricultural commodities; that is, some (such as sugar) compete with industrial countries while others (such as coffee or tea) do not. Export taxes have often been more detrimental to agricultural exports of developing countries than to the global trading regime itself. In the longer term, growth in developing countries needs to shift toward manufacturing and tertiary activities, since the long-run trend in agricultural commodity prices is downward. However, the path to growth must ensure that agricultural policies, either domestic or international, do not discriminate against developing country agriculture, since it is the surplus savings and labor in agriculture that have traditionally been instrumental in leading to balanced and sustained growth.

An important problem, increasingly recognized but still unresolved, is how to give poor developing countries an effective voice in the negotiating process. Beyond the problems associated with insufficient domestic analytical resources, most countries simply do not have the resources to be adequately represented in Geneva and in the other venues where the negotiations occur. Most of the industrial countries attend negotiations with a team of lawyers, economists, and diplomats, whereas many of the developing countries must rely by and large on one or two (if any) diplomats in residence in Geneva, and with many other tasks to undertake. Clearly (sets of) developing countries need to identify effective coalitions. Two successful coalitions come to mind, the Cairns Group of agricultural exporters, which includes both industrial and developing countries, and the Alliance of Small Island States, which groups the small island nations in an effort to influence the global warming discussions. Even if their overall impact has been limited, they have been successful in coordinating their approaches and providing a clear and consistent message for promoting their aims.

The interests of developing countries will be fostered by multilateral trade negotiations that ensure increased access for developing country commodity exports to the industrialized countries and reduce distortions in world food markets, especially by a reduction or elimination of export subsidies. A more open and transparent trading system has become increasingly relevant to development and growth.

Notes

1. The Cairns Group began in August 1986 in Cairns, Queensland, Australia, and is a coalition of 18 developed and developing agricultural exporting countries (Argentina, Australia, Bolivia, Brazil, Canada, Chile, Colombia, Costa Rica, Fiji, Guatemala, Indonesia, Malaysia, New Zealand, Paraguay, the Philippines, South Africa, Thailand, and Uruguay).

2. In addition, members submitted four technical notes or discussion papers. All can be consulted and downloaded from the WTO website (http://www.WTO. org). In Phase 2, the special sessions were devoted to in-depth consideration of the proposals made in Phase 1, and most of the additional documentation took the form of informal papers, largely devoted to elaborating or commenting on proposals made in Phase 1.

2

The New Trade Debate and Options for Developing Countries

Ian Johnson

The fourth ministerial meeting of the World Trade Organization (WTO) to launch a new trade round was held in November 2001 in Doha, Qatar. Many member countries support the launch of a new round of trade negotiations in Doha. One of the key issues will be the question of whether the multilateral trading system can become an effective vehicle for sustainable development and pro-poor growth in low-income countries.

As in Seattle, the member countries of the WTO face a complex challenge in building a consensus on a new trade agenda that both accommodates the diverse interests of industrialized and developing countries and broadens public support for the global trading system. The task will not be easy.

The new trade debate now includes complex issues. More than ever before, trade and the rules of the trading system intersect with an array of policies and issues—that is, from investment and competition policy to environmental, developmental, health, and labor standards. How should the world protect endangered species and the environment, and promote sustainable development? What system of intellectual property rules can promote science and technology development in developing countries? Should trade be linked to labor standards and human rights? Can we preserve cultural identities in an age of borderless communications? Can poverty be eradicated and thereby reduce inequalities and promote the rights of women? These and other issues are a world away from such "traditional" trade concerns as tariffs and quotas. And yet, all are, directly or indirectly, part of the new trade debate. To the public these issues appear linked and are many facets of a single issue, and all are expressed more loudly and insistently in an age when the images of starving children or burning rain forests come into our homes through television. People will demand answers, and rightly so.

We need to improve the understanding of the relationships between these issues and the trade system so as to respond to the desire for a coherent and balanced consideration of different policies and objectives. The ability to advance sustainable development and reduce poverty will hinge on the capacity to build a strong global trading system, to make simultaneous progress on the complex issues, and to address the legitimate concerns about the growing social inequality, rising costs during adjustment, environmental degradation, and human risks during globalization. How is this to be done? How can antiglobalization protesters become a force for constructive public support?

First, the next trade round must be "fair" and must truly reflect the interests of developing countries, especially poor countries. For trade to promote sustainable development that really benefits the poor, we have to focus on the needs of developing countries inside the trade negotiations. In parallel, we must advance a complementary development agenda outside the WTO. The president of the World Bank and others have called for a "Development Round" as the next round, and for this to happen the interests of developing countries in agriculture trade reform must be high on the agenda, with agriculture issues fully integrated in the overall negotiations. Trade in agriculture, food, and agro-based manufactures remains imperative for least-developed countries. And because most (70 percent) of the world's poor are employed in agriculture, how trade reform and globalization affects agriculture and the rural poor will critically influence its overall impact on poverty reduction.

Therefore, to maximize the potential benefits of the new trade round for the poor, action in the following areas is critical: (a) Grant full market access in goods produced by poor countries. This includes reducing tariff escalation and tariff peaks in agriculture and agro-based processed products, textiles and clothing, and other labor-intensive manufactures. Tariffs in agriculture in Organisation for Economic Co-operation and Development (OECD) countries are three times higher than those in manufactures, and this does not include agricultural subsidies. In addition, rich countries are applying new types of nontariff barriers such as protectionist use of standards (including new food safety standards beyond those required in international agreements, and other production process standards in food and agriculture). Numerous countries use blunt quarantine instruments that excessively restrict imports well beyond what is necessary for protecting the health of their plants and animals. For example, there are outright bans on imports of many products. The levels of protection involved are in some cases equivalent to tariffs of more than 100 percent. In addition, the new tariff quotas in agriculture have also introduced new types of difficulties and market distortions. (b) Implementation of trade agreements must be adapted to local capacities and development priorities; that is, poor countries should be granted greater flexibility to implement trade agreements in areas that require large investments to make them consistent with development priorities. (c) Provide increased aid and technical development assistance in key sectors such as agriculture and rural nonfarm sectors where most of the poor are dependent for their incomes and livelihood.

Second, the international community needs to enhance the trade capacity of developing countries. In contrast to decisions to liberalize access to markets, building trade capacity demands up-front investment of resources in order to reap longer-term gains. It is up to governments to work with the private sector and civil society to set priorities in the context of an overall development strategy and to allocate scarce resources. To pay for vital social benefits such as health and education systems in the future, a country may need to invest now in building trade capacity rather than in investing resources in other areas. These are difficult decisions. The challenge for development policy is to identify the areas where the net social return to domestic (and international) action is highest. The challenge for the international community is to ensure that the global trading system supports the realization of national development priorities.

Third, the international community must facilitate corporate accountability. Multinationals and private firms must contribute to social and sustainable development goals, and strengthen their contributions to mitigate the adverse impact of global market integration on the poor.

Fourth, the international community must look at the issues and challenges as pieces of a puzzle. Both nationally and internationally, we need to give more thought to how we can coordinate policy goals. People associate globalization with free trade, dazzling technologies, and global capital markets. As important as these realities are, they do not capture the full picture. We are linked by the exchange of ideas, images, and information, as well as by the exchange of goods, services, and capital. There is globalization not just of our economies, but in our hopes and fears. It is this human dimension of globalization that is forcing the international system to change. In every country the same questions and anxieties are expressed: people want the benefits from global trade and integration, but they fear the effects of globalization on the environment, wage levels, and cultural identities. They recognize the need for greater cooperation and coordination at the international level, but they instinctively resist interference in their domestic affairs. Hence, the challenge of the trading system involves more than the minutiae of technical details or negotiating positions. They involve broader questions about the kind of international system we want.

There is the opportunity to include the world's poor in capturing the benefits from trade and global market developments, and this requires a more concerted effort by the international community to provide complementary measures to support developing countries.

The international community should support developing countries with more aid and assistance to eliminate internal barriers to trade expansion, such as inadequate port infrastructure, poor regulatory framework, inefficient customs services, inadequate institutions, and know-how on the basics of trade development. This is particularly important since implementing WTO agreements can be costly, and developing countries need support. In implementing the Sanitary and Phytosanitary Agreement, countries are required to provide scientific justification for any measure that is more trade restricting than the appropriate international standard would be, and to assess formally the risks involved. More technical assistance is needed to help developing countries meet these new requirements and to meet the new standards imposed by OECD countries.

The international community should address global public goods issues—such as the environment or labor standards—through appropriate direct assistance to developing countries. Development cooperation will be more effective than the threat of trade sanctions in achieving the shared environmental and trade goals. Such sanctions can turn into covert protectionism.

Developing countries should take their trade and agricultural policy reform still further. Developing countries have already cut their average tariffs, but further liberalization will promote greater productivity and living standards. Again, international support will be necessary to mitigate any adverse impact during adjustments.

Finally, developing countries must capture the benefits from science and technology. For instance, what is the role of genetically modified organisms (GMOs)? How are developing countries affected? One issue is the ability to lower the cost of food production. The other is, of course, trade barriers because of consumer concerns in mostly OECD countries. GMOs may benefit those food-exporting developing countries that already have sound intellectual property law and enforcement (because seed companies would otherwise be wary of selling into or producing in such countries). However, countries that cannot make productive use of the new biotechnologies could see their competitiveness eroded on international markets as international food prices decline. On the other hand, net food importing developing countries could benefit from the fall in global prices, and perhaps even more so if OECD countries ban imports of GMO products. In sum, the likely impact remains clouded, and this is clearly an area that requires further empirical research.

Then there is the role of the Consultative Group on International Agricultural Research (CGIAR). Mobilizing science and technology to accelerate the fight against poverty is a priority. Advances in science and technology hold the greatest promise for improving the lives of the world's poor. Whether it is a vaccine that wards off disease or hardier plants that can grow in adverse climates and still yield a bountiful harvest, science and technology can improve the quality of people's lives in many ways. However, the disparities between rich and poor countries in scientific and technology capacity, both in terms of input and output, are significant: OECD countries spent more in research and development in 1998 than the total economic output of the world's 61 poorest countries (the low-income countries excluding China and India), or US$500 billion versus US$464 billion. The CGIAR is strengthening its overall science and technology strategy to meet new challenges. By making food more available at cheaper prices, the CGIAR is meeting the needs of the poor while contributing to stronger scientific capacity in developing countries.

Conclusions and Options for Developing Countries

The new trade round of negotiations offers the best prospects ever for developing countries in general—and their rural communities in particular—to secure growth-enhancing reforms. Traditional agricultural market access liberalization should be the priority issue in the next WTO round of multilateral negotiations given the enormous potential for global and developing country welfare gains from reducing agricultural protection. It is also critical for the European Union and the United States to honor fully the spirit of their commitment in gradually expanding market access for textiles and clothing. Substantial progress in freeing up more trade in both these sectors is essential if the new trade round is to be a genuine development round.

Such reforms could boost enormously the earnings of the world's poor, the vast majority of whom are in rural households of developing countries. All this suggests a potentially high payoff for developing countries acting collectively to push hard for greater market access for farm and textile products, and for technical and economic assistance to aid their reform process, in return for providing more access to developing country markets for goods and services.

From an agricultural development perspective, attention should also focus on reducing protection granted to other manufacturing and services industries. Protection in those sectors still bestows a significant anti-agricultural bias in many developing countries, making it more difficult for those countries to benefit from the agriculture and textile trade reforms of OECD countries. Those reforms can be done unilaterally, but the new WTO trade round offers an opportunity to obtain a quid pro quo, and can be a useful instrument through which to lock in such reforms domestically.

The next WTO round will, however, be conducted in an environment in which globalization forces (including ever-faster development and international transfers of information, ideas, capital, skills, and new technologies) will, by having ever-stronger impacts on domestic markets, simultaneously trigger isolationist policy responses. For example, further reductions in traditional measures of farm protection will meet significant resistance in numerous OECD countries as farm groups join with food safety and environmental groups to argue for new forms of agricultural protection. In these circumstances, the mercantilist nature of trade negotiations may require that the agenda of the next WTO round include not only other sectors but also some "new trade agenda" items so as to provide the potential for beneficial issue linkages and tradeoffs.

Finally, what else should developing countries do to help their own reform processes complement those abroad? Direct new economic and technical assistance funds toward reducing the underinvestments in rural infrastructures (human as well as physical), agricultural research and developments, and agricultural technology transfer. Liberalizing foreign investment rules and improving intellectual property law enforcement will enhance the prospects for both transfer of new technologies and their further development locally. Removing disincentives to farmers in the form of agricultural export taxes, manufacturing protection, and overvalued exchange rates remains essential.

Some of the rural poor may lose in the short term. For instance, those who are employed or produce in sectors that are highly protected, low-productivity sectors may have a hard time. Examples include maize in Mexico, wheat in Morocco, and various import-substituting crops in many developing countries. If the mobility of these rural poor is limited, then a reduction in the tariffs in that sector is likely to hurt that subgroup, especially in the short term, as prices of their output fall. Over time those losses can be minimized or become gains as farmers change their output mix and produce more of the crops where prices did not fall. In a study on the northeast of Brazil, one of the world's poorest regions, switching to more profitable crops after trade liberalization and devaluation was found to be important in dampening the real income effect of price changes to the point that the resulting negative real income effects for small farmers were found to be very small.

The ability to shift to the production of new products (possibly exportables whose price has risen) may depend on necessary complementary reforms. Shifting crops may require restructured land arrangements, some additional capital, or access to water. If markets for these factors are poorly developed, farmers may be unable to take advantage of new opportunities. Thus, important complementary reforms of these markets may be necessary to help poor farmers.

Given that poor farmers may be hurt in the short run, proper safety net procedures should be put in place. Strategic retraining may be needed. As far as trade reform itself is concerned, one option to consider is to phase down tariffs in the vulnerable sector gradually following a preannounced schedule. Experience shows that reforms with long transition periods (typically more than five years) lack credibility and provide lobbyists with time to defeat reform. Thus, such schedules should not extend beyond five years. Indeed, a true Development Round, supported by these complementary measures, could build strongly on this momentum and hasten progress toward a world free of poverty.

Part I

Lessons from the Implementation of the Uruguay Round

3

The Uruguay Round Agreement on Agriculture in Practice: How Open Are OECD Markets?

Dimitris Diakosavvas

Before the World Trade Organization (WTO), the rules that applied to agricultural primary products deviated from the general rules.[1] This resulted in a proliferation of impediments to agricultural trade by means of import bans, quotas setting the maximum level of imports, variable import levies, minimum import prices, and nontariff measures maintained by state trading enterprises. The Uruguay Round (UR) Agreement on Agriculture (AoA) has fundamentally changed the way agriculture was treated under the General Agreement on Tariffs and Trade (GATT). It imposed specific commitments to reduce support and protection in the areas of domestic support, market access, and export competition. It also strengthened and made more operationally effective rules and disciplines in each of these areas, including export prohibitions and restrictions. The AoA is being implemented over a six-year period (10 years for developing countries), and it began in 1995.

The market access provisions established disciplines on trade distorting practices while maintaining historical trade volumes and creating increased access opportunities in highly protected markets.[2] Most important, nontariff barriers, such as quantitative import restrictions, variable import levies, and discretionary import licensing, were banned. These barriers were converted to ordinary tariffs ("tariffication"). Existing and new tariffs were bound and subject to reduction. Developed countries agreed to reduce agricultural tariffs from their base period rates by a total of 36 percent, on a simple average basis, with a minimum cut of 15 percent for each tariff. Current access commitments were put in place to ensure that there was no erosion in market access as a result of the AoA. At the same time, countries also had to provide a minimum level of import opportunities for products previously protected by nontariff barriers. This was accomplished by creating tariff-rate quotas (TRQs), which generally impose a relatively low tariff (in-quota) on imports up to a specified level, with imports above that level subject to a higher tariff (over-quota).

The domestic support provisions are regarded as one of the major breakthroughs of the AoA insofar as they explicitly recognize the direct link between domestic agricultural policies and international trade. A key aspect of the provisions was the distinction between domestic policies that were deemed (a) not to, or only to a minimum extent, distort trade ("green box" measures) and (b) all other policies, that is, those that distort trade ("amber box" measures, "blue box" measures, and some other exempt measures). The provisions require countries to reduce agricultural support levels arising from those domestic policies, which most unequivocally have the largest effects on production, such as administered prices, input subsidies, and producer payments that are not accompanied by limitations on production. Domestic support reductions are implemented through a commitment to reduce the total aggregate measurement of support (AMS) for each country. The AMS is an indicator of the support associated with policies considered to have the greatest potential to affect production and trade. It has product-specific and non-product-specific elements, but the commitments themselves are not product specific but sectorwide applying to the total AMS.

Policies deemed to have no or minimal effect on production and trade are exempt from reduction commitments (green box). As a result of the Blair House Accord (1992), production-linked support related to production-limiting policies is exempt from the disciplines if such payments satisfy certain criteria (blue box).[3] However, the Due Restraint provision or "peace clause" renders actionable any increase in support, as measured by AMS, or arising from the "production-limiting programs," beyond the levels decided during the 1992 marketing year. Finally, support below a certain threshold is not required to be included in the calculation of reduction commitments. This is usually referred to as the *de minimis* provision. A WTO member shall not provide support in favor of domestic producers in excess of its commitments. Members who do not have a total AMS commitment shall not provide support to agricultural producers in excess of *de minimis* levels. Binding commitments on the level of support provided through domestic measures were an essential complement to the disciplines on market access and export subsidies.

The export subsidies discipline is considered to be an important accomplishment of the agreement as well and the one that was expected to have the most immediate trade implications. Not surprisingly, acceptance of a specific discipline on export subsidies was one of the most contentious issues not only in the agricultural negotiations but in the UR as a whole (Josling and Tangermann 1999). Before the AoA, export subsidies were an important policy instrument in agricultural trade, particularly for trade in grains and dairy products. The AoA did not outlaw agricultural export subsidies, but limits were established on the volume of subsidized exports and on budgetary expenditure. Countries that employed export subsidies are committed to reduce the volume of subsidized exports by 21 percent and the expenditure on subsidized exports by 36 percent. These reductions are to be made from the 1986–90 base period level over a six-year implementation period (10-year period for developing countries) on a product-specific basis. Moreover, export subsidies on products not subsidized in the base period are banned.

Though it is generally agreed that the AoA provisions represent a significant step in the direction of trade liberalization, it is also recognized that their actual impact on agricultural policies and trade would depend on the limited extent of the reductions and on the way in which they are implemented. The implementation period for the reductions to be made under the AoA is now completed, at least for the developed countries, and a new round of multilateral negotiations on agriculture has already started as mandated by Article 20 of the AoA. It is therefore pertinent to examine whether the AoA has been successful in liberalizing agricultural trade and to draw some lessons. An assessment of the implementation experience should provide valuable input to the new round of agricultural negotiations.

Overall Appraisal of Trade Developments

Whether the AoA has been successful in liberalizing trade in agricultural products depends on the expectations arising from the agreement. Some analysts emphasize the new rules and disciplines established in the AoA and point to their potential effect on future policymaking in world agriculture. Others argue that the quantitative commitments agreed under the AoA were so limited that they did not require major policy changes, and hence the AoA did not result in an actual liberalization of world agricultural trade.

The trade liberalization impact resulting from the AoA should be to expand market access and to reduce trade, consumption, and production distortions. The ultimate effects should be an increase in world import demand for agricultural products, and higher and more stable world market prices than otherwise would be the case.

However, identification of the combined effects of the three pillars and the separation of their effects from the influences of other factors are difficult tasks. The complexity of the AoA package, the linkages between the policy instruments that are subject to reform, and the options for their implementation by countries make quantification difficult, irrespective of the analytical tools used. Statistical evaluation of the trade impacts of the

AoA is fraught with difficulties. In particular, three stand out. First, what is the counterfactual evidence? Should we just assume a continuation of pre-existing policies and performance in the country concerned? In practical terms this may be all we can do, although it has an important shortcoming: How can the effects of trade reforms be disentangled from other policy shifts and exogenous shocks, such as technological change and the business cycle? Second, some pre-existing policies were likely to have been unsustainable and would have changed irrespective of the AoA. Third, supply responses and the process of adjustment will differ from economy to economy: How long should we wait before conducting an assessment? The implementation of the AoA is still under way, and the effects of the policies implemented are not instantaneous. Growth in agricultural trade will respond to liberalization with a time lag, which in itself will depend on a number of factors, including the way policies are being implemented, the extent of pre-existing distortions, and the flexibility of markets. With these caveats in mind, a preliminary appraisal of the evolution of a number of trade performance indicators is attempted. Two approaches are used: the so-called simple before and after[4] approach and a more sophisticated econometric model that takes into account some of the statistical pitfalls of the before and after approach.

Before and After Approach

The basic idea is to provide some empirical evidence on external openness to agricultural trade by comparing trade performance indicators for periods prior to and following the start of the implementation of the AoA. This is a difficult task that entails the choice of appropriate benchmarks as well as trade performance indicators. Both of these choices involve practical problems, and the results should be treated with caution and only tentative conclusions can be drawn. From the outset, it should be emphasized that it is vital not to equate liberalization with openness, as trade openness is a function of many factors, not just liberalization, such as technological change or reductions in transportation and communication costs. Clearly there are no straightforward indicators of liberalization, and trade openness and a number multiple indicators and criteria to identify liberalization are used. Broadly speaking, in the relevant literature, two types of measures of openness (trade barriers) have been used: incidence- and outcome-based measures (Harrison 1991; Pritchett 1996; Baldwin 1989).[5]

Each of these measures has its weaknesses and strengths. Incidence-based measures are direct indicators of trade policy, such as the level or dispersion of tariffs. Although these indicators are good proxies for inferring the trade policy of a country, they still have two shortcomings: first, they are imperfect because they cannot capture other types of intervention, such as nontariff barriers, and second, consistent data on tariffs are not available for many countries or for a sufficient number of years. However, outcome-based measures are widely used because they implicitly cover all the sources of distortion and are based on data that are more readily available. Outcome measures can be either price based, such as rates of protection or producer subsidy equivalents (PSEs) or trade flows based. An alternative aggregate measure of tariffs is the Trade Restrictiveness Index (TRI) developed by Anderson and Neary (1996). The TRI measures countries' overall tariff levels by using their underlying trade shares in production and consumption and their elasticities of factor substitution and import substitution as weights. This approach is arguably the most theoretically defensible of any single measure because it is based on the underlying consumer and producer behavior of a country that determines the trade effects of tariffs. However, empirical application of TRI is data demanding, and the results are sensitive to what assumptions are made.[6]

For the purpose of this chapter, the following commonly used indicators were calculated: (a) trade openness calculated as the average share of agricultural imports plus exports in agricultural gross domestic product (GDP), (b) import penetration ratios defined as the ratio of agricultural imports to consumption, (c) export performance calculated as the ratio of agricultural exports to production, (d) net trade performance defined as the ratio of exports minus imports to exports plus imports, (e) percentage producer support estimate (%PSE) and percentage consumer support estimate (%CSE) as measures of the cost of agricultural support and implicit tax on consumers due to agricultural policy, and (f) producer nominal protection coefficients (PNPCs) and consumer nominal protection coefficients (CNPCs) as measures of price distortions. Calculations were initially made either since 1986–2000, and in some instances to 2006, but to limit the effects of year-to-year fluctuations, more emphasis is given to results based on a six-year time span: 1989–94 and 1995–2000.

Trade Openness

The development of world merchandise exports relative to world production could provide some indication as to whether there has been an increase in market openness for world merchandise trade. As portrayed in figure 3.1, the share of trade in the output of world manufactures and agriculture has increased since the AoA, although agricultural trade expanded less rapidly (almost half). The growth of both manufactured and agricultural exports from Organisation for Economic Co-operation and Development (OECD) countries decelerated during the 1995–99 period when compared to the first half of the 1990s. In the first year of the im-

Figure 3.1 World Export Performance, 1989–99

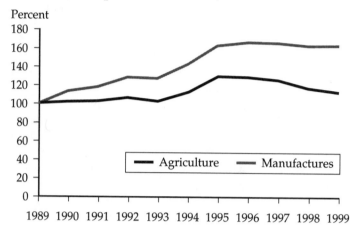

plementation of the AoA, world agriculture trade growth was strong, but actually declined in 1996 and 1997 when compared to the previous year.

The various indicators of trade openness that were calculated for the OECD countries suggest wide variation across countries and commodities. Overall, the import penetration rate was stable or increased for many commodities in the post-AoA era. However, absolute comparisons can be misleading. The significance of the difference between the pre-AoA and post-AoA periods was determined through use of parametric tests (that is, the paired sample *t*-test and the signs test) and nonparametric tests (that is, the Wilcoxon-Mann-Whitney (WMW) ranked-sums tests, Van der Waerden scores, and the Kolmogorov-Smirnov two-sample test). For clarity of presentation, only the significance levels reported in table 3.1 are based on the WMW procedure. For the AoA implementation period (1995–2000), the difference with the period five years prior to AoA (1989–94) is statistically significant only in a few cases. There are more significant results for the 2001–06 period, particularly for livestock products. In a number of cases, the indicators declined in the post-AoA era. The decline was statistically significant for import penetration for refined sugar (2001–06), export performance for wheat (2001–06), and net trade performance for butter and cheese (2001–06). Overall, these results provide support to the argument that for a number of agricultural commodities in the OECD countries, market openness in the post-AoA era is not discernibly different from that of the pre-AoA era.

Evolution of Agricultural Support and Protection Levels

The average total support to the agricultural sector as a whole (total support estimate [TSE]) for the OECD countries amounted to US$330.6 billion

Table 3.1. Relative Comparisons of Trade Performance Indicators in OECD Countries

	Import penetration					Export performance				
	1989–94	1995–2000	2001–06	Difference		1989–94	1995–2000	2001–06	Difference	
Commodity	(1)	(2)	(3)	(2) – (1)	(3) – (1)	(1)	(2)	(3)	(2) – (1)	(3) – (1)
Wheat	0.10	0.11	0.11	0.01**	0.01*	0.38	0.34	0.35	−0.04**	−0.03*
Coarse grains	0.11	0.11	0.11	0.00	0.00	0.18	0.17	0.18	−0.01	0.00
Oilseeds	0.31	0.32	0.31	0.01	0.00	0.28	0.30	0.31	0.03*	0.03**
Rice	0.12	0.14	0.13	0.02	0.01	0.18	0.21	0.21	0.03**	0.03**
Refined sugar	0.25	0.23	0.23	−0.02	−0.02***	0.27	0.28	0.29	0.00	0.01
Butter	0.05	0.05	0.06	0.01	0.02***	0.19	0.18	0.20	−0.01	0.01
Cheese	0.05	0.05	0.06	0.01	0.01***	0.08	0.09	0.09	0.01	0.01***
Skimmed milk powder	0.12	0.13	0.13	0.01	0.01	0.31	0.35	0.34	0.04	0.03
Whole milk powder	0.10	0.08	0.06	−0.02	−0.04	0.56	0.60	0.60	0.04	0.04***
Beef	0.13	0.14	0.17	0.01	0.04***	0.16	0.18	0.20	0.02	0.04***
Pork	0.04	0.05	0.06	0.01	0.02***	0.04	0.07	0.08	0.03	0.03***
Poultry	0.03	0.04	0.04	0.01	0.01***	0.06	0.12	0.12	0.06	0.05***
Sheep	0.18	0.18	0.20	0.01	0.02***	0.30	0.30	0.31	0.01	0.01**

(Table continues on the following page.)

Table 3.1. (*continued*)

Commodity	Net trade performance					Trade openness				
	1989–94 (1)	1995–2000 (2)	2001–06 (3)	Difference (2) – (1)	(3) – (1)	1989–94 (1)	1995–2000 (2)	2001–06 (3)	Difference (2) – (1)	(3) – (1)
Wheat	0.69	0.60	0.64	−0.09**	−0.05	0.45	0.42	0.43	−0.03**	−0.02*
Coarse grains	0.27	0.25	0.29	−0.02	0.02	0.29	0.28	0.29	−0.01	0.00
Oilseeds	−0.08	−0.04	−0.02	0.04	0.06***	0.60	0.63	0.62	0.04	0.02
Rice	0.20	0.12	0.08	−0.08	−0.12	0.31	0.38	0.39	0.07*	0.08***
Refined sugar	0.05	0.13	0.17	0.07	0.11*	0.52	0.49	0.49	−0.03	−0.03
Butter	0.66	0.60	0.59	−0.06	−0.08***	0.23	0.22	0.26	−0.01	0.03**
Cheese	0.28	0.26	0.23	−0.02	−0.05***	0.12	0.14	0.14	0.01***	0.02***
Skimmed milk powder	0.53	0.57	0.55	0.04	0.02	0.41	0.45	0.44	0.04	0.03
Whole milk powder	0.84	0.90	0.92	0.06	0.08*	0.61	0.63	0.63	0.02	0.02
Beef	0.12	0.13	0.12	0.01	0.00	0.29	0.32	0.36	0.03***	0.07***
Poultry	0.02	0.15	0.16	0.13***	0.14***	0.09	0.13	0.13	0.04***	0.05***
Poultry	0.32	0.49	0.52	0.17***	0.19***	0.10	0.16	0.16	0.06***	0.06***
Sheep	0.34	0.33	0.30	−0.01	−0.04*	0.45	0.46	0.48	0.01	0.03***

*** Indicates that difference between medians is significant at a 1 percent two-tail level.

** Indicates that difference between medians is significant at a 5 percent two-tail level.

* Indicates that difference between medians is significant at a 10 percent two-tail level.

Note: The null hypothesis is that the median of the variable for the post-URAoA period is the same as the median for the pre-URAoA (1989–94) period. This hypothesis is tested using a Wilcoxon-Mann-Whitney rank test.

in 1998–2000, accounting for 1.3 percent of GDP (%TSE), compared with a nominal US$271.2 billion or 2.2 percent of GDP in 1986–88. For the same period, support to producers (PSE) was US$250 billion and US$214.8 billion correspondingly. For the OECD as a whole, support to producers as a share of total farm receipts (%PSE) has exhibited a slow downward trend since 1986–88; it was estimated at 33 percent in 1995–2000, down from 37 percent in 1989–94 and 39 percent in 1986–88 (table 3.2, Appendix table A.1).

Table 3.2 also displays the evolution of PNPCs and CNPCs by commodity. The PNPC is an indicator of the nominal rate of protection for producers measuring the ratio between the average price received by producers, including payments per metric ton of output, and the border price (both measured at farm gate level). The CNPC is an indicator of the nominal rate of protection for consumers measuring the ratio between the average price paid by consumers and the border price (both also measured at farm gate level). The results suggest that although nominal protection has decreased in the OECD area as a whole over the last 14 years, domestic prices are still much higher than world prices. The PNPC, on average, declined for all commodities, except sugar and pork, between 1995 and 2000 and between 1990 and 1994. For the same period, the CNPC did not decline for rice, sugar, beef, and pork. Moreover, the decline in the PNPC for rice and in the CNPC for eggs is statistically insignificant. Thus, the level of the nominal protection coefficients remains very high for a number of agricultural products, particularly in the case of rice, sugar, and milk, which, over the 1995–2000 implementation period, exhibited nominal protection coefficients higher than 100 percent. Domestic prices are, on average, around 40 percent higher than world prices over the 1995–2000 period across the standard PSE commodities.

These results demonstrate that agricultural protection rates in OECD countries are still high. Moreover, although the composition of support has gradually shifted from measures that support higher farm prices financed by consumers to payments financed by taxpayers, market price support and output-related payments still dominate (Appendix table A.2). In 2000, the last year of the completion of the AoA implementation for developed countries, market price support and payments based on output represented 72 percent of overall support to OECD producers. These forms of support continue to insulate farmers from world markets and to impose a burden on consumers. They also have the greatest impact on production and trade, both for OECD and non-OECD countries.

A Cross-Section and Time-Series Analysis

Though it is easy to employ and is seemingly objective, the problem with the before and after approach is that it is based on a strict *ceteris paribus* assumption that factors such as technological change, weather conditions,

Table 3.2. Relative Comparisons of Support Indicators in OECD Countries

Commodity	% PSE				PNPC			
	1986–88 (1)	1990–94 (2)	1995–2000 (3)	Difference (3) – (2)	1986–88 (1)	1990–94 (2)	1995–2000 (3)	Difference (3) – (2)
Wheat	47.8	39.2	34.4	-4.7	1.7	1.4	1.1	-0.3***
Maize	40.0	27.4	23.8	-3.6	1.3	1.2	1.1	-0.1**
Other grains	51.2	46.3	42.9	-3.4	2.0	1.7	1.2	-0.4***
Oilseeds	26.3	22.3	16.0	-6.3	1.3	1.2	1.1	-0.1
Rice	80.7	79.2	77.6	-1.6	4.9	4.6	4.4	-0.2
Refined sugar	54.0	47.7	46.6	-1.0	2.4	1.9	2.0	0.1
Milk	57.5	55.9	49.5	-6.4**	2.7	2.3	1.9	-0.4**
Beef	32.9	32.3	34.8	2.5	1.4	1.4	1.3	-0.1
Sheep	55.0	53.8	44.7	-9.1**	1.9	1.6	1.2	-0.4**
Pork	13.9	17.8	19.7	1.9	1.2	1.2	1.2	0.0
Poultry	16.2	15.0	12.7	-2.3*	1.3	1.2	1.1	-0.1**
Eggs	15.1	14.0	11.3	-2.7	1.2	1.2	1.1	-0.1**
All PSE commodities	38.7	36.6	32.7	-3.9**	1.6	1.5	1.4	-0.1***

Wheat	−30.0	−21.4	−8.6	12.8**	1.8	1.5	1.2	−0.3***
Maize	1.1	2.0	8.5	6.6***	1.2	1.2	1.1	−0.1***
Other grains	−13.0	−10.6	−5.0	5.6***	1.9	1.6	1.2	−0.4***
Oilseeds	−3.3	−3.1	−1.4	1.7***	1.1	1.0	1.0	0.0***
Rice	−77.1	−74.8	−77.3	−2.5	4.5	4.1	4.6	0.5
Refined sugar	−58.5	−48.4	−50.1	−1.7	2.4	2.0	2.1	0.1
Milk	−56.8	−52.4	−44.4	8.0**	2.7	2.3	1.9	−0.4**
Beef	−27.8	−25.1	−22.4	2.7	1.4	1.4	1.3	0.0
Sheep	−52.7	−40.9	−22.6	18.3**	2.1	1.8	1.3	−0.4**
Pork	−16.0	−18.0	−16.5	1.5	1.2	1.3	1.3	0.0
Poultry	−17.9	−14.4	−8.2	6.1**	1.3	1.2	1.1	−0.1**
Eggs	−15.4	−13.4	−8.7	4.7**	1.2	1.2	1.1	−0.1**
All PSE commodities	−33.0	−30.3	−25.5	4.8**	1.6	1.5	1.4	−0.1**

*** Indicates that difference between medians is significant at a 1 percent two-tail level.

** Indicates that difference between medians is significant at a 5 percent two-tail level.

* Indicates that difference between medians is significant at a 10 percent two-tail level.

Note: %PSE = percentage producer support estimate; PNPC = producer nominal protection coefficient. The null hypothesis is that the median of the variable for the post-URAoA period is the same as the median for the pre-URAoA (1989–94) period. This hypothesis is tested using a Wilcoxon-Mann-Whitney rank test.

and business cycles do not change between the pre-AoA period and the between-AoA or post-AoA periods. This means that before and after estimates of AoA effects will typically be (a) biased, because this approach incorrectly attributes all of the changes in outcomes between the pre-AoA and AoA periods to AoA factors, and (b) unsystematic over time, because estimated AoA effects for a given year will often be dominated by specific non-AoA influences of that year. Thus, for example, if economic growth rises between the pre- and post-AoA periods, we might erroneously conclude that the AoA performed well and vice versa when economic growth falls.

These shortcomings of the before and after approach make it a poor estimator of the counterfactual, defined as the trade performance that would have prevailed in the absence of the AoA. The before and after approach is flawed as an estimator of the counterfactual because the situation prevailing before the AoA is not likely to be a good predictor of what would have happened in the absence of the AoA, given that non-AoA determinants can and do change from year to year. This is a nontrivial drawback because the counterfactual is perhaps the most appealing yardstick against which to assess AoA performance and the standard most widely employed in economics to define and measure the impact of government policies. However, the crux of the problem is that the counterfactual is not directly observable and must be estimated.

To deal with some of these deficiencies, a simple trade model was constructed. The modeling strategy adopted follows a pooling of a cross-section and time-series estimation approach where differences in both cross-country and intertemporal dimensions are captured. This approach is broader and incorporates the before and after approach as a special case. Following the work of Goldstein and Montiel (1986), Greenway, Morgan, and Wright (1998), Faini et al. (1991), and others, changes in trade performance indicators are postulated to depend on a vector of autonomous policy changes and on changes in the external environment.[7] Further to capture the impact of AoA liberalization effect, we introduce a dummy variable, which takes a value of zero for all pre-AoA years (1989–94) in a given country and a value of unity for all years thereafter (1995–2000). Thus, the optimal or equilibrium value of a trade indicator, y_{it}^*, is assumed to be a linear function of ρ exogenous or independent variables, $X_{i,t}$, an intercept, $\alpha_{\iota\tau}$, the dummy variable and an error term:

$$y_{it}^* = \alpha_{\iota\tau} + \sum_{\kappa=1}^{\rho} X_{i,t}' \beta_{\iota} + \gamma_{\iota\tau}(\text{DUMMY})_{i,t} + \epsilon_{\iota\tau}$$

$$\iota = 1, \dots N; \tau = 1\dots, T \tag{3.1}$$

where N is the number of cross sectional units, and T is the length of the time series for each cross-section.

It is also assumed that the trade performance indicators follow a partial adjustment process. In particular, the observed adjustment in a trade indicator, $y_{it} - y_{i,t-1}$, is a fraction, λ, of the optimal or long-term adjustment, $y_{it*} - y_{i,t-1}$:

$$y_{it} - (y)_{i,t-1} = \lambda \, [(y)_{it}^{*} - (y)_{i,t-1}] \quad 0 < \lambda < 1. \tag{3.2}$$

After substitution, equation (3.2) becomes

$$y_{it} = \lambda \alpha_{\iota\tau} + (1 - \lambda)(y)_{i,t-1} + \lambda \Sigma_{\kappa=1}^{\rho} X_{i,t} \beta_{\kappa} + \lambda \gamma (\text{DUMMY})_{i,t} + \lambda \epsilon_{i,t}. \tag{3.3}$$

This specification has obvious intuitive appeal in that it models trade performance in a dynamic way and so it captures not only the transitional effects of trade reform but also the longer-run impacts. The sample comprises all OECD countries (the 15 countries of the European Union considered as one country). Two trade performance indicators were employed: import penetration ratio (IPR) and export performance (XP). The exogenous variables include population (POP), real GDP per capita (GDPCP), real effective exchange rate (REER), production (Q), world price (PW), the CNPC for the case of import penetration specification, and the PNPC for the export performance specification. The REER index is an indicator of competitiveness that takes into account both export and import competitiveness. A fall indicates improvement in competitive position.[8] The CNPC is defined as the ratio between the domestic price paid by consumer and the border price (both at farm gate level) (OECD 2001b). The data are from the OECD PSE and AGLINK databases.

Estimates of the AoA effects consist of two components: first, in the form of an intercept shift, $\lambda \times \gamma$, which measures average annual change in import penetration ratio following the agreement, and, second, from AoA-induced changes in the CNPC variable as they captured in the term $\lambda \times \beta \times [\text{CNPC}]$.

The fixed effects model used to estimate equation (3.3) as the null hypothesis that the intercepts are the same across countries was rejected in all cases, both for the import penetration and export performance specifications. The fixed effects estimator allows $\alpha_{\iota\tau}$ to differ across cross-section units ($\alpha_{\iota\tau} = \alpha_{\iota}$) by estimating different constants for each cross-section. In some instances, to correct for the fact that the residuals were correlated, a mixed variance-component moving average model was estimated using the Da Silva method.

The results of estimating the above equation are reported in table 3.3 and table 3.4. Despite their preliminary nature, a couple of interesting points emerge. First, the coefficients of the lagged dependent variable and of production are significant in most of the cases and with the expected

Table 3.3. Import Penetration Model

Dependent variable	Wheat	Coarse grains	Oilseeds	Rice	Refined sugar	Butter	Cheese	Skimmed milk powder	Whole milk powder	Beef	Pork	Poultry	Sheep
Intercept	-0.152	-0.103	-0.381	0.741	0.634	-0.191	-0.254	-4.257	0.145	-0.326	-0.279	-0.181	0.524
	(-0.710)	(-0.600)	(-1.779)*	(1.299)	(2.088)**	(-1.048)	(-1.189)	(-1.962)*	(0.589)	(-1.844)*	(-2.635)***	(-2.180)**	(1.912)*
(IP)$_{t-1}$	0.138	0.106	0.117	0.553	0.151	0.048	0.729	0.068	0.168	0.258	0.742	0.710	0.339
	(1.934)**	(1.361)	(1.555)	(8.625)***	(1.725)*	(0.684)	(14.443)***	(0.899)	(2.791)***	(4.435)***	(12.989)***	(11.777)***	(3.139)***
(Q)	-0.108	-0.060	-0.054	-0.089	-0.246	-0.088	-0.028	-0.240	-0.053	-0.128	-0.017	-0.055	-0.175
	(-4.178)***	(-2.886)***	(-5.951)***	(-1.176)	(-5.191)***	(-5.597)***	(-5.299)***	(-3.009)***	(-3.768)***	(-6.394)***	(-1.801)*	(-3.441)***	(-3.815)***
(PW)	0.028	0.025	0.049	-0.008	0.086	-0.066	-0.021	0.556	-0.039	-0.033	0.020	-0.003	0.008
	(0.963)	(1.258)	(1.691)*	(-0.092)	(1.599)	(-1.764)*	(-0.456)	(1.248)	(-0.750)	(-1.175)	(1.535)	(-0.161)	(0.221)
(POP)	0.442	0.246	0.457	-0.588	-0.203	0.337	0.296	4.360	-0.055	0.657	0.265	0.213	-0.385
	(2.077)**	(1.543)	(2.281)**	(-1.036)	(-0.665)	(1.858)*	(1.452)	(2.025)**	(-0.230)	(3.706)***	(2.534)**	(2.411)**	(-1.484)
(GDPCP)	-0.027	-0.011	-0.037	-0.039	-0.003	0.017	0.007	0.120	0.055	0.031	0.001	0.038	0.003
	(-2.651)**	(-1.668)*	(-3.745)***	(-1.704)*	(-0.251)	(2.038)**	(0.701)	(1.253)	(4.820)***	(4.356)***	(0.163)	(1.289)	(0.040)
(GDPCP)^2	0.002	0.001	0.001	0.002	0.000	-0.001	0.000	-0.008	-0.005	-0.001	0.000	-0.011	0.013
	(3.086)***	(1.882)*	(2.577)**	(1.639)	(0.364)	(-1.895)*	(-0.453)	(-1.483)	(-8.636)***	(-3.750)***	(0.218)	(-1.202)	(0.798)
(REER)	-0.097	-0.007	-0.009	-0.009	-0.072	-0.0202	0.006	0.276	-0.004	-0.100	0.000	0.000	0.114
	(-2.605)***	(-0.261)	(-0.268)	(-0.103)	(-1.264)	(-0.647)	(0.161)	(0.799)	(-0.092)	(-3.694)***	(0.004)	(-0.009)	(2.786)***
(CNPC)	-0.004	-0.004	-0.004	-0.001	0.025	0.009	-0.001	-0.079	-0.022	0.011	0.024	0.003	0.012
	(-0.177)	(-0.325)	(-0.399)	(-0.043)	(1.186)	(0.855)	(-0.001)	(-1.248)	(-1.398)	(1.132)	(2.132)**	(0.760)	(0.998)
(DUMMY)	-0.008	-0.012	-0.005	0.049	0.010	-0.009	0.010	-0.400	-0.002	-0.022	0.002	0.011	0.048
	(-0.607)	(-1.149)	(-0.378)	(1.084)	(0.534)	(-0.716)	(0.678)	(-2.539)**	(-0.120)	(-2.104)**	(0.233)	(1.924)*	(2.958)***
DF	156	123	156	156	112	156	156	170	156	156	156	112	35
R^2-adjusted	0.968	0.987	0.982	0.895	0.887	0.922	0.938	0.101	0.925	0.947	0.925	0.983	0.987
F test	10.349***	12.478***	10.629***	2.837***	7.957***	11.998***	4.666***	2.295***	11.928***	12.357***	2.696**	2.959***	12.514***

*** Significant at 1 percent level.
** Significant at 5 percent level.
* Significant at 10 percent level.
The F test for testing the null hypothesis that the intercepts are the same across countries.

Notes: IP = import penetration indicator. The ratio of imports to consumption in volume terms; DUMMY = 0 for 1989–94 and 1 for 1995–2000; t values in parentheses.

Table 3.4. Export Performance Model

Dependent variable	Wheat	Coarse grains[a]	Oilseeds	Rice	Refined sugar	Butter	Cheese	Skimmed milk powder	Whole milk powder	Beef	Pork	Poultry
Intercept	1.093	0.460	0.282	0.516	0.154	0.583	-0.212	-0.709	0.361	-0.197	0.183	-0.017
	(4.659)***	(2.978)**	(0.805)	(1.841)*	(0.796)	(2.516)**	(-1.707)*	(-1.642)	(1.081)	(-1.007)	(-1.503)	(-0.252)
$(XP)_{t-i}$	0.057	0.329	0.546	0.294	0.317	0.461	0.635	0.251	0.526	0.493	0.467	0.632
	(0.700)	(4.811)***	(7.818)***	(2.489)**	(4.112)***	(6.847)***	(14.740)***	(3.241)***	(8.382)***	(7.669)***	(6.771)***	(13.411)***
(Q)	0.007	0.041	0.03	-0.045	0.143	0.033	-0.001	-0.024	0.015	0.073	0.117	0.007
	(0.259)	(2.128)**	(2.013)**	(-1.252)	(4.699)***	(1.710)*	(-0.472)	(-0.953)	(0.805)	(3.266)***	(4.407)***	(0.555)
(PW)	-0.049	-0.063	-0.084	0.054	-0.020	-0.113	-0.03	0.076	-0.001	0.020	0.021	0.012
	(-1.645)	(-3.335)***	(-1.765)*	(1.223)	(-0.747)	(-2.378)**	(-1.136)	(-0.85)	(-0.143)	(-0.657)	(1.327)	(1.134)
(POP)	-0.593	-0.399	0.115	-0.219	-0.261	-0.543	0.228	0.861	-0.25	0.161	-0.243	0.055
	(-2.712)***	(-2.699)**	(0.352)	(-0.819)	(-1.325)	(-2.364)**	(1.922)*	(2.034)**	(-0.773)	(0.824)	(-1.795)*	(0.765)
(GDCP)	-0.001	-0.004	-0.011	-0.005	0.021	-0.021	0.008	-0.009	0.005	0.005	-0.051	0.003
	(-0.108)	(-0.628)	(-0.737)	(-0.041)	(2.380)**	(-1.912)*	(1.418)	(-0.472)	(0.313)	(0.681)	(-1.270)	(0.870)
$(GDCP)^2$	0.000	0.000	0.001	-0.007	-0.001	0.001	0.000	0.001	0.000	-0.001	0.009	0.000
	(-0.520)	(0.087)	(0.775)	(-0.167)	(-2.502)**	(1.580)	(-1.092)	(0.633)	(-0.433)	(-0.418)	(0.698)	(-0.794)
(REER)	-0.022	0.0175	-0.169	0.100	-0.009	0.052	-0.004	0.000	0.041	-0.010	-0.031	-0.015
	(-0.563)	(0.692)	(-2.916)***	(0.442)	(-0.244)	(1.287)	(-0.181)	(-0.001)	(0.688)	(-0.362)	(-1.593)	(-1.394)
(PNPC)	0.002	-0.009	-0.018	0.009	0.002	0.000	0.004	-0.007	-0.026	-0.002	0.011	0.002
	(0.117)	(-1.561)	(-1.551)	(0.873)	(0.338)	(-0.010)	(0.493)	(-0.299)	(-1.337)	(-0.165)	(0.864)	(0.674)
(DUMMY)	0.034	0.018	0.013	0.006	0.002	0.029	0.0106	-0.059	0.000	-0.011	0.023	0.005
	(2.382)***	(1.811)*	(0.605)	(0.352)	(0.196)	(1.671)*	(1.191)	(-1.946)*	(0.003)	(-0.923)	(3.232)***	(1.202)
DF	145	170	134	57	123	156	156	156	156	156	145	156
R^2-adjusted	0.952	0.921	0.806	0.989	0.951	0.943	0.98	0.9	0.933	0.973	0.923	0.958
F test	9.131***	12.997***	3.040***	7.196***	9.284***	5.096***	3.260***	5.627***	4.284***	4.994***	4.811***	3.720***

*** Significant at 1 percent level.
** Significant at 5 percent level.
* Significant at 10 percent level.
The F test for testing the null hypothesis that the intercepts are the same across countries.
Notes: XP = export performance indicator. The ratio of exports to production in volume terms; DUMMY = 0 for 1989–94 and 1 for 1995–2000; *t* values in parentheses.
a. The errors component model was used estimated by the Fuller and Battesse method.

signs. A small estimate of $1 - \lambda$, the coefficient of the lagged dependent variable, implies a large λ, which would imply that the trade openness measure would adjust rapidly to changing economic conditions. Our estimates of $1 - \lambda$ in tables 3.3 and 3.4 suggest that imports adjust to economic conditions more rapidly than exports.

Second, on the import side, the AoA dummy variable is statistically significant for skimmed milk powder (SMP), beef, poultry, and sheep meat. The SMP and beef dummies have the expected sign (positive). On the export side, the AoA dummy variable is statistically significant for wheat, coarse grains, butter, skimmed milk powder, and pork. The wheat, coarse grains, butter, and pork dummies have the expected sign (that is, positive); the skimmed milk powder dummy does not have the expected sign. Third, in most cases, the coefficients of the policy variables (CNPC in the import penetration model and PNPC in the export performance model) are not statistically significant. An exception is the equation for import penetration of pork: the CNPC coefficient is significant, but of the wrong sign (its sign is expected to be negative). The coefficient of the PNPC variable in the export performance model is expected to be positive.

Overall, these results hint that for several commodities, the AoA did not have a significant impact on either increasing agricultural imports to or exports from OECD countries. We would need, however, to compute the total estimated impact of the AoA (that is, the impact of the dummies plus the impact through CNPC or PNPC). For example, in the cheese import penetration model, both the dummy and the CNPC coefficient have the expected signs (they are not statistically significant, though), and we could conclude that the AoA induced increased imports of cheese (if the cheese CNPC declined in the relevant period). In the sheep meat import penetration model, the dummy has the expected sign (and it is statistically significant), but the CNPC coefficient does not have the expected sign; thus, in this case, it is not clear whether the AoA induced increased imports of sheep meat. We need to compute the total impact.

Weaknesses of the Uruguay Round Agreement on Agriculture

Market Access

Disciplines on market access were significant accomplishments of the AoA, although its shortcomings are also obvious. In many instances, tariff bindings are at very high rates and offer limited market access opportunities.[9] The tariffication process allowed scope for considerable discretion, resulting in agricultural tariff bindings being sometimes far above actual protection rates.[10] Consequently, agricultural tariffs remain high and in addition there is substantial disparity among countries and across commodities. In contrast to manufacturing tariffs, many of which are now of the order of 5 to 10 percent, agricultural tariffs are, on average, 62 percent, with tariff peaks of over 500 percent (Gibson et al. 2001). Average commodity tariffs range from 50 to 91 percent, with the highest tariffs set for tobacco, meats, dairy, and sugar and sweeteners. The high tariffs currently existing in the agricultural sector restrict trade.

Another important aspect of tariff profiles that emerged from the AoA is that tariff rates vary over a wide range. Triple-digit tariffs are in place alongside zero tariffs. Increases in tariff dispersion can intensify the distortion effects of tariffs. Empirical evidence suggests that dispersion of tariffs as measured by domestic and international "spikes" increased for most OECD countries in 1996 relative to 1993 (OECD 2001a). Available evidence also suggests that tariffs tend to increase with the level of processing (tariff escalation[11]), although the extent of escalation differs greatly across countries. Moreover, agricultural bindings are not always transparent. Transparency and comparability of agricultural tariffs is impaired by the use of non–*ad valorem* tariffs such as specific or mixed tariffs. Twenty-five WTO members, from both developing and industrial countries, have non–*ad valorem* bindings on more than 50 percent of their agricultural tariff lines.

In OECD countries, tariff protection is very high in many sectors, including dairy (116 percent), grains (78 percent), livestock (82 percent), and sugar and sweeteners (64 percent). OECD tariffs in other sectors are relatively low. Because tariff spikes for sensitive commodities characterize OECD countries' tariff profiles, there is a large dispersion in their tariffs across commodities. Non-OECD countries tend to have higher average tariffs than OECD countries, although less disparity across commodity groups (Gibson et al. 2001). Non-OECD countries use mega-tariffs (more than 100 percent) more than OECD countries. However, particularly for developing countries, the tariffs actually applied may be considerably lower than the bound rates. For example, the 1998 applied rate for Latin American countries of 13 percent is less than one-third of their average final bound rate of 45 percent.

The market access provisions have, paradoxically, caused a proliferation of TRQs in agricultural trade, reflecting the high levels of tariffs prevailing in the agricultural sector. TRQs were introduced to establish minimum access opportunities where there had been no significant imports (less than 5 percent of domestic consumption) before the tariffication process or to maintain current access opportunities where the tariffication would otherwise have reduced market access conditions. TRQs are two-tier tariffs that allow some fraction of domestic consumption requirements to be imported at a low tariff (in-quota), while any imports above the minimum access commitments are charged a much higher (over-quota), and often prohibitive, tariff.

The distribution of TRQs among countries and product groups reflects the incidence of tariffication. More than 80 percent of all TRQs are concentrated in five of the 12 product groups concerned by tariff quotas (WTO 2000). More than one-quarter of all TRQs applies to fruits and vegetables alone; the four other groups most affected by TRQs are meat, cereals, dairy products, and oilseeds. Although TRQs cover only 6 percent of tariff lines, they are prevalent in the sensitive sectors of meats, dairy, sugar, and cereals. Only 37 of the 142 WTO members (September 2001) use TRQs. They are concentrated in a small set of countries and commodities. Three countries, Norway (17 percent), Poland (8 percent) and Iceland (7 percent), account for one-third of all TRQs and three commodity groups, fruits and vegetables (26 percent), meat (18 percent), and cereals (16 percent), for 60 percent of all TRQs (Appendix table A.3).[12] All OECD countries, except Turkey, have tariff quota commitments shown in their Schedules with a total of around 700 individual tariff quota commitments. The provision that allowed TRQs to replace former quantitative restrictions was critical to bringing the UR to a successful conclusion.

Although not as economically efficient as tariffs, TRQs are, in general, less trade distorting than are nontariff barriers. It can be argued that TRQs increase market access, since, in contrast to import quotas, there is no explicit ceiling on imports under this system. However, TRQs are second-best policy instruments because they retain many of the characteristics of nontariff barriers that might impede market access. Countries are not obliged to import quantities corresponding to the TRQs, and the "fill rate" of many of TRQs has been low. Between 1995 and 2000, on average, TRQs in OECD countries have been only two-thirds filled (figure 3.2). Moreover, the fill rate of tariff quotas has steadily decreased over time. The simple average fill rate for the OECD countries as a whole declined from 66 percent in 1995 to 59 percent in 1999 (Appendix table A.4).[13]

Tariff quotas may not be filled for various reasons. One reason could be that economic conditions, including deficient import demand and changing competitiveness in the importing country, have changed since the reference period. A second reason might be that the method by which TRQs are administered can also influence trade and the likelihood of being filled. Most licensing systems lead to the establishment of vested interests and built-in rigidities. In fact, the degree of TRQ utilization varies among methods of quota allocation (OECD 2001a). The precise method of administration of TRQ could operate as a second-tier level of protection over and above that provided through the tariffs. Further, TRQs are often allocated totally or partially to specific supplying countries under preferential agreements, thereby limiting market access by other countries.

Figure 3.2 Tariff Quota Fill Rates in OECD Countries (Simple Average), 1995–99

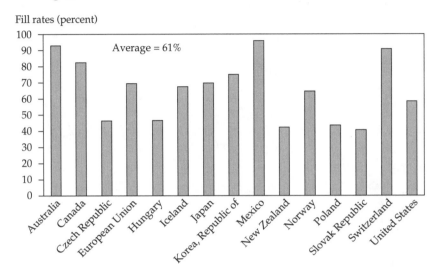

Frequency Distribution of Fill Rates

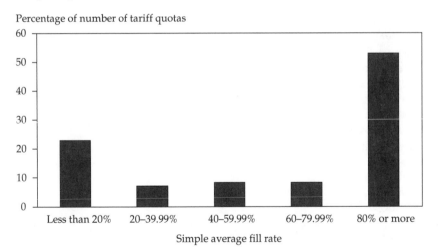

Another important possibility could be that the levels at which the in- and over-quota tariff rates are set too high. The difference between the in-quota and the over-quota tariffs is often so large as to prohibit any trade at the higher rate. If the over-quota tariff is high and the volume of imports within the tariff quotas remains restricted, then the tariff quota will exhibit many of the most market-distorting aspects of a nontariff barrier. Over-quota tariff rates for most commodities in many countries are at triple-digit levels. The average over-quota tariff for 25 countries out of 40 is higher than 62 percent (Gibson et al. 2001). Seven OECD countries have average over-quota final bound tariffs of more than 130 percent (table 3.5).

Table 3.5. Agricultural Tariffs
(percent)

Country	Tariffs (all lines)	In-quota tariff (TRQ lines)	Over-quota tariff (TRQ lines)	TRQ lines as a share of total
OECD				
Australia	4	10	25	2
Canada	23	3	139	22
Czech Republic	12	28	48	14
European Union	30	17	78	28
Hungary	29	26	40	50
Iceland	113	49	181	57
Japan	58	22	422	21
Korea, Republic of	66	19	314	25
Mexico	43	48	148	13
New Zealand	7	0	7	1
Norway	142	262	203	55
Poland	48	31	59	85
Slovak Rep.	13	30	42	21
Switzerland	120	75	210	42
United States	12	10	52	24
Non-OECD				
Argentina	35			
Brazil	37	7	42	1
Colombia	87	132	137	38
Israel	75	79	151	6
Morocco	65	148	115	20
Tunisia	110	26	109	17
Malaysia	25	106	248	10
India	114			
Indonesia	48	65	179	1
Pakistan	101			
Thailand	35	27	91	12

Note: Tariffs are bound most-favored nation (MFN) rates based on final URAoA implementation.
Source: Gibson et al. (2001).

In general, in-quota tariffs are less than 50 percent, but a few very high tariffs raise the simple average. Thus, the high in-quota and over-quota tariffs significantly impede agricultural trade. These results provide support to the argument that the establishment of tariff quotas could hamper market access and trade flows. Nevertheless, it should be pointed out that the fundamental issue is not the existence of TRQs per se, but rather the predominance of many very high tariffs (Tangermann 2001).

Domestic Support

The discipline on domestic support commitments, although deemed to be a major achievement, proved to be the least binding in most OECD countries. Of the current 142 WTO members (as of September 2001), 30 have total AMS reduction commitments. Domestic support is highly concentrated in a few OECD countries, with the European Union, Japan, and the United States accounting for 90 percent of total domestic support (that is, AMS, blue box, green box, *de minimis*, and special and differential treatment) for the OECD area as a whole. Based on information for the period 1995–98, the four years for which sufficient data are available, the evolution of total domestic support shows a downward trend. The value of support subject to reduction commitments in OECD countries declined significantly in the first four years of AoA implementation. The average value of the 1995–98 current total AMS for the OECD, US$100 billion, is equal to about 60 percent of the AMS level in the 1986–88 base period for these countries.[14]

Total AMS reduction commitments have generally not been binding, as current total AMS has been kept far below commitment levels (table 3.6). On average, current total AMS as a percentage of the AMS commitment level for the OECD was 56 percent in the 1995–98 period. Most countries have fulfilled their support reduction commitments by a large margin. The AMS commitments are close to becoming a binding constraint for only four OECD countries.

Although domestic support from policies with the greatest potential to affect production and trade has decreased since the AoA base period, a number of factors potentially limit the effectiveness of the AoA in trade protection.

First, the base period for support reductions is not representative of average support because it was a period of extremely high support for many commodities and countries. Moreover, many countries have availed themselves of a "credit" by adopting the 1986 level of AMS as the base period level for a commodity in cases where it exceeded the average level for the 1986–88 period. The effect, in many cases, is to significantly exaggerate the final bound level relative to what it would have been had the

Table 3.6. Ranges of Notified Current Total AMS Levels in OECD Countries, 1995–99

			Current total AMS as a percentage of total AMS commitment levels			
Year	*0–10 percent*	*11–49 percent*	*50–69 percent*	*70–89 percent*	*90–100 percent*	*>100 percent*
1995	Czech Rep., Mexico, New Zealand, Poland	Australia, Canada, United States	European Union, Hungary[a]	Iceland, Japan, Norway, Switzerland	Rep. of Korea	
1996	Mexico, New Zealand, Poland	Australia, Canada, Czech Rep., United States	European Union	Iceland, Japan, Norway, Switzerland	Rep. of Korea	
1997	Canada, Czech Rep., New Zealand, Poland	Australia, Mexico, United States	European Union	Iceland, Japan, Norway, Switzerland	Rep. of Korea	
1998	Czech Rep., New Zealand, Poland	Australia, Canada, Japan, Mexico	United States	European Union, Rep. of Korea,[b] Iceland,[b] Norway Switzerland Rep. of Korea		Iceland[c]
1999	New Zealand	Czech Rep.		Rep. of Korea	Norway	

Note: Data for 1998 and 1999 are incomplete.
a. *De minimis.*
b. With inflation adjustment.
c. Without inflation adjustment.
Source: OECD (2001b); author's calculations based on country notifications to WTO.

reduction commitment been applied to the 1986–88 average. In addition, inclusion of support in the base period that was subsequently exempted from reduction as blue box support overstates the initial AMS, thereby making it easier for countries that claim blue box exemptions to fulfill their commitments. Further, countries are not prevented from introducing new trade-distorting support measures as long as annual bound levels are not exceeded.[15]

Second, a relatively large set of domestic subsidies, covering a broad range of measures, is exempted from the reduction commitments, some of which are not trade and production neutral. In the OECD as a whole, almost 60 percent of domestic agricultural support in OECD countries is excluded from the domestic reduction commitments (figure 3.3). During the implementation period, the composition of some OECD countries' domestic support has changed. Reduction of total current AMS was simultaneously accompanied by an increase in exempt support, particularly in green box support. The largest increases in green box expenditures were recorded in the European Union, Japan, and the United States. On average, green box support in OECD countries doubled between 1986 and 1988 and 1995 and 1998. Over the 1995–98 implementation period, green box support was higher than AMS support.

The constraints on domestic support appear to have contributed to the reinstrumentation of domestic support away from the most trade-restrictive measures toward the less trade-restrictive ones. However, many exempt support measures, while less trade-distorting than price or output- and input-based supports, still have production and trade effects by reducing risk and keeping resources in agriculture. The total amount of the payment as well as the detailed design and duration of a program are critical factors for determining the impact of policies on production and trade. Several blue box and green box measures in WTO classification are included in the OECD PSE calculation and some of them as payments based on outputs (OECD 2001a). Blue box programs are considered to be less trade distorting and more transparent than price support measures. Nevertheless, these payments require farmers to produce in order to be eligible for the payment. Payments may be directly dependent on production so long the volume does not exceed 85 percent of production in the base period or based on fixed area and yields. Moreover, the level of support associated with these measures is very significant. For the European Union, for example, payments in the blue were on average US$25 billion or 23 percent of total domestic support over the 1995–98 period.[16]

Green box policies are assumed to have the smallest effects on production and trade. In fact, the fundamental criterion for green box exemptions is that they have "no, or at most, minimal" effects on trade and also "shall not have the effect of providing price support to producers." Thus,

Figure 3.3 Composition of Domestic Support, 1995–98

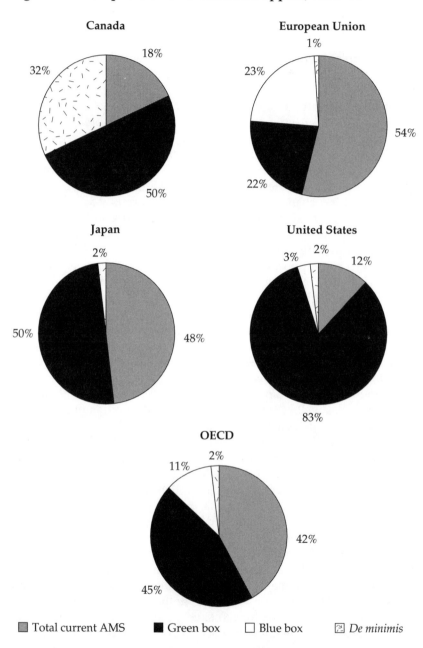

Source: WTO notifications and author's calculations.

changes in the mix of domestic policies away from reliance on AMS policies and toward more green box policies might lead to expectations of a reduction in production and trade distortions. However, the question of whether all payments reported in the green box have no, or at most minimal, trade and production effects requires further investigation. The eligibility criteria of the AoA for green box measures do not always ensure that no or minimal distortions to production and trade result. Although it is virtually impossible to design income support policies that do not have some effects on resource allocation through income, wealth, and risk effects, there is considerable scope for strengthening the disciplines to ensure that the exempt policies are minimally trade distorting. There is a need for designing more rigorous operational criteria for exemption from reduction commitments. The AoA provisions establishing criteria for green box policies focus attention on the way in which policies are implemented, but do not limit the amount of the subsidy. In addition, the interpretation of what is a "minimal" trade or production effect is not specified.

Third, the application of the *de minimis* provision has led to an exclusion of measures that are potentially highly distorting. The *de minimis* provisions are applied on both a product-specific and sector-wide basis. This creates the potential for the continued support of commodity production at high levels. In OECD countries, the *de minimis* provision includes product-specific support as well as non-product-specific support, particularly input subsidies. In Hungary, current total AMS is nil because all product-specific and non-product-specific support are *de minimis,* while in Canada *de minimis* support accounted for 30 percent of total support. In Canada, out of the 22 product categories with product-specific, nonexempt direct payments, 20 products are exempt under the *de minimis* provision, as was the non-product-specific AMS.

Fourth, the AMS is not an indicator in itself of production and trade distortions; that is, (a) the total AMS reduction commitments are sector-wide and not on product-specific AMS. This provides governments the chance to reduce support for some products while leaving support for others unchanged or even raised. A cursory look at countries' notifications shows that some of them have increased their support to certain specific products. In Iceland, for example, the current total AMS has declined by some 27 percent between the base period and 1997, while support to milk in nominal terms increased by 240 percent. (b) The market price support component of the AMS is based on the domestic administered support price and a fixed external reference price. The domestic administered support price may be a poor proxy for the domestic market price, while the fixed external reference price does not represent the actual border price, which brings into question the measure of price support as defined by the AoA. (c) The exclusion of price support in cases where no administered price exists provides wide flexibility to governments in choosing policy instruments.[17] (d) The AMS only includes support provided through domestic measures and does not capture distortions arising from trade measures that are excluded from the AMS provisions (for example, tariffs and export subsidies). Despite the reduction in the current total AMS, the level of agricultural support as measured by the PSE remains quite high, and the gap between the OECD PSE and the AMS is increasing over time (Appendix table A.5). Finally, the AoA does not provide specific criteria for determining a country's development status.

Export Subsidies

Export subsidies may take a wide variety of implicit or explicit forms, including direct export subsidies, export credits, state trading, and food aid. The proliferation of export subsidies in the years leading to the UR was one of the key issues addressed in the agricultural negotiations. Of the WTO's 142 members (in September 2001), 25 have scheduled export subsidy reduction commitments (Appendix table A.6). The main reduction commitments affect OECD countries, particularly the European Union, which is the major user, accounting for 90 percent of actual export subsidies notified to the WTO for the 1995–98 period (figure 3.4).[18]

The export subsidy discipline of the AoA proved to be the most binding of the three disciplines. The total amount of subsidized exports has been curtailed, and the number of products that were actually subsidized during the implementation period was much smaller than the number permitted to receive subsidies under the AoA.[19]

Figure 3.4 Notified Subsidized Exports in OECD Countries, 1995–98
(percent)

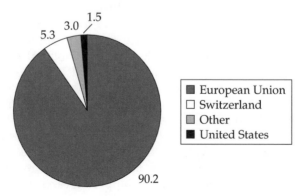

However, export subsidies are allowed to continue, and a number of policies with the potential to affect export competition—such as STEs, abuse of international food aid, officially supported export credits on agriculture, export restrictions, and revenue pooling arrangements—were excluded from the discipline. Further, in some cases, the rate of export subsidy remained high and there was a large degree of disparity among commodities. In addition, the provision to carry over unused export subsidies and to cumulate them with their annual commitments in subsequent years weakened the discipline when it did risk becoming binding.[20] Moreover, even if the use of export subsidies has been limited, then their potential impact is still significant for products such as wheat or some dairy products, and existing commitments would still allow a large share of world exports to be affected.

Conclusion

The AoA marked a historic point in the reform of the agricultural trade system. One of the main achievements of the AoA has been the development and implementation of a framework to address barriers and distortions to trade in three major policy domains (market access, domestic support, and export subsidies). New and operationally effective rules have been established, and quantitative constraints have been agreed upon for all three pillars. In addition, the AoA has provided an overall framework for the reinstrumentation of agricultural support toward less trade-distorting policies. Moreover, the AoA has provided the basis for further negotiations.

The experience to date from the AoA implementation period shows that agricultural policy reform has not been significant. Although the immediate trade impact specific to the implementation of the AoA in OECD countries is difficult to identify and distinguish from the impact of other events, the preliminary empirical evidence presented suggests that the overall effects have been moderate. Reductions in support and protection were limited largely because of weaknesses of many of the specific features of the AoA. Without underrating the achievement of the AoA in bringing agriculture into the mainstream of multilateral trading rules and securing some reform, limited progress has been made over the past six years in reducing agricultural protection and market insulation.

The ongoing WTO negotiations on agriculture, which commenced in March 2000, provide an important opportunity for deepening the process of agricultural reform and trade liberalization. The perceived areas of ineffectiveness in the AoA identify areas for progress in the next agreement. On market access, negotiations should be more straightforward than in the past as tariffication has already made the level of border protection more transparent. A major question for the current round is what process could be adopted to reduce agricultural tariffs that remain in many cases at a very high level. Related questions concern dispersion of tariff rates and the weighting system to be used for further tariff reductions. Several techniques could be used, each having specific economic features. On TRQs, if their elimination is not feasible, market access can be expanded by reducing their restrictiveness by either increasing import quotas, reducing over-quota tariffs, eliminating in-quota tariffs, or a combination of the three. In this case, more efficient methods of quota allocation could expand market access through increased fill rates of tariff quotas. Nevertheless, a proper assessment of the impact of each of the factors that could potentially affect TRQ fill rates is a difficult task and has not yet been seriously undertaken.

On domestic support, a significant reduction of trade distortions would require careful scrutiny of the following issues: addressing the various weaknesses of the AMS discipline identified in this chapter, including its sectorwide nature; better defining and strengthening the eligibility criteria for exempt policies to ensure that only the least trade-distorting programs are included; the role of the peace clause; and the role of special and differential treatment for developing countries.

Disciplines on export subsidies have been more effective than the other two disciplines. Further reduction in trade distortions could be achieved by strengthening the AoA export subsidy provisions. Nevertheless, several issues need to be addressed. In particular, the coverage of export subsidies would have to be broadened to embrace all those policies that have the potential to distort export competition. These include some aspects of parastatal trade agencies, revenue pooling arrangements, international food aid, export credits, export taxes, and export restraints. Moreover, the rules concerning "unused" export subsidy allowances and the definition of export subsidies, and in particular the issue of "cross-subsidization" among markets, merit re-examination and should be tightened.

There are a number of other potentially important issues for the next round of WTO negotiations, including environmental sustainability, rural development, structural changes in the agro-food sector, food security, food safety, food quality, and animal welfare. In addition to the more traditional issues addressed under the three pillars of market access, domestic support, and export subsidies, these "nontrade" concerns provide important challenges for the international policy agenda. The challenge is to define the characteristics of appropriate policies to accommodate nontrade concerns in ways that are targeted, transparent, and implemented in a minimally trade-distorting way. The Program of Work of the OECD Agriculture Directorate has a number of ongoing projects with the overall objective of defining such policies.

Table A.1. OECD: Producer Subsidy Equivalent by Commodity

Commodity	1986–90	1990–94	1995–2000	1997	1998	1999	2000
Wheat							
US$ (millions)	16,666	18,653	16,014	13,769	18,413	19,659	16,304
Euro (millions)	14,757	15,173	14,406	12,150	16,463	18,450	17,692
Percentage PSE	41	42	34	30	40	45	40
Producer NPC	1.54	1.46	1.1	1.04	1.19	1.24	1.11
Producer NAC	1.75	1.73	1.55	1.42	1.67	1.83	1.66
Maize							
US$ (millions)	11,212	9,972	9,312	7,003	10,880	12,960	13,359
Euro (millions)	10,011	8,091	8,605	6,180	9,728	12,163	14,496
Percentage PSE	35	28	24	18	29	34	34
Producer NPC	1.25	1.19	1.09	1.04	1.11	1.17	1.15
Producer NAC	1.55	1.39	1.33	1.22	1.40	1.51	1.51
Other grains							
US$ (millions)	10,159	10,659	9,544	8,859	11,166	10,033	7,505
Euro (millions)	9,004	8,681	8,442	7,817	9,983	9,416	8,144
Percentage PSE	46	49	43	38	53	51	41
Producer NPC	1.79	1.72	1.22	1.12	1.41	1.35	1.12
Producer NAC	1.93	1.98	1.78	1.60	2.11	2.03	1.69
Rice							
US$ (millions)	27,181	29,790	29,765	27,225	22,333	27,466	29,335
Euro (millions)	24,039	24,265	26,272	24,023	19,968	25,777	31,831
Percentage PSE	79	80	78	73	74	79	82
Producer NPC	4.63	4.68	4.36	3.47	3.64	4.50	5.43
Producer NAC	4.92	4.97	4.6	3.65	3.86	4.78	5.69
Oilseeds							
US$ (millions)	5,761	4,727	4,086	2,666	4,281	5,919	6,198
Euro (millions)	5,063	3,806	3,782	2,352	3,828	5,555	6,725
Percentage PSE	27	21	16	10	17	23	25

(Table continues on the following page.)

Table A.1. (continued)

Commodity	1986–90	1990–94	1995–2000	1997	1998	1999	2000
Producer NPC	1.29	1.14	1.08	1.02	1.07	1.17	1.18
Producer NAC	1.37	1.28	1.2	1.11	1.20	1.31	1.33
Sugar (refined equivalent)							
US$ (millions)	5,476	6,743	5,986	5,694	6,848	7,560	5,788
Euro (millions)	4,852	5,483	5,385	5,024	6,123	7,095	6,280
Percentage PSE	48	50	47	43	51	61	50
Producer NPC	2.08	1.98	1.98	1.77	2.10	2.69	2.04
Producer NAC	1.98	2.01	1.92	1.74	2.04	2.53	1.99
Milk							
US$ (millions)	47,275	53,185	44,844	42,060	50,443	45,333	39,125
Euro (millions)	41,693	43,214	39,787	37,114	45,101	42,545	42,454
Percentage PSE	56	57	50	47	56	52	48
Producer NPC	2.53	2.39	1.92	1.83	2.21	2.00	1.85
Producer NAC	2.33	2.34	1.99	1.89	2.26	2.07	1.92
Beef and veal							
US$ (millions)	24,175	28,293	28,754	30,760	28,896	29,902	25,425
Euro (millions)	21,354	22,957	25,555	27,143	25,836	28,063	27,589
Percentage PSE	32	33	35	37	37	37	32
Producer NPC	1.41	1.4	1.32	1.34	1.36	1.36	1.31
Producer NAC	1.47	1.49	1.53	1.59	1.59	1.58	1.48
Sheep meat							
US$ (millions)	5,113	5,728	4,821	4,079	4,443	4,733	3,489
Euro (millions)	4,475	4,643	4,207	3,599	3,973	4,442	3,786
Percentage PSE	56	53	45	37	45	47	40
Producer NPC	1.86	1.56	1.25	1.15	1.26	1.26	1.13
Producer NAC	2.28	2.15	1.83	1.60	1.83	1.99	1.67

Wool							
US$ (millions)	315	398	173	186	137	138	125
Euro (millions)	273	322	151	164	122	130	135
Percentage PSE	7	13	8	7	8	7	6
Producer NPC	1.01	1.04	1.02	1.02	1.03	1.02	1.02
Producer NAC	1.08	1.15	1.08	1.08	1.08	1.08	1.07
Pork							
US$ (millions)	7,556	9,735	9,885	7,250	7,058	13,284	10,251
Euro (millions)	6,579	7,969	8,827	6,397	6,310	12,467	11,124
Percentage PSE	15	18	20	12	16	32	22
Producer NPC	1.22	1.25	1.22	1.08	1.16	1.46	1.25
Producer NAC	1.18	1.22	1.25	1.14	1.18	1.46	1.29
Poultry							
US$ (millions)	4,282	4,759	4,745	4,058	3,059	4,905	6,819
Euro (millions)	3,718	3,871	4,299	3,581	2,735	4,603	7,399
Percentage PSE	16	15	13	11	8	13	18
Producer NPC	1.25	1.21	1.13	1.09	1.07	1.14	1.19
Producer NAC	1.19	1.18	1.15	1.12	1.09	1.15	1.23
Eggs							
US$ (millions)	2,388	2,406	2,069	1,829	1,961	1,874	1,388
Euro (millions)	2,115	1,956	1,798	1,614	1,753	1,759	1,506
Percentage PSE	15	13	11	10	12	11	9
Producer NPC	1.19	1.16	1.11	1.08	1.12	1.11	1.07
Producer NAC	1.17	1.16	1.13	1.11	1.13	1.13	1.09
All commodities—total							
US$ (millions)	240,392	279,542	253,684	227,140	253,661	273,552	245,487
Euro (millions)	211,903	227,315	225,937	200,428	226,798	256,729	266,378
Percentage PSE	37	37	33	29	34	37	34
Producer NPC	1.54	1.51	1.36	1.29	1.38	1.44	1.38
Producer NAC	1.59	1.59	1.49	1.41	1.51	1.58	1.52

Notes: US$ = U.S. dollar equivalents; PSE = producer subsidy equivalents; NPC = nominal protection coefficient; NAC = nominal assistance coefficient.

Source: OECD, PSE/CSE database.

Table A.2. Composition of Producer Subsidy Equivalent

(percent)

Country	1986–88	1989–94	1995–2000
Canada			
Market price support and output payments	66	67	62
Payments on area/animals, historical entitlements, and income	17	17	28
Payments on inputs	16	14	10
Miscellaneous payments	2	1	0
European Union			
Market price support and output payments	91	81	64
Payments on area/animals, historical entitlements, and income	3	10	26
Payments on inputs	6	8	11
Miscellaneous payments	0	0	0
Japan			
Market price support and output payments	93	94	94
Payments on area/animals, historical entitlements, and income	0	0	0
Payments on inputs	7	6	6
Miscellaneous payments	0	0	0
Korea, Republic of			
Market price support and output payments	99	96	95
Payments on area/animals, historical entitlements, and income	0	2	1
Payments on inputs	1	2	4
Miscellaneous payments	0	0	0
Norway			
Market price support and output payments	70	67	58
Payments on area/animals, historical entitlements, and income	9	12	11

Payments on inputs	21	21	31
Miscellaneous payments	0	0	0
Poland			
Market price support and output payments	15	−5	78
Payments on area/animals, historical entitlements, and income	25	13	0
Payments on inputs	59	92	21
Miscellaneous payments	0	0	0
Switzerland			
Market price support and output payments	83	79	65
Payments on area/animals, historical entitlements, and income	6	12	24
Payments on inputs	8	6	8
Miscellaneous payments	3	3	3
Turkey			
Market price support and output payments	65	71	67
Payments on area/animals, historical entitlements, and income	0	0	0
Payments on inputs	35	29	33
Miscellaneous payments	0	0	0
United States			
Market price support and output payments	53	54	53
Payments on area/animals, historical entitlements, and income	29	22	24
Payments on inputs	18	24	23
Miscellaneous payments	0	0	0
OECD			
Market price support and output payments	82	81	72
Payments on area/animals, historical entitlements, and income	8	8	17
Payments on inputs	10	11	12
Miscellaneous payments	0	0	0

Source: OECD, PSE/CSE database 2001.

Table A.3. Who Has Tariff-Rate Quotas?

OECD members	No. of tariff quotas	Non-OECD members	No. of tariff quotas	Non-OECD members	No. of tariff quotas
Australia	2	Barbados	36	Philippines	14
Canada	21	Brazil	2	Romania	12
Czech Republic	24	Bulgaria	73	Slovenia	20
European Union	87	Colombia	67	South Africa	53
Hungary	70	Costa Rica	27	Thailand	23
Iceland	90	Ecuador	14	Tunisia	13
Japan	20	El Salvador	11	Venezuela	61
Korea, Republic of	67	Guatemala	22		
Mexico	11	Indonesia	2		
New Zealand	3	Israel	12		
Norway	232	Latvia	4		
Poland	109	Malaysia	19		
Slovak Republic	24	Morocco	16		
Switzerland	28	Nicaragua	9		
United States	54	Panama	19		
Total OECD	842	Total non-OECD			529

Source: WTO (2000), Background Paper by the Secretariat, G/AG/NG/S/7.

Table A.4. Tariff-Rate Quotas by OECD Member

OECD members	Number of quota lines						Fill rates					
	1995	1996	1997	1998	1999	2000	1995	1996	1997	1998	1999	2000
Australia	2	2	2	2	2	2	99	98	90	91	89	92
Canada	21	21	20	20			78	85	82	85		
Czech Republic	24	24	24	24	24		44	50	47	45	46	
European Union	53	80	85	42	42	41	76	72	71	66	68	64
Hungary	66	68	67	67	65	59	55	52	45	43	41	45
Iceland	88	87	87				65	67	70			
Japan	18	18	18	18	18		69	72	70	67	71	
Korea, Republic of	67	67	67	64			78	76	76	70		
Mexico	11	3	3	3	3		80	100	100	100	100	
New Zealand	3	3	3	3	3		62	40	33	27	50	
Norway	224	222	221	221	221		68	64	62	65	64	
Poland	10	13	15	14	19	20	47	52	57	41	31	34
Slovak Republic	24	24	24	24	24	24	37	47	46	43	44	27
Switzerland	28	27	27	27			92	92	89	90		
United States	47	52	53	53	40		45	53	55	66	73	
OECD[a]	686	711	716	582	461	146	66	65	64	63	59	46

a. Average fill rate has been calculated from the number of notified quota lines.
Source: Author's calculations based on country notifications to WTO.

Table A.5. Evolution of Aggregate Measurement of Support and Producer Subsidy Equivalent
(US$ billion)

Country	1986–88			1995			1996			1997			1998	
	AMS (1)	PSE (2)	(1)/(2) (%)	AMS (1)	PSE (2)	(1)/(2) (%)	AMS (1)	PSE (2)	(1)/(2) (%)	AMS (1)	PSE (2)	(1)/(2) (%)	AMS (1)	PSE (2)
Australia	0.4	1.3	35	0.1	1.6	7	0.1	1.6	7	0.1	1.6	6	0.1	1.3
Canada	4.1	5.6	72	0.6	4.0	14	0.5	3.6	12	0.4	3.1	12	—	3.4
Czech Republic	1.2	4.6	26	0.0	0.6	8	0.1	0.6	10	0.0	0.4	9	0.0	0.8
European Union	80.7	94.6	85	65.4	123.2	53	64.7	113.9	57	56.9	100.7	57	52.2	110.3
Hungary	0.9	3.0	29	0.2	0.8	21	—	0.6	—	—	0.4	—	—	1.0
Iceland	0.2	0.2	106	0.2	0.1	131	0.2	0.1	129	0.1	0.1	117	0.3	0.2
Japan	33.8	53.4	63	37.3	78.4	48	30.6	62.4	49	26.2	50.5	52	5.9	50.1
Korea, Republic of	2.1	12.2	17	2.7	26.7	10	2.4	25.1	10	2.0	20.9	10	1.1	12.5
Mexico	9.6	−0.2	570	0.5	0.8	60	0.3	1.8	16	1.1	5.0	21	1.3	4.0
New Zealand	0.2	0.4	44	0.0	0.1	0	0.0	0.1	0	0.0	0.1	0	0.0	0.1
Norway	2.1	2.6	80	1.5	2.9	54	1.6	2.8	58	1.5	2.7	56	1.4	2.6
Poland	4.2	1.5	105	0.3	3.3	8	0.2	4.4	5	0.3	3.5	8	0.3	3.4
Switzerland	3.4	5.1	67	3.6	6.3	57	3.0	5.7	52	2.4	4.9	48	2.3	5.0
United States	23.9	41.9	57	6.2	22.8	27	5.9	29.6	20	6.2	30.5	20	10.4	48.9
Total	166.7	226.3	72	118.5	271.6	42	109.6	252.5	43	97.3	224.3	43	75.3	243.7

— Not available.

Notes: Mexico=1991 US dollars.

Source: OECD PSE Database; author's calculations.

Table A.6. Who Can Subsidize Exports?

OECD members	No. of products	Non-OECD members	No. of products
Australia	5	Brazil	16
Canada	11	Bulgaria	44
Czech Republic	16	Colombia	18
European Union	20	Cyprus	9
Hungary	16	Indonesia	1
Iceland	2	Israel	6
Japan	0	Panama	1
Korea, Republic of	0	Romania	13
Mexico	5	South Africa	62
New Zealand	1	Uruguay	3
Norway	1	Venezuela	72
Poland	17		
Slovak Republic	17		
Switzerland	5		
Turkey	44		
United States	13		
Total OECD	183	Total non-OECD	245

Source: WTO (2000), Background Paper by the Secretariat, G/AG/NG/S/5.

Notes

1. The GATT 1947 allowed countries to use export subsidies on agricultural primary products, whereas the use of export subsidies by developed countries on industrial products was prohibited.

2. Tariffication affected around 14 percent of OECD agricultural trade.

3. In addition to the exemption from disciplines for green and blue box policies, and de minimis exemption, developing countries also received "special and differential" exemptions for certain input and investment subsidies.

4. The before and after approach is popular, particularly in the literature of the effects of International Monetary Fund (IMF) and World Bank structural adjustments programs.

5. The most common of these measures is the trade openness of a country measured as the ratio of exports plus imports over GDP. Other outcome-based measures are obtained from deviations between actual trade and predicted trade; the predicted values are estimated according to some kind of theoretical framework, such as the Hecksher-Ohlin model or the gravity equations. Therefore, these types of indicators are subject to arbitrariness in the choice of relevant trade theory.

6. Bureau, Fulponi, and Salvatici (2000) use the TRI to measure the welfare effects of UR AoA tariff reductions for the European Union and the United States.

7. The impact of post-UR liberalization on trade has also been assessed using computable general equilibrium (CGE) models (see, for example, Hertel 2000).

8. The RER is a chain-linked index with base period 1995. It uses a system of weights based on a double-weighting principle, which, for each country, takes into account relative market shares held by its competitors on the common markets, including the home market, as well as the importance of these markets for the country in question. (A discussion of this methodology is given in Durand, Simon, and Webb 1992.)

9. The special agricultural safeguard that was put in place to help countries to cope with the effect of tariffication has been moderately used in the last six years. Of the 38 WTO members who have reserved the right to apply the special agricultural safeguard, only 8 have used it.

10. Available evidence suggests that the gap between bound and applied tariff rates on agricultural products is important in many developing countries, while in developed countries it is not significant.

11. Tariff escalation occurs when the tariff applied on a product "chain" rises as goods undergo further processing, resulting in a higher effective protection for the processing industry than otherwise would be the case.

12. However, 90 percent of TRQs in Norway and Iceland are administered as "applied tariffs" (that is, unlimited imports are allowed at the in-quota tariff or below). In fact, almost one-half of all TRQs notified to the WTO are administered on the basis of "applied tariffs," that is, unlimited imports are allowed at or below the in-quota tariff (that is, the quota is not enforced).

13. Caution should be exercised in interpreting the TRQ fill-rate results as all quotas, irrespective of size, are assigned the same weight. No allowance is made for differences in size between individual TRQs. A small TRQ is given the same weight as a large TRQ with the same level of fill. Likewise, the simple average does not differentiate between low-value and high-value products.

14. Certain support measures that are included in the base total AMS were excluded from the current total AMS during the implementation period because they met the blue box criteria. Blue box payments, however, were excluded from the AMS in the implementation period even though they were included in the base year. Including them would result in a smaller decline in domestic support. Combining the 1995, 1996, 1997, and 1998 blue box payments with the reported AMS increases the 1995, 1996, 1997, and 1998 support level to 77 percent of the base.

15. The AoA only requires that countries notify new or modified policies claimed as green.

16. As of September 2001, the following countries/regions have notified blue box programs to WTO: European Union, Iceland, Norway, and the Slovak Republic in 1996 and 1997; United States in 1995; and Japan in 1998.

17. For example, it opens up the possibility to alleviate the domestic support commitment by eliminating the administered price for those products that had an administered price in the base period, but continuing to provide the same level of support through border measures, provided that the specific commitments on tariff bindings and export subsidy are not breached.

18. The European Union is also the largest user of export subsidies of the 25 countries that have export subsidy commitments in their WTO schedules.

19. The start of the implementation period coincided with a marked rise in world market prices for cereals that allowed countries to fulfill their reduction commitments easily. In fact, the European Union even imposed a tax on cereal exports during that period.

20. Over the first four years of the implementation, six OECD countries have availed themselves of the roll-over provision (OECD 2001a).

References

Anderson, J., and P. Neary. 1996. "A New Approach to Evaluating Trade Policy." *Review of Economic Studies* 63(1):107–25.

Baldwin, R. 1989. "Measuring Non-Tariff Trade Policies." NBER Working Paper 2978. National Bureau of Economic Research, Cambridge, Mass.

Bureau, J. C., L. Fulponi, and L. Salvatici. 2000. "Comparing EU and US Trade Liberalisation under the Uruguay Round Agreement on Agriculture." *European Review of Agricultural Economics* 27(3):259–80.

Durand, M., J. Simon, and C. Webb. 1992. "OECD's Indicators of International Trade and Competitiveness." OECD Economics Department Working Papers 120. Paris.

Faini, R., J. De Melo, A. Senhadji, and J. Stanton. 1991. "Growth-Oriented Adjustment Programs: A Statistical Analysis." *World Development* 19(8):957–67.

Gibson, P., J. Wainio, D. Whitley, and M. Bohman. 2001. "Profiles of Tariffs in Global Agricultural Markets." ERS Report 796. ERS/USDA, Washington, D.C.

Goldstein M., and P. Montiel. 1986. "Evaluating Fund Stabilization Programs with Multicountry Data: Some Methodological Pitfalls." Staff Paper 2. IMF, Washington, D.C.

Greenway, D., W. Morgan, and P. Wright. 1998. "Trade Reform, Adjustment and Growth: What Does the Evidence Tell Us?" *The Economic Journal* 108:1547–61.

Josling, T., and S. Tangermann. 1999. "Implementation of the WTO Agreement on Agriculture and Developments for the Next Round of Negotiations." *European Review of Agricultural Economics* 26(3):371–88.

Harrison, A. 1991. "Openness and Growth." *Journal of Development Economics* 12: 59–73.

Hertel, T. 2000. "Potential Gains from Reducing Trade Barriers in Manufacturing, Services and Agriculture." Federal Reserve Bank of St. Louis. July/August.

OECD (Organisation for Economic Co-operation and Development). 2001a. *The Uruguay Round Agreement on Agriculture: An Evaluation of its Implementation in OECD Countries.* Paris.

———. 2001b. *Agricultural Policies in OECD Countries: Monitoring and Evaluation 2001.* Paris.

Pritchett, L. 1996. "Measuring Outward Orientation in LDCs: Can It Be Done?" *Journal of Development Economics* 49:307–55.

Tangermann, S. 2001. "Has the Uruguay Round Agreement on Agriculture Worked Well?" Paper presented at the International Agricultural Trade Research Consortium Meeting, May 18, 2001. Washington, D.C.

WTO (World Trade Organization). 2000. "Tariff and Other Quotas." Background Paper by the WTO Secretariat. Geneva.

4

Lessons from Implementation of the Uruguay Round Agreement on Agriculture: A Cairns Group Perspective

Simon Tucker

The Cairns Group is composed of 18 agricultural exporting countries, which between them account for one-third of the world's agricultural trade. Of that group, 15 are developing countries and the other three are industrialized countries. The members are Argentina, Australia, Bolivia, Brazil, Canada, Chile, Colombia, Costa Rica, Fiji, Guatemala, Indonesia, Malaysia, New Zealand, Paraguay, the Philippines, South Africa, Thailand, and Uruguay.

The overall objective of the Cairns Group is the creation of a fair and market-oriented international agricultural trading system. This means trade in agricultural products is to be treated in the same manner as trade in nonagricultural industrial goods. It also means stopping the damage done to efficient producers everywhere, particularly in developing countries, by the farm policies in some Organisation for Economic Co-operation and Development (OECD) countries. Our concern is to ensure that these objectives are achieved as soon as possible.

Specifically, in the context of the agricultural negotiations currently (2002) under way in Geneva, the Cairns Group has already tabled specific proposals calling for (a) the elimination and prohibition of all forms of export subsidies for all agricultural products, (b) deep cuts in trade-distorting domestic support, and (c) significant increases across the board in market access for agricultural products.

The Uruguay Round

The Uruguay Round (UR) and the UR Agreement on Agriculture (AoA) were significant for agricultural trade in that for the first time, trade in agricultural products was brought into the global trading system. In broad terms, the AoA accomplished three basic points:

- "Tariffication" conversion of a range of protection (quotas, voluntary restraints, minimum prices, and so forth) into bound tariffs. Some of these are shamefully high, but are now at least transparent and comparable. Given that tariffication led to tariffs for some products in the United States, the European Union, and Japan in the hundreds of percent, the 36 percent average cut guaranteed by the UR for 1996–2000 was a small step. The UR also agreed on a minimum access requirement of 3 percent of the market rising to a total of 5 percent of the market (note that tariffs can still be applied on the minimum access volumes).
- Disciplines on export subsidies on agricultural products: Commitment to no new subsidies, with some programmed cuts.
- Classification of domestic support into boxes of "green," "blue," and "amber," depending whether they are trade distorting, with some reduction commitments.

The key point is that while this integration itself was a significant strategic development, the actual gains in agricultural liberalization as a result of the UR were only modest. It was a step in the right direction, but only a step.

For example, tariffs on agricultural products currently average over 40 percent, compared to around 4 percent for industrial products. To quote some specific examples cited recently in *The Washington Post*: in the United States, there is a 244 percent tariff on sugar and 174 percent tariff on peanuts; in the European Union, the tariff on beef is 213 percent; and wheat in Japan faces a 353 percent tariff. On domestic support, James Wolfensohn, President of the World Bank, noted that the richest nations spend more than US$300 billion a year in subsidizing their farmers. This figure is roughly equivalent to the entire gross domestic product (GDP) of Sub-Saharan Africa. Trade in agricultural products still remains very heavily distorted across the globe.

The fact that the UR had only really made an initial start on agricultural liberalization was recognized through the creation of the "built-in agenda" as a specific outcome of the round. This guaranteed the commencement of further agriculture negotiations at least one year before the end of the implementation period. These new mandated negotiations commenced in 2000. The first lesson from the UR therefore was that there is still much work to be done on agricultural trade liberalization. It is difficult to judge the full effects of agricultural trade liberalization until the process is complete.

Impact of Ongoing Protectionism

Government support in the form of subsidization and trade restrictions on agriculture in developed countries continues to have a number of consequences. Subsidization and trade restrictions reduce agricultural imports, lower domestic consumption of certain products, increase production of certain commodities, and increase subsidized exports. This combination of factors acts to depress world market prices for many agricultural products. That is, industrialized country market interventions therefore have effects on developing countries (or countries with low levels of support) through reducing access to markets, increasing competition on world markets from subsidized products, and depressing and destabilizing world market prices.

Obviously, these negative effects are most apparent and most direct on agricultural exporting countries, but they are not confined to that group and also have negative effects on countries with the potential to develop agricultural export industries.

At the Cairns Group Farm Leaders Meeting in Banff, Alberta, Canada, in 2000, the impact of protectionism was discussed, and the following points were raised: (a) National treasuries or ministries of finance face the problem of finding tax revenue to fund direct payments to farmers. (b) Consumers end up paying a large proportion of the cost of farm support through higher food costs. (c) Importers of agricultural products and foodstuffs (with more and higher trade barriers), as well as agribusinesses, are not able to increase their market share, handle more volume, or increase profits. (d) Developing countries with preferential access agreements are limiting more investment, technology transfer, and higher growth than if they had freer trade. This lack of growth will also inhibit the ability of those countries to repay loans to international lending agencies. (e) Exporters bear the burden of import barriers because sales of their products are related to the ability of countries to earn foreign exchange. (f) Developing countries are less able to protect the environment and more likely to exploit natural resources, at a cost to the environment, when there is less economic prosperity because of trade barriers. (g) Protected farmers could benefit from agricultural reform by becoming more efficient. (h) Special and differential or preferential treatment risks locking a country into wasteful uses of its resources, cause politicians to preserve the status quo, and deflect attention from the country's own protective policies and other domestic weaknesses.

The Case for Agricultural Liberalization as a Development Tool

For most developing and least developed countries, including those that are net food importers, agriculture is the foundation of economic development and growth. Income generated by the export of agricultural produce is often the major source of employment, revenue, or foreign exchange, but neither countries that export nor those that produce primarily for domestic consumption can compete with unfair competition from export subsidies. This means that protection and subsidization has allowed some industrialized countries to take advantage of expanding agricultural trade opportunities at the expense of developing and least developed countries with a comparative strength in agriculture.

If trade in agriculture were liberalized, then developing countries are more likely to produce and export greater quantities of agricultural products. This means their incomes would rise as they realize more fully any comparative advantage. A recent econometric study by the Australian Bureau of Agricultural and Resource Economics has estimated that a further 50 percent reduction in agricultural support levels alone would amount to a US$53 billion a year increase in global GDP by 2010. The dynamic gains from greater competition, innovation, improved management, and greater technological advances are estimated to be worth at least this much again.

Obviously, direct gains are going to be the greatest in those countries that either produce or could produce and export those products that are most heavily subsidized or protected in developed countries. For net food importing countries, it is often assumed that there is nothing to gain from actions that can be expected to result in an increase in the world market price of agricultural commodities. In contemplating that argument, it is useful to consider why those countries are net food importers and the extent to which this is caused by the agriculture protectionism and subsidization described above. However, even for net food importers there are advantages from market price stability, as well as fewer direct benefits as aggregate world incomes increase and the demand for goods and services—in which they may have a realizable comparative advantage—increase also. Obviously, those indirect gains will be more quickly realized if trade reforms are expedited across as broad a range as possible.

Of course, lowering barriers to trade, while important, is not by itself a total panacea for economic development and poverty eradication. Governance, human and institutional capacity building, health, education, and basic infrastructure development are all important. But having fair trade rules will play a key part of any solution through their positive impact on productivity and economic growth.

The Way Forward

Agriculture nearly scuttled the UR and will clearly continue to be a difficult issue in the World Trade Organization (WTO). But the lessons from the UR experience, the implementation of the AoA, and the start of the current mandated negotiations on agriculture are clear: Do not oversell the degree of liberalization achieved by the UR. There is still a long way to go. The UR set some useful rules and structures, and now it is time to liberalize.

Wealthy, developed countries need to recognize that their ongoing use of agriculture support and protection is directly curtailing the development of poorer countries. At a minimum, the agriculture component of new WTO negotiations must address the most egregious distortions by export subsidies and agree to a time frame for their total elimination; that market-distorting domestic support must be significantly reduced; that deep cuts in tariffs, with mega-tariffs, must be cut by more than average; and that tariff-rate quotas must be expanded.

If rich countries want to pursue "nontrade concerns" sometimes referred to as multifunctional objectives, then this must be done in ways that do not distort prices or production volumes. Similarly, food safety and food security and environment issues must be pursued in a manner clearly nonprotectionist and nontrade distorting. Finally, special and differential recognition of the differences between developed and developing countries must be recognized as an important value in the trade negotiating process.

5

Agriculture and Other Items on the World Trade Organization Agenda

Hugh Corbet

Liberalizing agricultural trade has been postponed for half a century. In a number of industrialized countries, most notably in the European Union and Japan, there are agricultural interests that would like it postponed even further. So what has to be done to get around that resistance and set about, in a new round of multilateral trade negotiations, the substantial liberalization of trade and (trade-related) investment in agricultural products?

In the eighth and last conducted round under the General Agreement on Tariffs and Trade (GATT), an agreement was finally reached on bringing agriculture into the multilateral trade-liberalizing process. Alas, because it took so long to achieve the agreement, there was little time and patience left to negotiate much actual liberalization. So the agreement had to conclude with a commitment to resume the negotiations in 1999–2000. These negotiations were initiated in March 2000, along with negotiations on trade in services, this time under the aegis of the newly established World Trade Organization (WTO). The launch of the first WTO round was supposed to take place in Seattle at the end of 1999, but did not happen. Another attempt to launch the round was begun at the start of 2001 in the hope that an expanded program of negotiations, or at least a more concerted preparatory process, could be launched later in the year at the WTO's fourth Ministerial Conference, to be held in Doha, Qatar.[1]

Years of Malign Neglect

The long history of procrastination over agriculture's place in the rules-based multilateral trading system may convey a sense of why agricultural expectations are running high today. It also helps to explain why there are farming interests, on the periphery of the world economy, saying, in effect, that they're mad and they're not going to take it anymore.

After World War II, following the autarkic and discriminatory excesses of the 1930s, intergovernmental attention focused on restoring orderly conditions in international commerce, first by establishing a framework of internationally agreed rules, the GATT, and then by conducting rounds of multilateral negotiations to reduce border protection. But agriculture was treated as a special case, as an exception to the rules, in particular the GATT rules prohibiting import quotas and export subsidies.[2] As a result, the trade liberalization achieved in the first six GATT rounds, in the 20 years 1947–67, was limited for all intents and purposes to industrial products traded among industrialized countries. No impact was made on the rising trend of protection accorded to agricultural producers in the industrialized economies. Nor was anything done about liberalizing trade in products of export interest to developing countries, which soon saw the GATT system as a rich man's club.

Growth of Agricultural Protection

Extensive consultations on the GATT's Haberler Report on trade in primary products (Haberler 1958),[3] led to agricultural trade liberalization becoming a priority of the United States. But things took a turn for the worse in the 1960s, during the Kennedy Round negotiations of 1964–67, when the European Community gave priority to securing agreement on its common agricultural policy (CAP). The CAP consolidated, in a still more protectionist direction, the import-levy systems of farm support in the European Community's original member countries.[4]

As the sixth GATT round proceeded, it became evident that to liberalize agricultural trade, not only border restrictions but also the farm support policies behind them had to be tackled. Indeed, toward the end of the Kennedy Round negotiations, the European Community proposed a *montan de soutien* approach, but how seriously was never clear and, anyway, the U.S. administration's five-year negotiating authority (under the Trade Expansion Act of 1962) was running out.

Consequently, one of the goals of the Tokyo Round negotiations of 1973–79 was the reform of farm support policies, but it was vehemently resisted by the European Community's leaders, who insisted that "the CAP is the cement that holds the Community together" and pressed instead for market-sharing international commodity agreements. In 1978, with Washington's new "fast track" negotiating authority (under the Trade Act of 1974) running out, the United States and the European Community took agriculture off the negotiating table. They were at odds over agriculture as much as ever, saw no chance of reaching an agreement in the time remaining, and did not want to put at risk a trade-liberalizing "package" on industrial products, which included plurilateral codes of conduct on nontariff measures.

In the end the Tokyo Round agreements were modest. They did not halt the increasing resort to subsidies, "voluntary" export restraints, and other nontariff measures, instruments of the "new protectionism." As adherence to the GATT rules continued to deteriorate and the multilateral trading system neared collapse,[5] a "crisis" GATT Ministerial Conference was held in November 1982, but it also failed to get to grips with the mounting protectionist threat.

Uruguay Round Breakthrough

Thus began the four-year tussle in Geneva to launch a new GATT round in which agriculture was the make-or-break issue. Just before the GATT Ministerial Conference in Punta del Este, Uruguay, in September 1986 convened to finalize the negotiating agenda, an ad hoc coalition of smaller agricultural exporting countries suddenly appeared on the scene. The Cairns Group, led by Australia, became the third force in the ensuing Uruguay Round (UR) negotiations, holding the feet of the European Community and the United States to the fire until an agreement was reached on how to set about liberalizing agricultural trade. The complicated agreement was aimed at decoupling price supports from production decisions. Essentially, it laid out a framework for "substantial progressive reductions" in domestic support, export subsidies, and border protection. And to facilitate this framework, the agreement provided for the "tariffication" of nontariff barriers.

Critical Role of the Cairns Group

Clayton Yeutter was a central figure in the UR negotiations, first as the U.S. Trade Representative in President Ronald Reagan's cabinet and then as Secretary of Agriculture in President G. H. W. Bush's cabinet. He later wrote of the critical role that the Cairns Group played, first, in helping to launch the negotiations; second, in maintaining their focus on agriculture; and third, in pushing the major trading powers toward the WTO's UR Agreement on Agriculture (AoA):

> Time and again the Cairns Group provided a balance wheel in the ideological differences over agriculture between the European Community and the United States, nearly always leading to a constructive outcome. Throughout the negotiations the Cairns Group was catalytic, sensible, and pragmatic (Yeutter 1998, pp. 65–67).[6]

On the formation of the Cairns Group, Dr. Yeutter noted that "Australia [had] learnt a lesson from its bitter experiences in previous GATT discussions where it had too few allies and its proposals, however reasonable and well argued, were quickly isolated and ignored." Prior to the Punta del Este ministerial, the smaller agricultural exporting countries had held "talks about talks," and Australia was joined by Argentina, Brazil, Canada, Chile, Columbia, Fiji, Hungary, Indonesia, Malaysia, New Zealand, Paraguay, the Philippines, Thailand, and Uruguay. Together they accounted for roughly a quarter of world trade in agricultural products.

What Now on Agriculture?

The Washington Post (2001), in an editorial, said that for at least two decades U.S. administrations have been telling developing countries to export their way out of poverty. Instead of relying on aid, these countries should earn foreign exchange by selling to industrialized countries. Rather than building "white elephant" steel mills and aiming for industrial self-sufficiency, the developing countries should focus on producing goods for which they have a natural advantage, such as agricultural products. The editorial said:

> Even as the United States and other rich countries have preached this gospel, they have simultaneously made it hard to follow. Tariffs and quotas have barred developing countries' farm products from rich markets. And farm subsidies in rich countries have kept world production higher and prices lower than they otherwise would be, hobbling poor countries' chances of making a living from agriculture. The main reason for this scandal lies in politics. Even though agriculture accounts for less than 3 percent of the U.S. work force and only 5 percent or so in Japan and the European Union, farmers everywhere are adept at holding politicians hostage.

In gearing up again to tackle the politics of farm support policies, the Cairns Group countries have allies in the United States even if, all too often, they seem to lose sight of the forest for the trees. Although American support for liberalizing agricultural trade has been positive since the 1960s, it ebbs and flows as the farm lobby is diverted from time to time by other factors, such as buoyant commodity markets or an occasional budget surplus to chase.

It is so far, so good in the current WTO negotiations on agriculture. The preparatory stage was completed in March 2001, with 44 proposals submitted by 125 countries, and the second stage is proceeding.[7] In the first two years, however, the negotiations were chiefly a matter of wait and see until a new U.S. administration was fully in position and the prospects for a WTO round were clearer.

Another Confrontation Impending

When the first attempt to launch a new round came to grief at the WTO Ministerial Conference in Seattle, Washington, in December 1999, public opinion was left to believe that somehow 50,000 protesters were responsible for the failure. In fact, the failure was several weeks before in Geneva, where, after more than a year of preparatory talks, delegations could not get close to agreement on an agenda for a new round that had been approved in principle at the previous WTO Ministerial Conference, held in Geneva in May 1998. The protesters in Seattle simply turned the failure into the fiasco that was seen on front pages, television sets, and computer monitors all around the world.

The failure reflected the inability of the Quadrilateral Group to provide clear leadership, which can mostly be put down to the possible mistakes of the Clinton Administration in the United States. On agricultural trade the European Union and Japan were the foot-draggers. Political leaders in both did nothing to prepare public opinion for the fundamental changes in farm support policies that will be necessary for substantial progress to be made in liberalizing agricultural trade.

In subsequently pressing for the launch of a WTO round, the European Union and Japan have stressed the need for the agenda to address the interests of all WTO member countries, meaning the developing ones. They do not put the same emphasis on the interests of agricultural exporting countries. On agriculture much is made, instead, of its "multifunctionality," which the European Commission says is deserving of "special trade treatment."[8]

Positions of Key Players

It is evident that whenever the first WTO round is launched, there is going to be another major confrontation over agriculture between, on the one hand, the Cairns Group and the United States and, on the other hand, the European Union, Japan, and Korea, along with Norway and Switzerland. The alignments are much as they were in the UR negotiations. Perhaps the net food importing developing countries are getting into the picture more, and environmentalists, consumer groups, and food safety advocates are more involved in the public debate in North America and Western Europe.

The Cairns Group remains the most vocal in the WTO system, arguing for the reform of farm support policies and the trade restrictions required to sustain them. Since 1995, the coalition has been joined by Bolivia, Costa Rica, Guatemala, and South Africa, but Hungary has left in preparation for joining the European Union.

Farm support policies amount to the export of adjustment, making for the unemployment of resources in low-cost agricultural economies, and so the Cairns Group countries are looking for "a fair and market-oriented agricultural trading system," the stated objective of the AoA.[9] They have called for the elimination of "all forms of export subsidies, for all agricultural products," and for a substantial reduction in farm support provided through production subsidies and border protection.

Given that fundamental reform is an ongoing process, Article 20 of the AoA expects negotiations to *take into account* nontrade concerns, among other things. But the European Union has been pressing for "nontrade concerns" (that is, nonreform issues) to be treated on a par with reform issues. For that reason, lest attention be diverted from the AoA's principal objective, the Cairns Group is insisting on an elaborated mandate for the agriculture negotiations. Achieving fundamental CAP reform requires agreement among the 15 European Union member countries and cannot be done in a quiet way. Until there are signs that governments are taking the steps necessary to prepare public opinion in general, and farm opinion in particular, the Cairns Group and the United States cannot be satisfied with statements of good intentions.[10]

The position of the United States has not been very different from the Cairns Group's. In the current WTO negotiations, the U.S. administration has called for sweeping reform: the elimination of export subsidies and the substantial reduction of domestic support, plus significantly improved market access. This last element of market access can be expected to improve as subsidies are phased out.

Since the last GATT round, resistance to liberalizing agricultural trade in the European Union, Japan, Korea, and other industrial countries has been as great as ever. Their governments have been on the defensive, seeking to limit the degree of liberalization and putting great stress on the pursuit of environmental sustainability, food security, rural development, and food safety in ways, they say, that would not distort production and trade.

These are goals arising from the multifunctionality of agricultural production, but they are old goals in a new guise. The following points are well established in the literature: (a) The goals of multifunctionality can be achieved by more direct policy instruments that are less costly and avoid waste, but they are not pursued because they are too transparent, which is to say too easily subjected to public scrutiny. Farm lobbies in industrialized countries do not favor the limelight. (b) Agricultural subsidies induce intensive farming methods, employing fertilizers and pesticides extensively, adversely affecting the environment, and leading to the pollution of rivers, the clearing of bushes, and the erosion of topsoil. (c) Agricultural protection is not necessary to ensure food safety, for it reduces global flexibility in production, putting food safety at greater risk.[11]

Alleviating poverty in developing countries is one of the great issues of the day, and so some European and Japanese leaders have been calling for a "development round." After all, launching a WTO round requires developing country support, but when it comes to agriculture, they are in difficulty. Fifteen of the Cairns Group's 18 members are developing countries, and there are the *net food importing developing countries*, such as Egypt, which are similarly disadvantaged by the farm support policies of industrial countries. On the crops they grow most efficiently, their agricultural production and consumption decisions are heavily distorted by the imports from subsidized producers in those countries, which have knock-on effects throughout their fragile economies.[12]

Preparations for a WTO Round

Since liberalizing agricultural trade is seen to be part of a larger trade-liberalizing effort, it is hoped providing scope for tradeoffs,[13] what progress is being made toward launching the first WTO round? In August 2001 the preparations for the WTO Ministerial Conference at Doha on November 9–13 entered the crunch period. It was realized that by the end of September, or not much later, the General Council would have to determine whether it was on course to launch a new round at Doha or was courting another public debacle. This last is what the Director-General, Mike Moore, was aiming to avert when early in the year, as the European Union and Japan renewed the effort to launch a new round, he proposed that the General Council conduct a reality check at the end of July.

Post–Reality Check Situation

In conducting that reality check, it had to be noted that all year there was a huge gap between high-level calls to launch a WTO round, culminating in the Genoa Economic Summit's communiqué,[14] and what was happening at ground level in the preparatory work in Geneva and in capitals on what is necessary to restore momentum in the WTO system. The report for the General Council's informal meeting on July 30–31 alluded to that gap and made for somber reading.[15] The report said, however, that "bridging the substantial gap . . . in a very short time" would not be impossible, provided there was "a strengthening of the political will to find consensus solutions" that can be converted into negotiated outcomes.

In his report for the meeting, prepared in cooperation with the Director-General, the General Council's Chairman, Stuart Harbinson, stressed the need for "a sense of the positive connections and trade-offs among issues and positions." In some cases "our work may be close to the limits of what is possible in terms of building consensus on specific issues *in the absence of convergence on the broader picture"* (emphasis added).

Changes in the WTO System

Until recently, the WTO system was drifting badly, with the United States taking a back seat and the other majors apparently not sure about the directions. Observers repeatedly remarked on the lack of leadership, a factor in the earlier failure of governments to agree on a negotiating agenda, prior to the WTO Ministerial Conference in Seattle. Since then, little has changed, for in the major trading powers, including the United States, political leaders are still not speaking up in support of the rules-based trading system. Sound bites about free trade are hardly enough. At the end of July 2001, then, governments did not appear to be any closer to agreement on a negotiating agenda than they were before the Seattle debacle.

After Seattle there was a hiatus as everybody waited for something to turn up. Only at the start of 2001, as a new U.S. administration took up residence, was the effort to launch a WTO round renewed. Much is expected of the Bush Administration, but settling into office, thinking through a new round, and securing trade negotiating authority all at once was bound to be hard.

At the end of July, the new U.S. administration was not quite in a position, with trade negotiating authority in hand, to provide clear leadership. So consensus building in Geneva was still being held up by uncertainties about the position of the United States, where on key issues, the Bush Administration differed from the previous one, especially over workers' rights and the environment. The need to provide guidance to other governments was complicating the efforts in Congress, on behalf of the Bush Administration, to secure a "clean" negotiating authority, one that has to be free of internationally unacceptable demands if negotiations are to proceed.

Unfortunately, there is a tendency in Washington to discount the multilateral consensus-building process, as if agreement between the European Union and the United States is all that matters. Sure, without agreement among the majors, accounting for two-thirds of the world economy, there can be no progress at the multilateral level. There can be no overlooking, though, how much the new WTO system is different from the old GATT system, before the UR negotiations were concluded.

By contrast to earlier GATT rounds, a new round has to take into account the interests of developing countries, four-fifths of the WTO membership. Today those countries recognize their stake in the WTO system, as they did not in the GATT system, and have to be persuaded that proposals for further change are going to be in their long-term economic interests.

As developing countries got nowhere in the 1970s with their demands for a "new international economic order," they were urged to participate more fully in the GATT system, which became an unstated goal of industrialized countries in the UR negotiations and was substantially achieved. In that eighth and last GATT round, the developing countries made multilateral market-opening commitments for the first time and, having agreed to the negotiations being conducted as a "single undertaking," they have become parties to all the agreements reached, as they did not with the agreements reached in the Tokyo Round negotiations.

Differences among the Key Players

The problems in launching a WTO round derive to a large extent from the failure of the major trading powers to rise to the challenges posed by the WTO system. Indeed, with the United States not out in front, the key players have been at cross purposes: The *European Union* supports a comprehensive round, provided it covers environmental issues and the extension of WTO rules to investment regulations and competition laws. Japan, too, favors a comprehensive round, provided it covers extending WTO rules to investment and competition, as well as antidumping reform.

The *Cairns Group* also favors a comprehensive round. It accepts that the European Union and Japan need to achieve progress on investment regulations and competition laws in return for progress in liberalizing agricultural trade. But it opposes the inclusion of labor and environmental standards on the agenda of a WTO round.

The *Like-Minded Group* of developing countries, which includes India, Pakistan, Malaysia, and Egypt, has been insisting that the "implementation problem" arising from the UR agreements has to be resolved before a WTO round can be launched. Besides opposing labor and environmental standards in trade agreements, the group is against the extension of WTO rules to investment and competition, but it at least supports market access negotiations. Outside interpretations of the group's position vary. It is a bargaining position. It is a rearguard action against the single-undertaking commitment. It is disingenuous because some have not tried to implement agreements.

As for the *United States*, other countries have been waiting to see what sort of negotiating authority President Bush obtains, perhaps mistrustful of the evenly divided Congress. President Clinton insisted on a remit to press for labor and environmental standards in trade agreements, which the Congress effectively denied him in 1994, 1995, 1997, and 1999. He also opposed the inclusion of investment regulations, competition laws, and antidumping reform on the agenda of a WTO round.

The European Union and the United States are aligning their positions. Pascal Lamy, the European Union's Commissioner for Trade, and Robert

Zoellick, the U.S. Trade Representative, issued a joint statement in Washington on July 17, 2001, that was 90 percent rhetoric, aimed at the media and political community. The focus was on nonagricultural trade, but it said nothing new, not even on investment and competition, for the United States had earlier indicated a readiness to support a limited approach. On these it indicated that the European Union and the United States were fully committed to launching a WTO round at Doha, and, with personal careers depending on it, the pressure on other countries was expected to mount.

The statement was silent on agriculture, but the majors probably take the view that at Doha they can convey enough on agriculture, without getting into details, to persuade Cairns Group ministers to go along with a short declaration that the round is launched. Intellectually, they may understand that the developing countries have to be carried along, but with a belief that might is right, they probably reckon those countries can be logrolled.

Impediments to a WTO Round

Securing agreement on a negotiating agenda requires a degree of give and take. In preparing to launch the last GATT round, ministers acknowledged in the end that all proposals had to be included. If some items were found in the course of negotiations not to engage much interest, they would simply fall by the wayside. That is what happened with the U.S. interest in a comprehensive investment agreement.

The impediments to launching a WTO round are not so much over the specific trade issues as over the development of the multilateral trading system per se. In this respect there are three major impediments. One is whether labor standards have a place in the WTO system. Another is dealing with the fundamental implementation problem through trade-related "capacity building." The third is institutional reforms. All are having an adverse effect, both on the conduct of "core business," including the work program, and on public support for the WTO system.

Labor Standards in the WTO System?

U.S. labor leaders and sectional interests have been pushing for a "social clause" in the WTO system. Behind the push is the old pauper-labor argument for protection, popular in America since the 1920s, which said that because of low wages in developing countries, with an abundant supply of cheap labor, industries in industrialized countries should be protected by tariffs that counteract the lower costs of those foreign suppliers.[16] During the Tokyo Round negotiations, the argument was resurrected in "human rights" clothing by President Carter,[17] and during the UR negotiations it was raised by President Clinton. A more recent variant of the argument is characterized as "the race to the bottom." It expresses the fear that the need to compete with imports from developing countries with low wages and standards will reduce wages and standards in industrialized countries.[18]

The issue was raised again by the United States in preparations for the first WTO Ministerial Conference in December 1996. In their concluding declaration, however, ministers renewed the commitment of WTO member countries to adhere to core labor standards, agreed that the International Labour Organisation (ILO) is the competent body to deal with them, affirmed their support for the ILO's work, and noted that the WTO and ILO "will continue their existing collaboration." The ministers rejected the use of labor standards for protectionist purposes and agreed that the comparative advantage of countries, particularly low-wage developing countries, must in no way be put in question. Moreover, they endorsed the view that economic growth and development, fostered by increased trade and further trade liberalization, contribute to the promotion of core labor standards.

At the Seattle Ministerial Conference there was a provisional trans-Atlantic agreement on a working group to examine the "social dimension" of trade liberalization, but it was killed when President Clinton suddenly went public with his support for trade sanctions if countries did not comply with core labor standards. He confirmed the suspicions of many developing countries that U.S. demands on the subject were intended to put new limits on their trade.

Critical to the launch of a WTO round at Doha, then, was a recognition that labor standards, along with sanctions to enforce them, have no place in the multilateral trading system. They are overwhelmingly opposed by WTO member countries. To include in U.S. trade negotiating authority a remit to press for enforceable labor standards in trade agreements would have been a launch breaker. There is no willingness to negotiate with the United States on such terms.

On trade and labor standards, the Organisation for Economic Cooperation and Development (OECD) Ministerial Conference in May 2001 agreed, in its communiqué, that the issues need to be addressed through dialogue, drawing on the expertise of all relevant international institutions, including the WTO. But the nature of the dialogue has not been settled. One possibility was raised at the ILO's board meeting in June when its Director-General, Juan Somavia, proposed the creation of an international commission on "the social dimensions of globalization," carrying a stage further the working party it has had on the subject for four years. The proposal was put down for discussion at the ILO annual meeting in November.

In the United States, the labor unions represent only 13 percent of the work force (9 percent outside the public sector), but they are a significant source of electoral support for the Democratic Party, financially and in getting out the vote. After the UR negotiations, the U.S. Congress declined four times to renew the "fast-track" trade negotiating authority for the administration because President Clinton, in response to the AFL-CIO (The American Federation of Labor and Congress of Industrial Organizations) and special interests, insisted on including in it a requirement to press for labor (and environmental) standards in trade agreements.[19]

Since then, positions on Capitol Hill have not changed. In a speech on August 2, 2001, Representative Richard Gephardt, the Minority Leader in the U.S. House of Representatives, said he is "optimistic Congress can reach a deal on legislation giving the president trade-negotiating authority that makes labor, environmental, and human rights central to U.S. trade agreements."[20]

Neglect of the "Implementation Problem"

Many developing countries have been reticent about a WTO round because of problems they are having in implementing their commitments in the UR agreements. Toward the end of the negotiations, industrial countries talked of technical and financial assistance to help developing countries meet the kind of obligations they were assuming for the first time, but those were nonbinding assurances and nowhere near enough has come of them.

At the second WTO Ministerial Conference, in May 1998, a number of developing countries argued that implementation problems should be addressed as part of the WTO work program. By the Seattle meeting, they were being encouraged to set out the problems, and, after the debacle, the Like-Minded Group took over the issue in the WTO General Council's implementation work program. Failure by the majors to pay attention turned an issue into an impediment.

The documents now list a hundred problems, [21] but the bulk of them, implying the renegotiation of UR agreements, can only be addressed in the context of a WTO round. There is no objection in principle to renegotiations. Many agreements reached in the UR negotiations specifically provide for their review as part of the built-in agenda. But the industrialized countries are not about to enter into piecemeal renegotiations.

On the implementation problem, the debate among WTO member countries has avoided identifying genuine problems and exploring what to do about them, which has degenerated into an argument over sorting out the problems before or during a WTO round. At a technical level, the issues need to be clarified to put them in perspective, so a technical analysis needs to be carried out as soon as possible.

What about the assurances of technical and financial assistance? At its spring meetings in 2000, the World Bank agreed, in response to the UR declaration on "global coherence in policymaking," to promote trade-related capacity building in developing countries. Something similar was agreed at the spring 2001 meetings. But action is needed to make something of that new readiness to leverage trade for development on the one hand and to encourage trade ministers in developing countries to make something of it on the other.

At the Genoa Economic Summit, the leaders said, "Capacity building is essential to integrate developing countries into the trading system, and we are intensifying our efforts in this area, including with international institutions." The next question is, What is being done, not only in the World Bank but also in other institutions, to put *new* resources into those efforts?

Question of Institutional Reforms

The antiglobalization demonstrations in Seattle drew attention to the inability of governments to agree on an agenda for the first WTO round. Observers put the stalemate down to an unwieldy negotiating process, the intransigence of some countries, and lack of leadership by the major trading powers. At the Seattle meeting, much was also made of a lack of transparency and accountability in the WTO system, dissatisfaction with the decisionmaking process, and the exclusion of nongovernmental organizations (NGOs) from the dispute settlement mechanism. Since then, there have been concerns that the WTO's dispute settlement function, although working well, is infringing on its rule-making function and that its informal and formal consultative processes have become "UN-ized."

Eschewing these issues is not making it easier to conduct WTO business or to secure agreement on a WTO round. These kinds of issues cannot be resolved in negotiations. They need to be tackled through the WTO's permanent institutional machinery—its councils, committees, and working groups—and by the membership and Secretariat.

One way would be to move away from each WTO agreement or topic having its own formal proceedings, which would allow the number of meetings, itself a major problem for small delegations, to be greatly reduced and allow many issues to be broached in a more cross-cutting way. Another way would be to dispense with ministerial declarations, which occupy the Secretariat and delegations for 6 months out of every 18 months to two years, are unnecessary and have no status under WTO legal provisions.

Regarding the WTO's decisionmaking processes, the European Commission has proposed returning to something like the Consultative Group of Eighteen, which operated in the GATT system from the mid-1970s to the start of the UR negotiations. Such a representative group may work in some circumstances, but open-ended informal consultations are probably the only way to address specific issues, enabling all member countries to participate in discussions affecting their national interests.

Prospects for a WTO Round?

Nearly all WTO member countries, with India apparently a notable exception,[22] accept that the working hypothesis for the Doha ministerial was the launch of an expanded program of negotiations. There are still huge differences over the scope of a new round. Besides liberalizing trade in agriculture and services, there is a readiness for the agenda to cover industrial products, the focus in previous rounds. There have been proposals to abolish tariffs under 5 percent ("nuisance tariffs") and the usual proposals to reduce tariff "peaks" and tariff "escalation." And recently there have been proposals to eliminate all remaining industrial tariffs in order to get rid of the different rules of origin associated with preferential tariffs in about 150 bilateral or regional trade arrangements. Beyond those three major items, though, there are problems over other proposals for the negotiating agenda where, in the course of six months, there has not been much progress.

Extending the WTO System

Looking ahead, the WTO system has to keep abreast of emerging problems with the continuing integration of the world economy, not only border restrictions and nontariff distortions of international competition but also other impediments within markets to international businesses investing and doing business in them.

On *investment regulations*, no country is arguing for a WTO round to cover the wide range of issues addressed in the OECD attempt to negotiate a Multilateral Agreement on Investment, which was abandoned in 1997. Many investment issues are already covered in WTO agreements, including the General Agreement on Trade in Services, the Agreement on Trade-Related Investment Measures, and the Agreement on Trade-Related Aspects of Intellectual Property Rights. It is argued that, in the interests of systemic coherence, public policy issues having to do with foreign direct investment need to be codified in a WTO agreement.

International competition is often restricted inside countries, as with regulations limiting entry to some industries, such as telecommunications. In some countries, governments have taken insufficient interest in enacting or applying competition laws to prevent private companies restricting competition. No country is arguing for a WTO round to cover all the aspects of *competition laws* that are covered in the United States, the European Union, and other industrial countries. It is argued, as more and more developing countries introduce competition laws, that the issues should be addressed in sequence, beginning with a code on competition standards.

Including investment and competition on the agenda continues to be a problem. The European Union has lowered its "level of ambition" on both, which has brought the United States on board, but it has been saying that the two sets of issues are acceptable. This may seriously underestimate the opposition among developing countries.

On extending the WTO system to *environmental standards*, no one knows what the European Union really wants, let alone what is its bottom line. It might be satisfied if the main issues—the "precautionary principle," eco-labeling, and multilateral environmental agreements—could be addressed in reviews of the WTO agreements on technical barriers to trade and on sanitary and phytosanitary measures. The United States and the Cairns Group remain skeptical about the issue, which is seen as a potential launch breaker, especially when it is linked with agriculture.

Regarding other new issues, *trade facilitation* continues to be unsettled, with many developing countries objecting to more binding rules in this area. Including transparency in *government procurement* is possible, but the European Union is still talking, at least tactically, about adding a "market access" dimension, but that is considered to be a nonstarter.

Coherence of the WTO Escape Clauses

On another vexing subject, as a result of recent findings by dispute settlement panels, the reform of *antidumping laws* is already on the WTO agenda. More countries are introducing antidumping laws, far beyond the four traditional users (Australia, Canada, the European Union, and the United States), and are basing them on Brussels and Washington practices that are heavily criticized.

Many argue that antidumping laws are being misused as selective safeguard measures, which are banned, along with voluntary export restraints, under the Agreement on Safeguards reached in the UR negotiations. It is argued, therefore, that a WTO round should review all escape clause provisions (emergency protection, subsidy countervailing, balance-of-payments, and antidumping actions) in the context of competition policy with a view to achieving coherence among them.

Need for a Positive Outcome

As governments got ready for the last phase of the preparatory work for the Doha Ministerial Conference, the U.S. Congress had not passed trade negotiating authority, which the Republican leadership had hoped could be done before the August recess. That meant the question of enforceable labor standards in the WTO system, which was not featured in the preparatory work, was still out there as a potentially explosive issue, especially if left to the last minute. At a minimum, the European Union and some others were arguing for a reference to what the ILO was doing, with a link to the WTO for further discussion.

There was still a danger of ministers going to Doha with too many issues unsettled, including the implementation problem, which could not be settled without agreement on a broad agenda. After the reality check at the end of July 2001, those close to the preparatory work in Geneva were circumspect, but believed there was still time to get close to agreement on a negotiating agenda.

The majors appeared fully committed to the launch of a WTO round at Doha, but for negotiations to yield worthwhile results there had to be confidence among participants, and as things stood, confidence was seriously lacking among WTO member countries. Besides looking for reassurances on U.S. trade negotiating authority, the developing countries were generally reluctant to embark on negotiations that would lead to their undertaking new commitments that many did not have the administrative capacity to implement.

An inconclusive ministerial meeting in Doha would have been bad enough. Launching a WTO round with a short declaration, by press release as it were, devoid of economic and business content, could have been just as bad and possibly worse. Officials would have returned to Geneva to find that they were no further forward. They would have had to mark time, by embarking on a preparatory stage, while waiting for the decks to be cleared of impediments.

If the launch of a WTO round at Doha continued to look doubtful, then enough time must be left to prepare a fallback position, for the WTO system could not afford a repetition of the Seattle debacle.[23] If ministers could not agree on a negotiating agenda, then they could initiate a serious preparatory process that addressed, among other things, the three major impediments in the way of restoring WTO momentum.

Notes

1. In January 2001 some ministers and officials met informally in Frankfurt (Germany), Davos (Switzerland), and Rome at the invitation of the European Commission and Japan to consider the prospects for resuming efforts to launch a new round. See the *Financial Times*, January 29, 2001.

2. In public discussion, it is often said that the GATT did not cover agriculture, but it was covered from the outset in Article XI, on quantitative restrictions, and in Article XV, on subsidies, and in two other articles.

3. For a review of those consultations, see Fernon (1968, pp. 55–60).

4. For an authoritative analysis of the evolution of the enormous distortions in agricultural trade, see the seminal work of Johnson (1991).

5. On the parlous state of the GATT system in the early 1980s, see Croome (1995, pp. 8–12).

6. Also see Yeutter (1999).

7. For a review of the state of play, see WTO (2001).

8. It was reported that Pascal Lamy, the European Union's Commissioner for Trade, speaking at the London School of Economics, said that "the EU would continue to insist that agriculture was different from other industries and *deserved special trade treatment*.... However that did not mean continuing to maintain artificially high prices, extensive trade protection and export subsidies, but moving to policies based on income support for farmers" (emphasis added). See de Jonquieres (2001).

9. Preamble, GATT (1994).

10. In August 2001 the British Prime Minister, Tony Blair, made statements on the need for the fundamental CAP reform in Latin America, where he could expect to get no argument. It is in the European Union—in Brussels, Munich, and Paris—that the debate has to be conducted.

11. Two other points of interest to industrial countries ought to be made in case they get overlooked as the protectionist farm lobbies try to make "multifunctionality" the issue. One, the chief burden that results from agricultural protection is borne by exporters, especially those in manufacturing and service industries. Two, slow progress by the industrial countries in liberalizing agricultural trade will mean, as mentioned, slow progress in liberalizing trade in services.

12. On this, see the address by Yousef Boutros Ghali, Egypt's Minister of Economy and Foreign Trade, at the Cairns Group meeting in Banff, Alberta, Canada, on October 11, 2000.

13. What that scope might be is hard to tell. The substantial liberalization of agricultural trade has not been a serious possibility in previous rounds.

14. G7 Statement, issued in Genoa, July 20, 2001, paras. 6–9.

15. "Report by the Chairman of the General Council, in cooperation with the Director-General, on the Current State of Preparatory Work," JOB(01)/118, WTO Secretariat, Geneva, July 24, 2001, para. 4.

16. The flaws in the argument are well known, pointed out long ago in Haberler (1936, pp. 251–53).

17. For a critique of the argument, see Lal (1981).

18. On the merits of these fears, see OECD (2000) and also Drezner (2000).

19. President Clinton first sought the remit in the UR implementing legislation in 1994 and again in proposed legislation in 1995 and 1997 that did not come to a vote. After announcing in his State of the Union Address in February 1999 that he would try again, he said on June 12, 1999, during his University of Chicago commencement address, "I want Congress to give me the ability to use trade talks to protect the environment and workers' rights," but again got nowhere.

20. Address to the Carnegie Endowment for International Peace, August 2, 2001, Washington, D.C.

21. "Implementation-Related Issues and Concerns," JOB(01)/4, WTO Secretariat, Geneva, February 20, 2001, a compilation of outstanding issues prepared for the WTO General Council. In June, seven WTO delegations—Argentina, Mo-

rocco, New Zealand, Norway, Switzerland, Thailand, and Uruguay—circulated a paper, "Proposals on Implementation," suggesting how the issues might be addressed before, at, and after the WTO Ministerial Conference in Doha.

22. During the discussion of a new round, India's Minister of Commerce and Industry, Murasoli Maran, said on numerous occasions that the implementation issues has to be cleared first, which has been the main demand of the Like-Minded Group in Geneva.

23. Reuters reported on August 24, 2001, that in an interview in the Finnish business magazine *Talouselama*, Helsinki, the former U.S. Trade Representative, Charlene Barshefsky, said it is "best to have a positive meeting and a continuation of the process than a second failure." The failure to launch a new round at the Seattle Ministerial Conference was because Europe and ultimately the United States were not ready. "The [Seattle] talks did not fail because of the riots. The streets could have been completely quiet and the talks would still have failed. The call for the round was premature."

References

Croome, John. 1995. *Restoring the World Trading System*. Geneva: World Trade Organization.

Drezner, Daniel W. 2000. "Bottom Feeders." *Foreign Policy* 1:73–102.

Fernon, Brian. 1968. *Issues in World Farm Trade: Cooperation or Chaos*. London: Trade Policy Research Centre.

GATT (General Agreement on Tariffs and Trade). 1994. "Agreement on Agriculture." In *The Results of the Uruguay Round of Multilateral Trade Negotiations: The Legal Texts*. Geneva: GATT Secretariat.

Haberler, Gottfried. 1936. *Theory of International Trade*. London: William Hodge.

———. 1958. *Trends in International Trade*. Geneva: GATT Secretariat.

Johnson, D. Gale. 1991. *World Agriculture in Disarray* (2nd ed.). New York: St. Martin's Press.

de Jonquieres, Guy. 2001. "Bush Urged to Back New Trade Round." *Financial Times*, February 2.

Lal, Deepak. 1981. *Resurrection of the Pauper-Labour Argument*. Thames Essay No. 28. London: Trade Policy Research Centre.

OECD (Organisation for Economic Co-operation and Development). 2000. *International Trade and Core Labor Standards*. Paris: OECD Secretariat.

The Washington Post. 2001. Editorial: "The Farm-Subsidy Scandal." January 12.

WTO (World Trade Organization). 2001. "Agriculture Negotiations." Press release. WTO Secretariat, Geneva.

Yeutter, Clayton. 1998. "Bringing Agriculture into the Multilateral Trading System." In Jagdish N. Bhagwati and Mathias Hirsch, eds., *The Uruguay Round and Beyond*. New York: Springer.

———. 1999. "Critical Role of the Cairns Group in Liberalizing Farm Trade." In Andrew Stoeckel and Hugh Corbet, eds., *Reason versus Emotion: Requirements for a Successful WTO Round*. Canberra: Centre for International Economics.

Part II

Evaluating the Benefits of Liberalization to Date for Developing Countries

6

The Role of the World Trade Organization Accession in Economic Reform: A Three-Dimensional View

Craig VanGrasstek

Accession to the World Trade Organization (WTO) or its predecessor, the General Agreement on Tariffs and Trade (GATT), has long been a key step in the economic reform programs of many developing and transitional economies. Joining this international organization can aid a country not only in securing access to global markets but also in integrating its trade commitments with other reform initiatives. The accession process can nevertheless be quite lengthy and difficult, with the existing WTO members setting ever higher standards for the new applicants to meet. The members sometimes approach these negotiations as yet another opportunity to advance issues of interest to them, a fact that can undercut the potential benefits of accession for the aspiring members. The accession process can be seen as almost a reverse form of Special and Differential (S&D) Treatment for developing countries. While the GATT rules negotiated in the 1960s and 1970s provided for various forms of preferential treatment for developing countries, including enhanced access to industrialized countries' markets and less rigorous application of rules and disciplines, the new environment of the WTO is much more demanding. It sometimes obliges them to shoulder burdens that are not shared by other countries that joined in earlier decades.

This chapter reviews the evolving character of the GATT and WTO accessions, as well as the changing approaches taken toward developing and transitional economies in the global trade regime. It does so by examining the shifting emphasis upon three distinct dimensions of the system: the height of global tariff walls and other border measures, the width of country membership in the system, and the depth of issues that fall within its jurisdiction. It is this report's argument that after the major industrialized countries had all joined the GATT, their policies regarding the width of the regime (that is, accession) were largely determined by their priorities along the other two dimensions. Concerns over the height of the tariff wall dominated trade negotiations among the industrialized countries from the 1950s through the 1970s, and depth has been their main concern since the 1980s. Accession was relatively easy when height was the chief concern, and the small markets of the developing countries attracted little attention. Quite the opposite is true today, now that new issues are under debate and the major players miss no opportunity to set a precedent. This desire to set precedents can greatly complicate the accessions of new countries. The demands made in each successive negotiation tend to increase, irrespective of the specific status or conditions of the acceding country.

This is not to say that countries have been frightened away from accession. Quite the contrary: The number of countries that now seek accession appears impervious to the law of supply and demand, with applications rising at least as fast as the increasing costs of admission. What began in 1947 as a contract among 23 countries has grown into an international organization in which 142 countries are members, another 30 are currently negotiating for their accession, and several others are expected to seek accession soon. The only countries of significant economic or demographic size that are neither in the WTO nor actively seeking accession are Iraq, Libya, and the Democratic People's Republic of Korea.[1]

While the WTO is approaching universal membership, its approach toward accession is far different from that of most other international organizations. These institutions generally operate under a principle by which, in the absence of truly egregious problems or especially intractable diplomatic difficulties, all sovereign states have a presumptive right of membership. There may be agreements to sign, dues to pay, and other obligations to meet, but the process of accession is neither burdensome nor lengthy. It will generally involve little or no formal scrutiny of the country's existing laws and policies, and even fewer demands for changes in these laws and policies (at least as an initial condition of membership). Examples of such universalist institutions include the United Nations, the International Labour Organisation, the World Bank, the International Monetary Fund, and the World Health Organization.

By contrast, the WTO operates more like a club to which countries can claim no presumption of membership, and must instead meet whatever standards and demands might be set by the existing members. In this respect it is more akin to the Organisation for Economic Co-operation and Development (OECD). Even the club metaphor may be too gentle from the perspective of acceding countries' diplomats, for whom accession to the WTO can sometimes seem more like the hazing rituals of college fraternities. Perhaps the only international economic body that places higher demands on prospective members is the European Union, which generally requires major realignments of a country's laws, policies, and institutions, and that can take more than a decade to negotiate.

The process of acceding to the WTO is a deliberately one-sided affair, with all of the requests and demands coming from the existing members and the full burden of adjustment falling on the acceding country. The applicant is not entitled to request additional benefits or concessions in excess of those stipulated in the WTO agreements, nor can it seek tariff concessions or services commitments from the members. WTO Article XII and its GATT predecessor (Article XXXIII) offer deliberately spare language that establishes a framework within which accession negotiations are conducted. It provides that "any state or separate customs territory possessing full autonomy in the conduct of its external commercial relations . . . may accede to this Agreement, on terms to be agreed between it and the WTO." The provision does not specify the precise commitments expected from acceding countries, nor does it establish clear standards for which compliance is sought to identify the scope and extent of demands that could be made. The rules are marked by ambiguities that place the entire accession process in a negotiating context. This ambiguity is in some sense positive, insofar as it allows for a degree of flexibility, but—for reasons to be discussed below—the leading members of the institution are much less inclined to employ that flexibility now than they were in decades past.

Put this way, it might be rhetorically asked why countries are willing to subject themselves to such a process. The costs and benefits of acceding to the WTO can be properly understood only if the advantages of membership are viewed in their larger context. It can be somewhat misleading and even disheartening to employ the common terminology of trade negotiators, in which the commitments that countries make are deemed to be "concessions" and hence imply that the country is surrendering something of value. These unfortunate terms seem to cast trade relations in a zero-sum, neo-mercantilist framework in which any one country's gain can come only at another country's loss. The ultimate objective of accession is to enhance a country's competitiveness within a global economy that—notwithstanding the archaic terminology that negotiators employ—offers opportunities for mutually beneficial trade and investment. However, it may be legitimately questioned whether the current approach adequately balances the needs of the regime with the capacities of the acceding countries and whether it encourages or complicates the process of economic reform.

The Evolving Geometry of the GATT and WTO Accessions

The global trading regime's treatment of developing countries and nonmarket economies has changed markedly over the years since World War II, primarily in response to the changing priorities in trade relations

Figure 6.1. The Three Dimensions of the GATT/WTO System

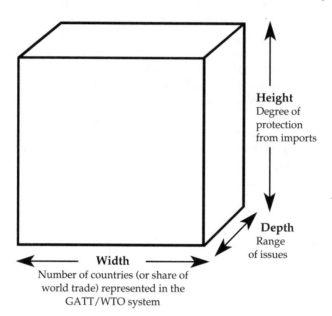

Height
Degree of
protection
from imports

Depth
Range
of issues

Width
Number of countries (or share of
world trade) represented in the
GATT/WTO system

among the industrialized countries. Those changes can be illustrated in geometric form.

As portrayed in figure 6.1 the shape of the WTO regime is like a three-dimensional object whose facets are analogous to the height, depth, and width of a cube. The first of these dimensions is the most traditional. It can be thought of as the tariff wall, although tariffs are not the only type of barrier at issue. The various border measures that countries impose on imports, as well as beyond-the-border measures through which governments intervene in markets, can be portrayed as either high (more restrictive or interventionist) or low (less restrictive or interventionist). The principal aim of most trade agreements is to bring down the height of this wall. The second dimension is the width, which measures the extent of WTO membership. It can be either narrow (many countries remain outside the system) or wide (most or all counties are in). The third dimension—the depth—is defined by the range of issues that fall within the jurisdiction of trade rules. This dimension can be either shallow (trade is defined solely as the cross-border movement of goods) or deep (trade is defined expansively to include a greater range of issues and measures).

Three of these dimensions have changed over the course of the GATT and WTO history. To simplify, the major focus of attention has shifted from the first dimension to the third. Trade policy was once devoted solely to the regulation of border measures, whether unilaterally or through international agreements. The GATT negotiations concentrated primarily on the height of the tariff wall, and the earliest talks made the most dramatic progress toward its reduction. Attention began to turn toward other matters by the mid-1960s, but it was not until the Uruguay Round (UR) (1986–94) that the depth of the system became more important than height to the major players. Both in the early and the late history of the GATT, however, these two dimensions mattered more to the leading countries than did the width of the system. The GATT started with fewer than two dozen countries that nevertheless accounted for the majority of trade in a world recovering from war. The countries inside the system have always been responsible for more trade than countries outside of it, and in most cases the individual applicants have been quite small. This smallness has had very different implications for the treatment of applicants at different periods of the GATT/WTO history.

When Height Mattered Most: Accession and Succession, 1949–79

The illustration in figure 6.2 emphasizes the principal direction of the GATT negotiations in the early years of the regime, when much of the detritus that accumulated in the pre-war years had yet to be removed. Average tariff rates in the years immediately following World War II were much higher than they had been just after World War I, and the most immediate task—in addition to reconstruction and addressing the "dollar

Figure 6.2. The Key Dimension of Height in Early GATT History

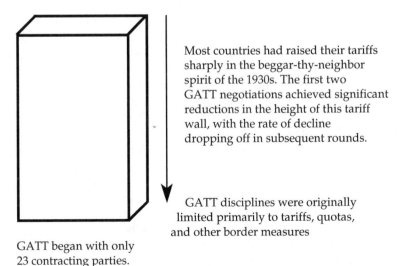

Most countries had raised their tariffs sharply in the beggar-thy-neighbor spirit of the 1930s. The first two GATT negotiations achieved significant reductions in the height of this tariff wall, with the rate of decline dropping off in subsequent rounds.

GATT disciplines were originally limited primarily to tariffs, quotas, and other border measures

GATT began with only 23 contracting parties.

shortage"—was to bring tariffs below confiscatory levels. The GATT was more successful in this enterprise than many feared it would be, and on a percentage basis, the tariff cuts in the first few years were much greater than those achieved in the ensuing decades.

The GATT accessions during those early years were conducted as might be expected in a system dominated by considerations of height: The countries that accounted for larger shares of actual or anticipated trade attracted much greater attention than did the smaller states. This was especially true before the Kennedy Round (1964–67) and the advent of the formula-cut approach to tariff negotiations. When talks were still conducted under the labor-intensive method of request and offer, the rational negotiator in Geneva would be well advised to concentrate on larger and wealthier countries. It was in the interests of the larger original GATT countries such as Canada, France, the United Kingdom, and the United States to set relatively high standards in the accessions of other large countries such as Italy (acceded in 1949), Sweden (1949), West Germany (1951), and Japan (1955). They had much less incentive to bargain hard with smaller acceding countries.

The first set of accession negotiations was conducted in the Annecy Round in 1949, when 10 new countries sought adherence to the GATT. The applicants were obliged in their protocols of accession to accept the rules of the GATT, abide by additional commitments made by contracting parties in the Annecy Round, and negotiate with existing contracting parties to establish their own schedules of concessions. The accessions negotiated in the Annecy Round set two important precedents. In the great majority of the GATT accessions, the applicant's "entry fee" was negotiated concurrently with one of the eight rounds of multilateral trade negotiations conducted under the auspices of the GATT. This eased the domestic politics of accessions for many countries, insofar as their negotiators could seek tariff concessions or other commitments from the existing countries as soon as their own accession negotiations were completed. (That same rule has not applied in the WTO for the simple reason that there has not yet been a round conducted by the new organization.) Furthermore, the concessions made by the Annecy Round applicants were not particularly onerous, involving relatively small numbers of tariff concessions. Most of the accessions through the end of the Tokyo Round (1973–79) followed a similar pattern, and were comparatively easy for smaller applicant countries.

Over the ensuing half-century of GATT experience, the contracting parties developed a fairly regular process for the GATT accessions. The basic outlines of this process remains in effect today; that is, from a procedural standpoint, the only major difference is that a wider array of issues are subject to negotiation in the WTO than was the case in the GATT. The process has both multilateral and bilateral components. The multilateral aspects begin with the formation of a working party, composed of existing GATT contracting parties (now WTO members), to which the applicant country submits a memorandum outlining its trade policy. The working party then examines this memorandum and addresses a series of questions to the applicant. In these communications, the working party acts collectively to negotiate the nontariff aspects of the applicant country's terms of accession. When the working party is satisfied with the arrangements, these are recorded in a protocol and a working party report. Taken together, these two documents lay out the terms under which the country acceded.

 ̄ There are also bilateral tariff negotiations conducted concurrently with the working party's activities. The applicant country also negotiates a schedule of tariff concessions with interested contracting parties; that is, since the advent of the WTO, it has also negotiated schedules of commitments on services and agriculture. Once the talks are concluded, the protocol of accession is opened for signature by the acceding government and the contracting parties. The rules formally provide that a two-thirds majority is required for acceptance, but in actual practice accessions—like virtually all other GATT decisions—came to be conducted on the basis of consensus. This meant that each of the existing members of the club had the ability to blackball any new applicant. This rule effectively blocked the attempted Soviet and Bulgarian accessions to the GATT during the Cold War, and Iranian accession to the WTO is similarly prevented today. In all three cases it was the United States that exercised the veto.

Accession negotiations were relatively painless for most of the countries that joined the GATT through the end of the Tokyo Round in 1979. Indeed, one scholar who reviewed the accessions at the midway point of this period opined that the process was "biased in favor of newcomers" (Curzon 1965, p. 36). Accession soon became an issue only for developing and nonmarket economies, as nearly all industrialized countries had joined the GATT within a decade of its establishment. The only laggard was Switzerland, the GATT host country that finally acceded in 1967. Most negotiations with developing countries during this period were tempered by pragmatism and compromise, in which the major players were accommodating to requests for S&D Treatment. Special terms were also developed for the few nonmarket economies that acceded prior to the end of the Cold War.

The majority of developing countries that joined the GATT did not actually *accede* at all, but rather *succeeded* to GATT status. Many of the countries that gained their independence from colonial powers in the post-war period—which included most of the Caribbean and Africa, as well as parts of Asia—had the option of entering the GATT under the special terms of Article XXVI:5(c). This provision, which now has no equivalent in the WTO, offered an easy route by which former colonies of the GATT contracting parties could acquire de facto GATT status upon their achievement of independence. A country could then convert this de facto status into full GATT contracting party status by succession, a process that involved much less stringent scrutiny of its trade regime and fewer new commitments than did the ordinary accession process of GATT Article XXXIII. Of the 128 countries that joined the GATT, fully half (64) did so through accession. Some countries succeeded to the GATT shortly after gaining independence, while others waited years before taking this step.[2] Several of the countries that are currently negotiating for accession to the WTO must now regret that they did not take advantage of this option. Some of them rejected the GATT and/or the succession route on ideological grounds, viewing both as vestiges of colonialism. The Lao People's Democratic Republic and Vietnam formally renounced their status as de facto contracting parties, and Algeria opted not to employ the succession route when it first applied for GATT accession in 1987.[3]

The arrangements made with certain nonmarket economies during this period also demonstrated the willingness of GATT countries to adapt the rules to special cases. The most significant of these adaptations was the acceptance of countries' nonmarket status. The GATT system met these countries halfway. These countries were nevertheless obliged to make pledges that were outside the normal scope of commitments. When Poland acceded to the GATT in 1967, for example, it made an undertaking to increase the total value of its imports from GATT contracting parties by not less than 7 percent each year. Poland also agreed to a special bilateral safeguard clause, which permitted the other contracting parties to maintain quantitative restrictions against imports from Poland during an undefined transitional period. Such safeguard actions would not be bound by the terms of the ordinary GATT safeguard mechanism, as defined under GATT Article XIX. Romania made comparable commitments in its 1971 accession, including a pledge to increase its imports from the contracting parties "at a rate not smaller than the growth of total Romanian imports provided in its Five-Year Plans" and a special bilateral safeguards clause. Hungary was not obliged to make an imports undertaking in its 1973 protocol of accession, but did accept a selective safeguard clause.[4] Special arrangements of this sort are no longer sought from acceding countries, nor are accessions based on the assumption that nonmarket status is a permanent condition.

When Depth Became Critical:
Accessions since the Mid-1980s

Figure 6.3 illustrates the shift in focus of the GATT negotiations from the height of trade barriers to the depth of the system in the later years of the

Figure 6.3. The Key Dimension of Depth in Recent GATT/WTO History

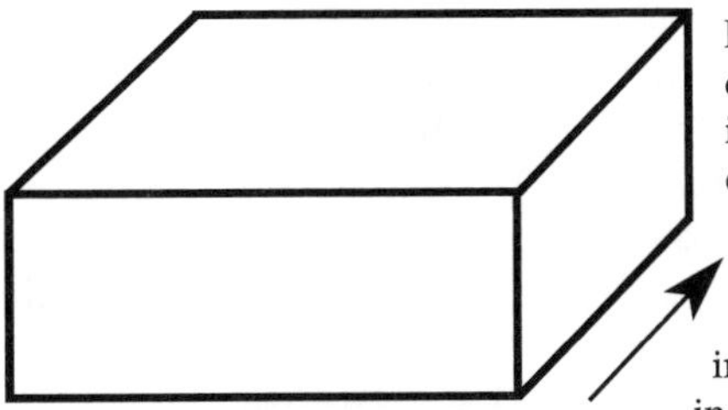

Most industrialized countries' tariffs on products other than labor-intensive items were cut to low levels by the end of the Tokyo Round phase-in period.

The GATT regime first handled services. intellectual property rights, and investment in the Uruguay Round, and dealt effectively with agricultural trade and subsidization for the first time.

By 1990, the only major economies outside of GATT were China, Taiwan, the ex-U.S.S.R., and several oil states.

regime. What had started as a contract among countries to reduce tariffs eventually became a much deeper regime that goes beyond border measures, covering such diverse economic activities as services, intellectual property rights, and agricultural subsidies. The proposed expansion in the scope of trade disciplines was not universally accepted in the 1980s, and disagreements erupted not only between industrialized and developing countries but also among the industrialized countries. Countries had once agreed on the basic principle that tariffs must be reduced, but bargained hard over how this principle should be implemented for tariffs on specific items; the new negotiating environment led to more profound disagreements over the principles themselves.

This change had major implications for the conduct of accessions. The smallness of most acceding countries meant obscurity and inattention when the principal focus was on reductions in the height of tariff barriers and other border measures that restricted trade. Even a huge reduction in a small country's tariff wall would have less practical effect than a seemingly small reduction in the tariffs imposed by a large country, and negotiators allocated their time and political capital accordingly. Their calculations are quite different in a depth-dominated system, in which the principal point of contention between the major players is over what issues will come within the scope of the regime. Put another way, countries that are highly unequal in their economic size will nevertheless enjoy a juridical equality when it comes to the precedents that they might set. A very small economy may account for a negligible share of global trade, and thus attract a commensurately small amount of attention from negotiators, but those same negotiators may devote a great deal of attention to an accession when it appears to offer a good opportunity to set a good precedent or block a bad one. The result is that acceding countries come under much more intense scrutiny, and the terms of their accessions are correspondingly strict.

These new developments were further reinforced by three other critical developments in the 1980s and 1990s: further erosion of already tenuous support for the S&D principle, the end of the Cold War, and the establishment of the WTO. All of these developments served to elevate the perceived importance of accession negotiations and the demands made on developing and transitional countries.

The decline of the S&D principle coincided with a growing understanding that many developing countries had been ill served by the trade strategies they had adopted in the 1960s and 1970s. The extension of special privileges was perceived to contribute to a growing free-rider problem in the GATT, in which developing countries were seen not only to be shirking their own responsibilities in trade liberalization but also to be isolating themselves from the benefits of a global market. Nor can the changing status of the S&D principle be attributed entirely to the declining interest of industrialized countries in granting it. In the early 1980s developing countries "began to perceive that the positive discrimination received under S&D Treatment had become outweighed by increasing negative discrimination against their trade," and they turned toward "defend[ing] the integrity of the unconditional MFN [most favored nation] clause, obtaining MFN tariff reductions, and strengthening the disciplines of GATT" (Gibbs 2000, p. 75). Developing countries also came to realize that in actual practice this principle generally produced very limited concessions that amounted to little more than tokenism. These views were reflected in the changing approach to S&D Treatment in the UR, where negotiators avoided special derogations and dispensations from generally applicable rules. They instead approved various provisions that allow longer periods for implementing obligations, more favorable thresholds for undertaking certain commitments, and greater flexibility in the implementation of agreements and procedures. Emphasis is now placed on the special needs of the *least*-developed countries, for whom many more exceptions are now provided. The principle of a single undertaking, or "package deal," further reinforced this aspect of the UR agreements. In contrast to prior rounds, developing countries could not avoid the regime's obligations either by invoking a general principle of S&D Treatment or by opting not to implement specific agreements that they considered to be incompatible with their development strategies.

Many of the countries that acceded to the GATT during the 1980s found the process to be more demanding, owing in large measure to a change in policy on the part of major trading countries. Negotiators from these countries—most notably the United States—grew increasingly insistent during the 1980s upon using the GATT accession process as a means of ensuring that the country's trade regime was consistent with the rules and principles of the system.

The Mexican example is a perfect case in point to appreciate the differences between the GATT accession practices before and after the change in policy. Mexico had negotiated for accession during the Tokyo Round, decided in 1980 not to implement the protocol of accession that it had negotiated the year before, and then changed direction once again in the mid-1980s. The protocol of accession that was negotiated in 1985 was more exacting than its 1979 predecessor. Whereas the earlier protocol consisted of little more than a list of tariff concessions, the latter agreement entailed (a) binding the entire tariff schedule at 50 percent, (b) agreeing to 373 concessions on tariffs below this ceiling (more than half of which were made in response to U.S. requests), and (c) making several other nontariff commitments, including pledges to adhere to the GATT codes relating to subsidies and countervailing measures, licensing procedures, antidumping, standards, and customs valuation. The second protocol was also less permissive than the earlier document with respect to certain sectoral exclusions that Mexico sought.

The negotiation of the second Mexican protocol can be seen as a real turning point for the GATT system. Coming a decade before the establishment of the WTO, which further institutionalized both the emphasis on depth and the decline of S&D, this negotiation set the pattern for the 12 developing countries' accessions that were concluded during the UR.[5] These accessions were more difficult than those conducted during the 1949–79 period, but less comprehensive than accessions to the WTO. The principal difference is that the GATT regime had not yet incorporated the new issues that were under negotiation in that round, and hence the acceding countries were under no obligation to make commitments on services, intellectual property, and investment or on agricultural issues other than tariffs. That did not, however, prevent some negotiators from raising these issues in the talks.

The end of the Cold War is another key development that coincided with these changes in the trade regime. The collapse of Communism had many direct and indirect consequences for the system, not the least being the applications for accession that soon came from Eastern Europe and most of the states of the former Soviet Union. The change was not merely quantitative, but qualitative: The operating assumption of older GATT accessions had been that a nonmarket economy was seeking a modus vivendi for trade with market economies, but now negotiations were con-

ducted on the principle that the acceding country was in an irrevocable
transition from nonmarket to market economy status. Those countries,
now known as economies in transition (EIT), are thus required to adopt
all of the same commitments that apply to other countries. While some
temporary accommodations might be made to the needs of the EIT, the
applicant would bear most of the burden of adjustment.

The end of the Cold War also led to accession negotiations with two
countries of considerable size. While most of the countries that acceded to
the GATT during the 1970s and 1980s were quite small (with some notable
exceptions such as Mexico, Thailand, and Venezuela), the same cannot be
said for China and Russia. Together with Taiwan and Saudi Arabia, these
are among the few acceding countries that individually represent significant shares of global trade. The prospect of negotiating with these countries may have reinforced the industrialized countries' stance in the accessions of smaller countries, on the expectation that any precedents set
with these countries—no matter how small they might be—could then be
applied to negotiations with major trading countries such as China and
Russia.

The Expanding Depth and Width
of the WTO Regime

Following the conclusion of the UR, the array of issues in the system—
and hence the scope for commitments in accession negotiations—has become much deeper. The intensification of accession negotiations that
began in the mid-1980s reached a new level with the inauguration of the
WTO in 1995. In addition to being subject to the same demands that
faced countries that acceded to the GATT, applicants to the new organization are obliged to make commitments on intellectual property rights,
services, agriculture, and (to a limited extent) investment. (See figure
6.4.)

The width of the WTO is expanding at least as rapidly as the depth.
Fourteen countries have acceded since the establishment of the organization: Ecuador and Bulgaria in 1996; Mongolia and Panama in 1997; the Kyrgyz Republic in 1998; Latvia and Estonia in 1999; Jordan, the Republic of
Georgia, Albania, Croatia, and Oman in 2000; and Lithuania and Moldova
in 2001. More countries and territories are negotiating for their accession.[6]
All of these applicants are either developing countries or economies in
transition. The data in figure 6.5 illustrate the relative weights of WTO
members and acceding countries in the global trading system. It shows that
while there are four applicants of relatively large size, all of the other countries that have acceded to the WTO or are currently negotiating for their accession represent very small shares of world trade. For reasons discussed

Figure 6.4. The Three Dimensions in Current WTO Relations: Both Depth and Width Are Expanding

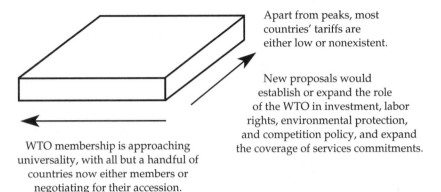

Apart from peaks, most countries' tariffs are either low or nonexistent.

New proposals would establish or expand the role of the WTO in investment, labor rights, environmental protection, and competition policy, and expand the coverage of services commitments.

WTO membership is approaching universality, with all but a handful of countries now either members or negotiating for their accession.

above, however, this does not mean that the existing WTO members are disposed toward giving these countries a free pass into the organization. Even the smallest country is important when precedent matters.

The diplomacy of accession has grown more contentious, with applicants and recently acceding countries having raised concerns over the

Figure 6.5. Relative Size of Countries by WTO Status: Countries' Shares of Global Exports, 1999

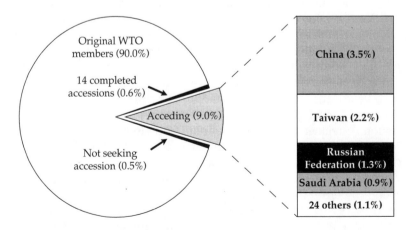

Source: Calculated from data from the United Nation's Conference on Trade and Development (UNCTAD).

process and its consequences. In a review of the debate among member countries over the accession process, a note by the WTO Secretariat (WTO 2000, p. 6) stated that:

> It was pointed out that the accession process was often lengthy and too demanding for certain acceding governments; the fact-finding stage, particularly, appeared to be unduly long, inquisitorial, and frequently repetitive. Many speakers said that many accessions were moving too slowly, some adding that the process should be simplified. Other speakers acknowledged that few accessions had taken place recently but said that this did not mean that the system was not working.... However, it appeared generally agreed that the WTO should look for ways to expedite the current accession processes so that applicants are not kept waiting longer than necessary.

The process is much more time consuming than it was in years past. The average WTO accession thus far has had an elapsed time of just over five years from the establishment of a working party to membership. This figure masks the considerable range of experience among acceding countries, where negotiations have ranged between 3 and 10 years, and fails to take into account the much longer periods experienced by some of the countries that have not yet completed the process. China began to seek accession back in 1986 (at a time when it hoped that this could be handled as a simple "renewal" of its former GATT status), while Algeria and Nepal have been at it since 1987 and 1989, respectively.

Developing country applicants are especially concerned over the apparent invalidation of established S&D principles in specific WTO agreements. Some aspects of the UR agreements provide for S&D Treatment for developing countries, but these rules are more limited in scope than the older GATT provisions. Many of the more substantive provisions of the WTO agreements provide for longer transition periods for developing countries, but do not provide for permanent exemptions. Some provide for two-year transitions (the Sanitary and Phytosanitary Agreement and the Import Licensing Agreement), and others for five years (the Customs Valuation Agreement, the Agreement on Trade-Related Investment Measures, and the Agreement on Trade-Related Aspects of Intellectual Property Rights). In accession negotiations conducted so far, however, developing and transitional countries have found their partners extremely reluctant to permit them to use these transitional provisions. The United States in particular takes the position that only original WTO members are entitled to use the transitional periods, while some other members are willing to consider transitional periods as negotiable possibilities.

The Perspectives of the Quad Countries

The stricter approach taken toward accession is ultimately attributable to a policy decision on the part of the four WTO members that compose the Quad. The United States is *primus inter pares* within this informal leadership group, which also includes Canada, the European Union, and Japan. Together with Australia and a few other countries, they account for the great majority of the questions that are posed to the acceding countries and the demands that are made of them. The United States especially treats accessions negotiations in a regime context, meaning that the commitments that it seeks from each acceding country are viewed in the broader context of the rules that the U.S. negotiators want to see applied uniformly to all WTO members. This sometimes leads negotiators to emphasize certain matters that may appear to be relatively unimportant in the bilateral relationship per se but are instead of great importance in U.S. relations with other countries that are either WTO members or are negotiating for their own accession.

Perhaps the most difficult position in which an acceding country can find itself is in a dispute between Quad countries over the place of an issue in the trading system. France convinced Albania to withdraw audiovisual commitments that it had made to the United States by threatening to block the country's WTO accession. French officials were reportedly concerned that the Albanian concession "could provide a back-door entry into Europe for U.S. productions" (Evans 1999). While Albania ultimately made commitments on cinema theater operation services and four other cultural sectors, it made none on cinema or television production.

In their case study of Vanuatu's accession, Grynberg and Joy (2000) were critical of a U.S. negotiating approach that stemmed not from the negligible American trade interests in that country but instead from Washington's desire to ensure that all countries make certain commitments. In this respect, they turned around the usual meaning of the term "concession" to argue that "any concession the United States might offer to Vanuatu [in the way of exceptions] might be used as a precedent for extension to other more significant WTO applicants." They nevertheless pointed a finger as well to the other major *demandeurs*:

> Given that the United States places the greatest demands upon acceding countries—and this is well known among accession negotiators—assumptions have developed regarding U.S. behavior that allow WTO members to play what accession negotiators now term "good cop-bad cop." Other Quad members and the Cairns Group, aware that the United States will take a hard line with applicants, are able to make less

strident demands. This strategy will minimize the political costs of attempting to extract concessions from acceding countries, some of whom are close political allies.

The European Union has also drawn a sharper distinction between the *less* developing countries and ordinary developing countries than has the United States. This might be partly attributable to the fact that five of the nine less developing countries that are currently seeking accession are former European colonies (that is, Cambodia, Cape Verde, the Lao People's Democratic Republic, Samoa, and Vanuatu).[7] They might have had the option of simply succeeding to the GATT, but under WTO rules and practice they are subject to the same accession procedures as all other countries. Whatever the reason, the European Union proposed in 1999 that a fast-track procedure be established to facilitate the accession of developing countries. This proposal suggested that the accession "could be expedited by agreeing with other WTO working party members on a range of minimum criteria" and a "flexible, streamlined approach" that would "[speed] up the process for them all without discrimination." Under this proposal the following criteria would apply:

- *Industrial tariffs:* Developing countries could bind at a level something like 30 percent across the board over a maximum five-year period (that is, to January 1, 2004), with the possibility remaining to agree to a limited number of higher tariffs on "exceptional" products.
- *Agricultural sector:* Developing countries could aim at 40 percent across the board and should not be asked to undertake reduction commitments as regards domestic support and export subsidies. Their commitments in these areas should be inscribed directly in their schedules. Any problems of specific products of should be addressed in a flexible manner.
- *Services:* Developing countries could be asked to make commitments in at least three services sectors. As far as horizontal commitments are concerned, the European Union does attach great importance to good commitments in mode 3 (commercial presence), in particular on foreign capital participation and employment requirements, and in mode 4 (movement of personnel).
- *Alignment with WTO rules:* WTO members could agree on the automatic applicability of transition periods agreed in the UR for developing countries toward full compliance with WTO agreements. Candidate countries would, however, be expected to provide a work program for the completion of legislative alignment. Technical assistance efforts should be intensified to ensure compliance is achieved.[8]

The proposal did not get far, owing to opposition from the United States. The U.S. negotiators take the position that while other WTO members are free to establish their own policies toward the accession of developing countries, including reduced demands upon these countries, they should not be granted substantially easier terms of accession. The only area in which the U.S. negotiators seem prepared to be lenient toward the developing countries is in the number of working party meetings, which they believe can be held to two or three. They otherwise insist that these countries be required to provide all of the same information that other applicants submit, and that developing countries be obliged to make commitments bringing their regimes into conformity with WTO rules. Even in some areas where the WTO agreements explicitly provide for special treatment, such as the transition period for intellectual property rights or the exemption from commitments on agricultural subsidies, they are likely to request that developing countries undertake disciplines that go beyond the letter of the WTO agreements.

The laws and policies of the United States pose a further complication in the case of most EITs. While the United States demands that these countries make substantial commitments in an accession, there is no guarantee that the United States will finally recognize the country's status as a WTO member. This policy stems from the Jackson-Vanik Amendment, a Cold War law under which the extension of MFN treatment (now known as normal trade relations) to certain countries is conditioned upon their emigration practices. It is a well-established principle of trade law that the Jackson-Vanik conditions are inconsistent with U.S. obligations under GATT Article I, which requires that WTO members extend MFN treatment to one another on an unconditional basis. This inconsistency requires that the United States make a choice whenever a country that is subject to Jackson-Vanik accedes to the WTO. One option is to graduate the country from Jackson-Vanik, and thus allow the full establishment of WTO relations between the United States and the acceding country. The other option is to maintain that country's status under Jackson-Vanik, which then obligates the United States to invoke a "nonapplication" clause that permits an existing contracting party to deny the application of the GATT and WTO rules to a new entrant (and vice versa).

Nonapplication is purely bilateral in nature and does not affect the relations between the new entrant and countries that did not invoke the clause. This clause is now provided under WTO Article XIII, which differs from its GATT predecessor (Article XXXV) in only one important respect. Whereas GATT Article XXXV had provided that a country could not invoke the nonapplication clause if it had engaged in tariff negotiations with an applicant country, there is no such prohibition in WTO Article XIII. In other words, the United States now has the capacity to negotiate with applicant countries in an area that had previously been out of bounds. It is still U.S. policy to invoke the nonapplication clause upon the accession of any country that is subject to the Jackson-Vanik law. The

United States is the only country that has invoked WTO Article XIII, which it has done for each acceding country that was (at the time of accession) subject to the Jackson-Vanik law. Those invocations remain in effect for just one country that is still subject to the law (Moldova), while the invocations for three countries (Georgia, Kyrgyz Republic, and Mongolia) were withdrawn after the U.S. Congress enacted laws removing these countries from the Jackson-Vanik law. In the special case of China, Congress enacted a law in 2000 that will graduate the country from Jackson-Vanik upon the completion of its accession to the WTO.

Two Perspectives for Acceding Countries

Accession to the WTO is clearly a difficult undertaking, and one that has become more complex and lengthy over time. How might the countries that are currently seeking accession best handle the negotiations? One approach would be to protest against the apparent inequities of the system, and to insist that countries that are undergoing major economic and (in many cases) political transitions should not be expected to meet all of the standards that industrialized countries have reached among themselves over more than half a century of negotiations in the GATT and WTO. While it is understandable that the acceding countries would feel this way, and may indeed get an empathetic response from others that have recently gone through the same difficulties, it is hard to find fault with the observation by Grynberg and Joy (2000, p. 173) that only the "extraordinarily naïve would believe that the system of accession will be reformed." The more demanding approach that is now taken toward acceding countries is a natural consequence of the three-dimensional evolution of the trading system, and it is to be expected that precedent will be given a high priority in a rules-based system. Those rules are defined primarily by the larger and more influential countries in the system, and those countries show little proclivity to change course.

It seems inevitable, therefore, that the accession process will remain demanding. If the acceding countries cannot expect to change the process itself, how might they best position themselves in it? There are two essential points of view that negotiators might adopt: alternatively approaching these talks from the perspective of a diplomat/trade lawyer or as an economist/reformer. While each of these approaches offers a valid means of assessing options and devising strategy, the latter perspective may be the most appropriate.

The Diplomat/Trade Lawyer's Approach

One option is to treat accessions as an exercise in diplomacy and law, emphasizing both the political dignity and the legal rights of the country.

Membership in this key international organization is now an important issue of international status, such that any country that remains outside of the WTO carries a taint of second-class citizenship in the global community. The acceding country may therefore adopt an approach that stresses the political necessity of early entry while also insisting that its commitments be limited.

This approach is commonly adopted by countries, often in response to impasses that they have reached in a negotiation over particularly difficult points. These impasses have often been attributable to the hard line taken by the United States. Trading partners sometimes hope that their disputes with U.S. negotiators can be solved by taking matters to the highest levels of government. When their chief executive meets with the president of the United States, they reason, he or she can reach a political understanding that breaks through the difficulties that have been reached at the working level. An attempt might be made either to negotiate the issues at the highest level or to win a political commitment that these matters will be resolved by a certain date. Though commonly attempted, this approach has never yet been successful in accessions. Presidents are unlikely to disagree with the positions adopted by their subordinates, especially when they have been forewarned that a foreign leader is likely to raise the matter. Perhaps most surprising for U.S. trading partners, however, are the real limitations on the powers of the president. "Presidential power is the power to persuade," according to one widely read analysis of American politics (Neustadt 1990). Presidents must persuade other actors when they seek to advance their agendas. The most immediate and powerful counterbalance to presidential power is the Congress, and the legislative branch in turn is influenced to a great degree by the positions adopted by interest groups in the private sector. This is especially important in the Jackson-Vanik cases discussed above.

Quite to the contrary, the effort to "kick a negotiation upstairs" can work more to the benefit of the existing countries than the acceding country. If they know that their interlocutor is under strong political pressure back home to secure accession at any cost, then the negotiators in Geneva will feel even more secure in setting that price at a high level. A country might theoretically conclude an agreement over accession on a much faster schedule, provided that it were prepared to accept without hesitation or revision all of the requests made by the members of its WTO accession working party. The end results, however, might be hard for the negotiators to explain to their masters. The Kyrgyz accession negotiation was the quickest on record, taking just 34 months, but it also led to the adoption of many commitments that have proven difficult to fulfill.

It is not surprising that many acceding countries approach these negotiations in the same manner that lawyers will approach a contract negotiation. When viewed through the eyes of a trade lawyer, a country's ac-

cession process might be compared to negotiations over a purchasing contract, a divorce, or other legal proceedings in which each side seeks to attain maximum advantage at minimum cost. Seen from this point of view,
the goal is to ensure that a country makes as few commitments as possible and is bound by the least onerous conditions. This approach is clearly
reflected in the terminology that trade negotiators employ, in which the
commitments that countries make are deemed to be "concessions." This
word implies that the country is surrendering something of value whenever it agrees to a specific condition in its accession, or otherwise makes a
commitment in a WTO-sponsored negotiation. The trade lawyer's advice
to accession negotiators would be simple: Concede as little as possible to
the countries with which you negotiate, make those concessions only after
ensuring that they are unavoidable, and try if possible to construe any
commitments narrowly.

The principal problem with this approach is that the typical acceding
country has little or no leverage over the existing WTO members. The applicant will almost always feel much greater pressure in these negotiations than do its negotiating partners, and while the applicant may greatly
desire to win its seat at the table, those who are already there perceive no
urgency in setting another place. Many of the usual tools in the negotiator's bag are rendered ineffective in this environment, where stonewalling
merely means delaying the process while the price of admission continues to rise.

The Economist/Reformer's Approach

An alternative approach is to look past the apparently unfair nature of the
accession process, and to concentrate more on the ends than the means.
This means viewing accession as an opportunity to reinforce the economic
reform process. This view is more readily adopted if policymakers look
past the usual terminology of trade negotiators. When all commitments
are described as concessions, trade relations appear to be defined in a
zero-sum, neo-mercantilist framework. To a liberal economist it is seriously wrong to suggest that one country's gain can come only at another
country's loss. It is important to bear in mind throughout the process that
the ultimate objective is to enhance a country's competitiveness within
a global economy that—notwithstanding the archaic terminology employed by negotiators—offers opportunities for mutually beneficial trade
and investment. The reformer's approach is based more on economic than
political/legal considerations, but also requires that negotiators make a
realistic assessment of what can be achieved.

The costs and benefits of acceding to the WTO can be properly understood only if the advantages of membership are viewed in their larger context. From this vantage point, the most critical consideration is not the sum

of rules by which an economy operates but instead what they mean for a country's investment, productivity, and competitiveness. These factors can be enhanced only if a country can attract and maintain the confidence of investors. To appreciate the importance of instilling confidence in domestic and foreign investors, compare the examples of market-oriented Asian economies such as Singapore (which acceded in 1973) and the Republic of Korea (which acceded in 1967) with the protectionist policies followed by many Latin American countries during the 1950s through the early 1980s. The Asian countries had few resources other than people, and neither enjoyed more favorable market access than other developing economies, but they have grown at phenomenal rates in the past half-century. This success is often attributed to the confidence that domestic and foreign investors felt in the permanence of their free-market policies. By contrast, most Latin American countries either adopted policies that were perceived to be hostile toward investors or failed to persuade investors that their market reforms were irrevocable. Even when these countries began to reform almost 20 years ago, based largely on the realization that they had fallen so far behind their Asian competitors, investors doubted the commitment to these policy changes until they were enshrined in trade agreements.

The solution that many Latin American countries adopted was to make their reforms permanent by incorporating them in international agreements. National economic reforms are made more credible when they are bound by such pacts. The agreement gives assurance to domestic and foreign investors that the improved business climate is not an ephemeral development that might be abandoned as quickly as it was adopted. By negotiating multilateral accords such as the GATT accession in the mid-1980s and the North American Free Trade Agreement (NAFTA) in the early 1990s, these countries gave convincing evidence that they would not revert quickly to more protectionist policies. In the case of NAFTA, for example, the agreement actually made relatively few changes in Mexico's access to the U.S. market, but made a huge difference in the perceived openness of the Mexican economy, the permanence of the Mexican reforms, and the degree of official U.S. support for these changes. By entering into an agreement with major trading countries such as the United States, a country can enhance the private sector's confidence in the permanence of economic reforms, and encourage new foreign investment. An economist may even suggest that negotiators should welcome the opportunity to make numerous commitments in an accession negotiation. In some countries—especially democracies—it can be difficult to win approval for economic reforms from the legislative branch. It can sometimes be easier to sell reforms to legislators when they are presented as commitments that were made in international negotiations, and that the country is honor bound to implement.

WTO accessions and other trade negotiations may play a similar role for other acceding countries. Any economic reforms that they have en-

acted can be incorporated into the terms of the WTO accession commitments, and be further supported through additional pledges made in response to the demands of existing WTO members. Viewed in this context,
the commitments that are made in the course of accession to the WTO
should not necessarily be deemed to be "concessions." From this perspective, it might be more accurate (and politically palatable) to conceive
of them as *investments,* insofar as they are payments made today in the expectation that they will produce rewards in the future. The liberal economist's advice to negotiators would therefore be quite different from what
a trade lawyer would advise. A country should approach its accession negotiations as an opportunity rather than a risk, and be prepared to make
whatever changes are appropriate—and not merely those that are necessary—in order to take full advantage of this opportunity.

A reformist perspective must also take due account of political reality.
If the trade lawyer's approach is followed to the letter, a country may find
that its accession negotiations last for many years. While a good bargain
can be worth the wait, that delay can prove costly. Conversely, blind adherence to the liberal economist's approach can leave a country too vulnerable to external shocks. The economic perspective thus requires some
tempering. A country should try to retain some leverage for those negotiations that will take place after its accession, and also reserve the flexibility to adjust its economic policies in response to future contingencies.

In place of urging that a country make either minimum or maximum
commitments, the reformer's perspective suggests that countries attempt
to devise a reasoned package of commitments that complements the national reform program. Negotiators should enter talks with clear notions
of what they might be asked to do and how far they are willing to go in
their commitments. Negotiators should neither oppose all requests from
the outset, nor should they cave in too quickly. Ideally, they should enter
the talks with a plan that distinguishes between the types of commitments
that a country might be asked to make. Beyond identifying those commitments that are mandatory (that is, represent truly minimal adherence
to WTO principles), negotiators should consider what types of commitments might complement a country's reform plans and what commitments might complicate those plans, and be prepared to respond accordingly. Above all else, negotiators should devise an overarching plan in
which the relationship between national economic objectives and international trade commitments is clearly understood.

Notes

1. Iran is a special case. While Tehran has sought to accede since 1996, the
United States has blocked the initiative.

2. The experience of countries under GATT Article XXVI:5(c) varied considerably. The Gambia succeeded to the GATT just four days after achieving independence in 1965, while Lesotho allowed more than 11 years to pass between the acquisition of de facto GATT status and its succession to GATT. GATT Secretariat, "De Facto Status and Succession: Article XXVI.5(c); Note By The Secretariat," MTN.GNG/NG7/W/40 (1988), *passim*.

3. The case of Cambodia is especially convoluted. Although the country enjoyed de facto status as a GATT Contracting Party, Cambodia made a serious effort to accede to the GATT on its own by negotiating under GATT Article XXXIII. The country concluded negotiations over its protocol of accession, but never completed the domestic ratification procedures. Like its Indochinese neighbors and other former colonies, Cambodia is now negotiating for accession under the more rigorous rules and procedures of the WTO.

4. The complex political economy of accessions by Poland, Romania, and Hungary are reviewed in Haus (1992).

5. Note that this figure counts only the accessions concluded under GATT Article XXXIII. There were also 26 successions to GATT under the terms of Article XXVI:5(c) during the UR.

6. Algeria, Andorra, Armenia, Azerbaijan, the Bahamas, Belarus, Bhutan, Bosnia and Herzegovina, Cambodia, Cape Verde, China, the Federal Republic of Yugoslavia (Serbia and Montenegro), the Former Yugoslav Republic of Macedonia, Kazakstan, Lao People's Democratic Republic, Lebanon, Nepal, the Russian Federation, Samoa, Saudi Arabia, Seychelles, Sudan, Taiwan (negotiating as the Separate Customs Territory of Taiwan, Penghu, Kinmen, and Matsu), Tonga, Ukraine, Uzbekistan, Vanuatu, Vietnam, and Yemen.

7. Bhutan, Nepal, Sudan, and Yemen are least developing countries seeking accession that would not have had the option of succeeding to the GATT.

8. "Accessions to the WTO: Communication from the European Communities," WT/GC/W/153 (March 8, 1999).

References

Curzon, Gerard. 1965. *Multilateral Commercial Diplomacy*. London: Michael Joseph.

Evans, Robert. 1999. "Croatia Blasts EU for Blocking WTO Entry Talks." Reuters.

Gibbs, Murray. 2000. "Special and Differential Treatment in the Context of Globalization." In *A Positive Agenda for Developing Countries: Issues for Future Trade Negotiations*. UNCTAD/ITCD/TSB/10. Geneva: UNCTAD.

Grynberg, Roman, and Roy Mickey Joy. 2000. "The Accession of Vanuatu to the WTO: Lessons for the Multilateral Trading System." *Journal of World Trade* 34(6): 167–68.

Haus, Leah A. 1992. *Globalizing the GATT: The Soviet Union's Successor States, Eastern Europe, and the International Trading System*. Washington, D.C.: The Brookings Institution.

Neustadt, Richard. 1990. *Presidential Power and the Modern Presidents: The Politics of Leadership from Roosevelt to Reagan* (3rd ed). New York: The Free Press.

WTO (World Trade Organization). 2000. "Technical Note on the Accession Process." WT/ACC/7/Rev. 2. Geneva.

7

Small Developing Economies in the World Trade Organization

Richard L. Bernal

The Issue

Small developing economies have structural and institutional character-istics that affect the process of economic growth, constrain their ability to compete, increase their vulnerability to external events, and limit their ca-pacity for adjustment. These characteristics are sufficient to identify small economies as a distinct type of economy.

Given the high degree of openness of small economies, external events and developments have a significant effect on their economic growth. The way in which these economies participate in the world economy and their internal economic management and structural adjustment are the critical determinants of their economic progress. The benefits of sound economic management can only be realized if international economic arrangements are complementary and do not frustrate these efforts (for example, by protectionist barriers to export markets).

Therefore the participation of small states in international trade ar-rangements is critical to their economic development and is an issue that must be examined and adequately addressed. In this regard, the treat-ment of small developing economies in the World Trade Organization (WTO) agreements is particularly important.

Context

The majority of states in the world are small; indeed, the number of small countries has increased significantly in recent decades. At the time of World War I, there were 62 independent countries. By 1946 that number had risen to 74, and currently (2002) there are 193. Of this total 87 coun-tries have a population of fewer than 5 million, 58 have fewer than 2.5 million, and 35 have fewer than 500,000. The proliferation of small states is a trend that could continue if states fragment as they have in recent years in Eastern Europe and Africa.

Recognition

The political integrity and security of small states have long been recognized as important issues in international relations, and hence are reflected in many academic and policy studies. More recently there has been a growing awareness of the critical question of the economic viability of small countries. The Commonwealth Secretariat has kept this matter under review and the Commonwealth Ministerial Group on Small States has emphasized "the need for the international community to recognize the multidimensional nature of the vulnerability of small states" and called for action to ensure that small states fully share in the benefits from globalization, regionalism, and international trading arrangements, and were not marginalized. The Free Trade Area of the Americas (FTAA) process, since its inception, has included a Working Group on Small Economies. At the second WTO Ministerial Conference, the ministers were deeply concerned over the marginalization of "certain small economies," and they recognized the urgent need to address this issue. The draft document, which was the basis of the aborted negotiations at the Seattle Ministerial in 1999, included references to small economies.

Small economies as a distinctive genre of economy attracted the interest of academics in the 1960s. Subsequently several technical studies of a policy-oriented nature have been carried out on small economies and in particular small island states by the Commonwealth Secretariat, the World Bank, the United Nations Conference on Trade and Development, and the FTAA Working Group on Small Economies. There is a general consensus in these studies that small economies have characteristics that distinguish them as a particular genre of economy and these features are constraints on their capacity for trade and development.

Importance

Small economies more than any other group of countries need a rule-based multilateral trading system, and it is in their vital interest that rule making be conducted within the WTO, where their limited leverage in bilateral negotiations with larger countries is not an impediment.

The effective participation of small economies in the WTO agreements would help to establish universal membership in the WTO, and ensure that all countries are conducting international trade under mutually agreed upon rules and disciplines. It will also promote trade liberalization in the global economy to the benefit of economic development in these countries and the global economy as a whole. The absence of small economies from the WTO could cause disruptions in international economic transactions, which would hamper the growth of international trade and investment and the emergence of a seamless global economy.

Definition of a Small Developing Economy

There is no single definition of a small developing economy, undoubtedly because size is a relative concept. Definitions based on quantitative criteria vary considerably because they employ different criteria and select different defining figures.

Various international organizations classify countries into categories according to selected indicators for operational and analytical purposes. The classifications used by international organizations mainly relate to per capita income levels, indicators of development status, and some selected concept of "size." While the main classification criterion used by institutions such as the International Monetary Fund, the World Bank, and the United Nations for establishing country categories is the level of per capita income, these institutions also classify countries by aggregate income levels, the types of goods exported (for example, fuels, nonfuel primary products, manufactures, or services), and by fiscal structure. The World Bank also groups economies with populations fewer than 1 million in a separate table of the *World Development Report*. The WTO follows the U.N. country classification, and for budget purposes also makes use of the income criterion adopted by the World Bank. Under the WTO classification, countries with less than US$1,000 of per capita income may consider themselves as falling in the "least developed" category in terms of the obligations and disciplines set out in the Uruguay Round (UR) Agreement on Agriculture (AoA).

The definition of what is a small developing economy is an issue that can be resolved technically and should not be allowed to delay substantive discussions on the appropriate treatment of small developing economies. The definition of "small" in relation to economic size is usually based on one or more of the criteria: population, land area, and gross domestic product (GDP), and could be arrived at by consensus. In addition, the principle of "self-selection" can be applied as it has been done for development status under the General Agreement on Tariffs and Trade (GATT) system and now under the WTO.

Characteristics of Small Developing Economies

Small developing economies have certain characteristics, such as a high degree of openness, limited diversity in economic activity, export concentration on one to three products, significant dependency on trade taxes, and small size of firms.

High degree of openness. External transactions are large in relation to total economic activity, as indicated by the high ratio of trade to GDP. There is heavy reliance on external trade because of a narrow range of resources and the inability to support certain types of production, given the small scale of the market. Economic openness is measured by imports and exports of goods and services as a percentage of GDP.

Export concentration. The limited range of economic activity in small economies is reflected in the concentration on one to three exports, accompanied in the majority of cases by a relatively high reliance on primary commodities. In extreme cases, one primary product export accounts for nearly all of exports (for example, in 1991 bananas accounted for 92 percent of total exports in Dominica and 87 percent in St. Lucia).

Export market concentration. Export concentration is compounded by the dependence on one or two export markets (for example, Britain absorbs 80 percent of Dominica's bananas and 90 percent of St. Lucia's).

Imperfect markets. The small size of markets in small developing economies results in market structures, which are characterized by substantial imperfections. These derive from the limited number of participants and, in many cases, there are monopolies and oligopolies. Even where there are a large number of producers or traders, one or a few firms effectively dominate the operation of markets both in the financial as well as the real sector.

Small size of firms. Firms from small countries are small by comparison with multinational corporations and firms in large economies. Small firms are at a disadvantage in the global marketplace because they cannot realize economies of scale, are not attractive business partners, and cannot spend significant funds on marketing, research, and development. Comparing 1996 total sales of the largest national firms, General Motors (United States, US$164 billion) is 9 times larger than Petrobas (Brazil, US$17 billion), which in turn is 35 times larger than Neal & Massey (Trinidad and Tobago, US$0.5 billion). Sales and employment of some multinational corporations are larger than the GDP and population of many countries.

Dependence on trade taxes. There is a high dependence on trade taxes as a percentage of government revenue in small developing economies. Trade taxes account for more than one-half of government revenue in St. Lucia, Belize, and the Bahamas, and more than one-third of government revenue in Guatemala and the Dominican Republic.

Physical vulnerability. One of the peculiarities of small developing countries, particularly small islands, is the fragility of their ecologies, the prevalence of natural disasters, and their susceptibility to the environmental impact of economic development. The World Bank has estimated that the impact of a natural disaster on a small economy and its financial sector can be far more devastating than it is on a large economy, where the damage is relatively localized. For example, the damage to Jamaica from Hurricane Gilbert in 1988 amounted to about 33 percent of GDP, to Antigua from Luis and Marilyn in 1995 to about 66 percent of GDP, and to Montserrat from Hugo in 1989 to about 500 percent of GDP. In comparison, the damage to the United States from Hurricane Andrew in 1992, while much larger in an absolute financial terms, amounted to only 0.2 percent of GDP.

Implications of Size

There is no direct correlation between size and rate of economic growth and level of development. This is evident in the fact that many countries, which are small in terms of standard indicators such as population, land area, and GDP, are ranked favorably according to levels of GDP per capita and the United Nations' Human Development Index. Nevertheless, small size has implications for the international trade of these countries.

Volatility

Small developing economies have traditionally experienced economic volatility because of instability of export earnings resulting from acute dependence on a few primary product exports. This instability is heightened when exports depend on a few external markets, because exports are exposed to fluctuations in demand and price, and changes in market access policy in importing countries.

It has been suggested that many small economies can reduce export instability by shifting to services, particularly tourism and financial services. Some studies, however, have indicated that the change in export composition toward the service industry has been accompanied by higher instability in export earnings.

Vulnerability

The high degree of openness and the concentration in a few export products, particularly some primary products and agricultural commodities whose prices and demand are subject to fluctuations in world markets, make small developing economies vulnerable to external economic events.

Substantial dependence on external sources of economic growth makes small developing countries acutely vulnerable to exogenous shocks. The exposure of small developing economies to real shocks is much greater than in larger economies, which are usually more diversified in structure and exports.

Economic vulnerability can be a feature of an economy of any size and level of development, but it is compounded by size, degree of openness, export concentration, susceptibility to natural disasters, and remoteness and insularity. The extent of vulnerability of an economy can be measured by a "vulnerability index." Different vulnerability indexes have been employed by researchers, the Commonwealth Secretariat, and the United Nations, and all may differ in which variables are included and the methodology of weighting. All vulnerability indexes reveal a relationship between vulnerability and size, with the smallest countries being the most vulnerable.

Suboptimal Resource Use, Allocation, and Mobilization

Small markets are imperfect markets, and this type of market situation has several implications for resource use allocation and mobilization. (a) The narrowness of the market—that is, a limited number of participants and/or the dominance of one institution—reduces the efficiency with which resources are allocated and leads to distortions in resource use. (b) The lack of market-driven competition leads to inefficiency and higher costs, as firms are not driven by the dynamics of competition to optimize efficiency and to introduce new technology and improved production systems. A firm's international competitiveness depends on its capacity to continually innovate in production techniques and products. The national market conditions in which the company operates is a significant variable in its drive to develop its competitive advantages. (c) The small size and skewed structure of the market inhibits the ability of small developing economies to garner resources from external sources, in particular from private foreign investment. Investors often are unaware of or do not find small developing economies worthwhile as investment locations because of the limited size of the national market. Even investment for export tends to be biased in favor of larger economies, no matter if they are low income and less developed. (d) The high import content of production and consumption, undiversified economic structure, and the lack of competitive markets in small developing economies means that there are rigidities in resource allocation. This makes the adjustment process more difficult and, of necessity, slower than the adjustment process in larger, more developed economies.

Lack of Competitiveness

It is firms, not countries, that conduct international trade, and firms in small economies are small by global standards. Small developing economies have severe constraints on their material and labor inputs, both in amount and variety, because of their limited land area, narrow resource base, and small populations. These constraints prevent the attainment of economies of scale for a wide range of products and lead to high unit costs of production. Small market size also tends to cause high costs because there is often a lack of competition; that is, in many instances the markets are oligopolistic or controlled by their monopolies.

Firms in small economies, especially small developing economies, are at a major disadvantage in comparison with large firms. These firms are small and cannot attain either internal economies of scale (where unit cost is influenced by the size of the firm) or external economies of scale (where unit cost depends on the size of the industry, but not necessarily on the size of any one firm). A small economy, and by extension small industries (including export sectors), is unlikely to foster the competitive dynamic necessary for firms in small economies to achieve competitive advantage. Competitive advantage is more likely to occur when the economy is large enough to sustain "clusters" of industries connected through vertical and horizontal relationships.

Firms in small developing countries have severe difficulties in attaining "economies of scope" (that is, economies obtained by a firm using its existing resources, skills, and technologies to create new products and/or services for export). Exposure to global competition requires small firms to invest heavily just to survive in their national market, and more so in order to export. Larger firms are better able to generate new products and sources from existing organization and networks. Very large firms, such as multinational corporations, operate internationally in ways very different from small firms.

A small developing economy is an aggregation of firms that are small in the world market and are therefore "price-takers"; that is, they exercise no influence on world market prices for goods, services, and assets. Inputs, including imports, cost firms in small economies more when compared with large firms, thereby making firms in small economies relatively less efficient.

Small developing economies pay higher transportation costs because of the relatively small volume of cargo. Small economies pay an average of 10 percent of the value of merchandise exports as freight costs, which is considerably higher than the world average. Small developing economies spend more on transportation and freight costs as a percentage of exports than do large countries. The figure is 4.3 percent for the Organisation for Economic Co-operation and Development countries and 7.5 percent for Latin America and the Caribbean.

The public sector in small developing economies accounts for a larger share of GDP, which reflects a certain indivisibility of public administration structures and functions; that is, every country, no matter how small, has a head of a state, a parliament, a police force. The growth of the public sector has also been due in part to attempts to compensate for the absence of the private sector and certain economic activities and the financing of large infrastructure projects.

The small size of the market and the prevalence of small firms make it difficult for small economies to attract private foreign investment and joint venture partnership even when policy regime and economic fundamentals are better than competing locations. The result is that both the public sector and the private sector composed of small firms pay higher interest rates and other costs increasing the cost of production.

Small developing economies and their small markets are unlikely to foster the competitive dynamic necessary for firms (including export sectors) to achieve global competitiveness. The attainment of competitive advantage is more likely to occur when the economy is large enough to sustain "clusters" of industries connected through vertical and horizontal relationships and where there is a network of related and supporting industries. A firm working together with world-class local suppliers can benefit from cross-fertilization opportunities. Related industries can also be an important source of innovations and provide strategic alliances and joint ventures.

Limited Adjustment Capacity

The high import content of production and consumption and the rigidity inherent in the undiversified economic structure of small developing economies severely hampers resource allocation, which make the adjustment process more difficult and slower than in larger economies. In many situations, adjustment requires resource creation as well as resource allocation.

There is a high degree of openness in small developing economies, the consequences of which include the overall domestic price level dominated by movements in the price of imports. The prices of nontraded goods also tend to adjust rapidly through the impact of foreign prices on wages and other costs. Exchange rate charges do not have the desired effect on the balance of payments because of low import and export price elasticities.

Stabilization policy must be designed specifically for small developing countries. The structure of markets and the nature of their operations must be recognized. The uncompetitive nature of these markets, particularly where monopolies and oligopolies exist, and the limited number and type of institutions make resource utilization and allocation more problematic than in large developed economies. These types of market situations are characterized by rigidities, which make the adjustment process more time consuming, and which diminish the efficacy of conventional policy measures such as open market operations and recalibration of economywide prices such as the exchange rate. Furthermore, structural adjustment, like stabilization, is a more difficult process in small developing economies because the inherent rigidities in the structure and operation of markets complicate the process of resource reallocation. The nature of these small markets also restricts the ability of private sector entities and the government to mobilize additional resources, both within these economies and from external sources.

Small developing economies have structural features that need to be changed if these economies are to cope with the rapid and profound changes associated with globalization. Adjustment will not suffice to enable these economies to cope with changes in the global economy since adjustment implies marginal and incremental modification to an economic structure that is fundamentally sound and conducive to sustainable economic growth. Economic transformation goes beyond the resource utilization, reallocation, and mobilization intrinsic in stabilization and structural adjustment to incorporate resource creation over the medium to long term. Transformation in the current and future global economy will entail the ability of small developing economies to facilitate the rapid and frictionless international mobility of goods, services, finance, capital, and technology, which is the essence of a seamless global economy.

Treatment of Small Economies
in the International Trade Agreements

Conventional trade theory assumes that international trade takes place between countries in an environment of perfect competition and that trade occurs because of differences in comparative advantage, which in turn derive from differences in resource endowment or technology. In this paradigm the effects of size of country and size of firm are not taken into account. However, in reality, size of country and size of firm have important implications when taking into account economies of scale. The size of a country and the size of a firm become important considerations because large firms can achieve economies of scale and market dominance (including oligopoly and even monopoly), which put small firms at a disadvantage.

While the WTO agreement does not recognize small economies as a distinct category, it explicitly recognizes that they are different types of economies and that these economies require rules and discipline that are specifically designed to take account of their needs. The preamble of the WTO UR AoA recognizes that there is need for positive efforts designed to ensure that developing countries "[s]ecure a share in the growth in international trade commensurate with the needs of economic development." The AoA includes provisions for developing member countries, and there are some concessions to the least developed countries, net food importing countries, and those with incomes below $1,000 per capita.

The effect of small size has been recognized in national economic policy because all countries have policies specifically designed to promote the viability of small businesses and small farms. This tenet needs to be applied to the global arena in the context of multilateral trade agreements, given the disparities in size between firms and countries. More generally, small and/or vulnerable participants (both firms and households) in national economies are afforded appropriate treatment by compensatory policy measures. These compensatory measures are fiscal transfers or enabling programs (for example, subsidies or low-cost finance or rules that discriminate in their favor, such as quotas or prevention of market dominance by larger firms). In a global economy increasingly dominated by the global market and where international trade is increasingly regulated by multilateral rules, there is no multilateral entity that provides fiscal transfers or enabling programs, and hence inequity and adjustment must be addressed by multilateral trade rules.

Differentiated Treatment

Differentiated treatment is a well-established concept and practice in multilateral, regional, and bilateral trade agreements. This has usually been based on differences in levels of development with three categories being recognized: industrialized and developing countries and least developed countries. Differentiated treatment had its origin in the colonial trade arrangement, and the principle has continued in various forms in agreements between countries at different levels of development (for example, the Lomé Convention, through which the European Union provided preferential treatment for a select group of developing countries). Differentiated treatment became universally recognized when the GATT was formed. Although the initial premise underlying the GATT (1947) was parity of obligations between all trading nations, the concept of permitting differentiated treatment existed from the outset. This took the form of preferential treatment to developing countries in the form of preferential access to industrialized country markets through tariff preferences and exemptions from GATT rules. In 1965 the special status of a developing country in the multilateral trading system was established with the adoption of a new Part IV of the GATT, which embodied what was termed "Special and Differential (S&D) Treatment." This treatment was defined as nonreciprocity for developing countries.

The principal of differentiated treatment in the form of permanent or temporary nonreciprocity is embodied in several trade agreements and integration arrangements such as the Caribbean Common Market (CARICOM) and the Central American Common Market. It is included in the Caribbean Basin Initiative, the Andean Trade Preferences Act, the CARICOM-Venezuela Agreement, the CARICOM-Columbia Agreement, and the Andean Pact.

S&D Treatment is embodied in the WTO agreements in 147 provisions, of which 107 were adopted at the conclusion of the Uruguay Round, and 22 apply only to least developed member countries. These measures are incorporated in the Multilateral Agreement on Trade in Goods, the General Agreement on Trade in Services (GATS), the Agreement on Trade-Related Aspects of Intellectual Property (TRIPs), the Understanding on Rules and Procedures Governing the Settlement of Disputes, and in several ministerial decisions. There are 12 provisions in four agreements and one decision, which are aimed at increasing the trade opportunities of developing country members. There are 49 provisions under which WTO members should safeguard the interests of small developing countries. However, both measures to promote trade opportunities and safeguards are for the most part best attempts that are not enforceable and have not been fully implemented.

Proposed Provisions for Small Developing Economies

The design of measures to address the concerns and interests of small developing economies should not be limited to measures that avoid putting these economies at a disadvantage and nor should they be confined to best endeavor commitments to promote trade opportunities and safeguard the interest of these economies. For example, Article IV of the GATS specifies measures aimed at increasing the participation of developing countries in the global trade in services through specific commitments in relation to strengthening their domestic services' efficiency, capacity, and competitiveness. It also requires industrialized member countries to facilitate the access of developing countries' service suppliers to information related to market access.

Measures to promote growth and development of small developing economies should be proactive, meaningful, and enforceable. Appropriate provisions for small developing economies can be grouped under six headings.

A Lower Level of Obligations

Small developing economies should be required to undertake commitments and concessions to the extent consistent with their adjustment capacity, development, financial and trade needs, and administrative and institutional capabilities for implementation. This should be negotiated on an issue-by-issue basis and, where appropriate, on a product-by-product basis.

Consideration could be given to the inclusion of an "enabling clause" for smaller economies, which would allow for the differential application of rules in the levels of obligation for smaller economies within the developing country framework.

Asymmetrically Phased Implementation Timetables

Given the small size of firms in small developing economies and the small scale of production and limited size of the market, export sectors will require a longer period of adjustment than larger firms and larger, more developed economies. Hence, there must be asymmetrically phased implementation of rules and disciplines, permitting a longer adjustment period for smaller economies. For example, in agricultural trade, in particular food items, small developing economies should be allowed the flexibility to implement their commitments in reducing protection and domestic support over a longer period than the implementation period prescribed for larger economies.

Provision for such differentiated phase-in schedules was included in both the Agreement on Textiles and Clothing (ATC) as well as the TRIPs agreement. In the ATC, small suppliers were allowed longer phase-out periods. Under the TRIPs agreement, developing countries and least developed countries were allowed the longest phase-in period for implementation of their TRIPs obligations.

Exemptions from Commitments in Certain Areas

Given the vast disparities in size, the extremely small size of some economies, and the human, financial, and institutional cost involved in implementing the trade agreements, smaller economies should be permitted some exemptions. This would not only address the question of disparities but also avoid delays, which may occur because smaller economies, despite their best efforts, are not able to meet certain requirements and timetables. For example, if, as is likely, exports subsidies are outlawed, smaller economies should be exempt from this requirement, or standardizing technical requirements through national organizations and participation in international standardization processes where these have no applicability because of lack of production or importation or exports. Where complete exemptions are not feasible, *de minimis* provisions would be helpful.

An example of this type of measure is the provision that exempts developing countries from the disciplines in two types of export subsidies. This type of provision should be included in other aspects of the WTO agreements. For example, in government procurement agreements the very small developing countries of the eastern Caribbean should have their government procurement markets exempt from coverage, given their very small size.

Flexibility in Application and Adherence of Disciplines under Prescribed Circumstances

Small developing economies are highly open economies and are therefore more susceptible to balance of payments problems. This is particularly the case for small developing countries where balance of payments deficits tend to be persistent because of their structural origins.

These provisions are not confined to any particular type of country, but all members may avail themselves of the right resort to these provisions under the circumstances prescribed. Because of their vulnerability to balance of payment problems, small developing economies should be permitted additional facilities to enable them (a) to maintain sufficient flexibility in their tariff structure to be able to grant the tariff protection required for the establishment of a particular industry and (b) to apply quantitative restrictions for balance of payments purposes that take full account of the continued high level of demand for imports likely to be generated by their programs of economic development.

The agreement on safeguards could enable the small developing economies to take such action in the case of balance of payments difficulties.

Enabling Access to Mediation

The Understanding on Rules and Procedures governing the Settlement of Disputes is currently under review in light of the experiences of the past few years. The problems that have been identified with the operations of the dispute settlement mechanism include (a) the limited capability of small developing countries to make use of the mechanism because of their inadequate expertise and institutional capacity to implement panel findings and (b) the high cost and administrative difficulties of using the dispute settlement mechanism.

There are provisions in the Dispute Settlement Office that provide for technical assistance to developing countries. This needs to be extended to smaller economies and made more effective.

Technical Assistance and Training

The promise of technical assistance to the small developing economies is widely accepted. Such assistance could (a) contribute to efforts by small developing economies to undertake the structural, institutional, and legislative adjustment; (b) promote the development of adequate institutional capacity by training technicians and negotiators to improve their participation in trade negotiations and the implementation of the international trade agreements; and (c) assist small developing economies in fulfilling their obligations under the various international agreements, particularly commitments under the WTO.

Technical assistance is provided for in 14 provisions across six agreements and one ministerial decision. The major difficulty has been ensuring that these provisions are given practical effect and that the presently inadequate funding be substantially increased.

Summary

It is now customary that national economic policies and international trade agreements recognize that firms and countries differ in structure, income levels, and developments. However, one of the most important differences, variations in size, has not received sufficient attention. While attempts have been made to address this disparity in national economic policy, this issue has not been addressed at the international level. Given the number of small developing economies, the intensification of globalization, and the progressive liberalization of international trade and investment, there is an urgent need to tackle this question.

Small developing economies have characteristics that affect their capacity to participate in and benefit from international trade. Given that they constitute a large part of the membership of the WTO and given that their effective participation will enhance both their own development and that of the global economy, international trade agreements must take account of their circumstances. The WTO as the multilateral framework for international trade must incorporate in its objectives, disciplines, and schedules measures specifically designed to facilitate the effective participation of small economies.

None of the proposed measures of differentiated treatment, a well-established principle in trade agreements of all types, will set a precedent in the WTO agreements. S&D Treatment must be designed specifically to address the characteristics of small developing economies. This will entail meaningful implementation of the type of special and differential measures that already exist in the WTO and the development of new measures. The recognition of the category of small developing economies involves agreeing on a definition, a technical task that can be solved by the science of economics. If a new category has to be acknowledged, then so be it, as was done in the case of "transition economies" and "highly indebted poor countries." The obstacles are not technical but political, but the fact that small developing countries constitute a very small share of world trade and the biggest single category in the WTO may be a salutary factor.

8

Evaluating Benefits
of Liberalization to Date
for Developing Countries

Usha Jeetah

In the middle of the last century, the implosion in Europe that was World War II saw the end of the colonial economic system that had dominated the world for over 400 years. The decades following the collapse of the European colonial powers saw the rise of scores of newly independent countries of all shapes and sizes, ranging from behemoths like India, which today boasts more than a billion people, and Brazil, to tiny countries such Mauritius, which has a population of just over 1 million.

The colonial experience also deeply shaped the newly independent countries. In some cases, particularly in Africa, these countries were pure geographic creations of the colonial powers who sat down at the map in Berlin in the 1880s and carved up the continent into artificial entities cutting across natural, religious, and ethnic boundaries. In the case of Mauritius, itself, it was a complete creation of colonialism, for there were no native Mauritians apart from the dodo, and we know its fate. Peoples from every continent, cultural background, and religion were thrust together on a tiny island in the middle of nowhere to sink or swim together.

The colonial powers not only created these artificial countries but also imposed their economic dominance and model on them. Their *raison d'être* was to provide the raw materials for the colonial center. In the case of Mauritius, this was the monoculture of sugar. The British wanted Mauritius, like many other small islands or countries with ports, for its strategic position. But, of course, the British were unwilling to pay for their colonial presence themselves and thus used the resources of those countries to pay for their administration. At the time of independence in 1968, 95 percent of Mauritian exports and its source of foreign exchange was the monocrop of raw sugar sold to the British sugar refiners. Mauritius's case is mirrored in scores of other cases throughout Africa and the Caribbean.

Not only were post-colonial economies skewed, but in many cases, particularly in Africa, the local economy, especially private enterprise, administration, and civil society, were deliberately destroyed in favor of the colonial state and the expatriates of the colonial powers. Today Mauritius, a major sugar producer, has no refinery, nor Mali, the major African cotton producer, any spinning factory.

After World War II, Bretton Woods sought to bring a new harmony to the international economy but based again on the model of the developed countries that made up the principal members of these international financial institutions. The failure of the International Monetary Fund's "one model fits all" Structural Adjustment Programs in Africa has been well documented even by the World Bank.

It is only when the specificities of the developing countries are taken into consideration that appropriate development plans can be implemented. This is why it is essential that the concept of Special and Differential (S&D) Treatment must be integrated into world economic discussions. In fact, when S&D Treatment has been properly utilized in economic programs, these have been successful. For example, there are three such programs that have proved to be successful for developing countries.

Special and Differential Treatment

In Mauritius, the Yaoundé Convention,[1] then the Lomé Convention,[2] and now the Cotonou Convention[3] have been vital to its economic success. Since independence and owing to complete reliance on sugar, every Mauritian government has sought to diversify its economic base. Through the market preferences that were offered into the European Union, Mauritius was able to attract investors who set up a now-thriving apparel industry. This has become a major employer, a principal source of foreign exchange, and has permitted Mauritian entrepreneurs to invest in Madagascar, Mozambique, Botswana, and Tanzania, and thus has helped the regional development so necessary for a solid regional renaissance.

The duty-free and quota-free access to Europe has enabled Mauritius to compete with traditional textile and apparel producers from the Indian subcontinent and from Asia. Mauritius's isolation, high freight costs, long lead times, limited labor pool, and lack of textile history would have rebuffed possible investors had it not been for the guaranteed market access to the European Union.

Access to the European Union did help greatly to spur the economy of Mauritius, and if more developing countries did not utilize these preferences, it was for other reasons than any fault in the Lomé Convention. In fact, in 1974, when the world price of sugar had reached astronomical prices, Mauritius negotiated under the Lomé Convention for a guaranteed market access at a lower price calling upon both the S&D case of Mauritius and the multifunctionality of sugar in its economy. Under the Sugar Protocol, Mauritius was provided with a major preferential access to the European Union. The price of sugar plummeted in 1977, but Mauritius maintained its economic stability through the special provisions of the Lomé Convention.

The Generalized System of Preferences

The Generalized System of Preferences (GSP) is yet another program that recognizes S&D Treatment and which has been of great help to those developing countries that have developed a manufacturing sector. This is particularly true for the countries of Asia that have benefited considerably from the GSP for access to Europe and the United States. While Africa, because of its lack of manufacturing capability, represents only about 2 percent of the GSP used in the United States, under the new African Growth and Opportunity Act (AGOA), there is a Special Africa GSP for eight years, which does allow for almost all exports from Africa to enter quota- and duty-free to the United States. Now shoes and leather goods can be duty exempt. Recently a major U.S. company has set up in Ghana for the export of tuna, benefiting from the AGOA.

The African Growth and Opportunity Act

The AGOA is another example of a successful use of S&D Treatment. In 2005, the end of the Multi-Fiber Agreement will free the world textile and apparel giants from quota limitation placed on them by the industrialized countries. Furthermore, since in most of these countries the quota is tight, it is actually sold and adds a quite considerable factor to the price of clothes. With no quota, there will be no quota price, and so developing countries will be able to flood the markets of the industrial countries. As a result, small countries like Mauritius and those in the Caribbean and the infant industries in Africa would be destroyed.

The AGOA does, by recognizing the specificities of Africa, provide the preferences that will permit Africa to continue to compete. Not only will the AGOA save Mauritius in the U.S. market, but it will allow Mauritius to invest in its neighbors to help develop their industrial base. Eight years ago the main export of Madagascar to the United States was vanilla. Today Madagascar is the fourth-biggest apparel exporter to the United States, and in two years will overtake Mauritius itself. This has meant the creation of employment, inflow of foreign exchange and investment, and, most encouragingly, a return inflow of Malagasy investment into the island nation.

So there are clear examples that a better understanding of the specificities of different countries does make for more economic sense. Even the World Bank recognizes this. In the past the World Bank provided loans based on the gross domestic product (GDP) per capita basis that simply took the country's GDP and divided it by the population. This created the mathematical fallacy that with a population of only 60,000, the Seychelles had a GDP more than twice that of South Africa, Botswana, or Mauritius. The World Bank did not take into account the other factors in a country's ability to pay back its loans.

After the campaign by small states, together with the Commonwealth Secretariat, the World Bank is studying the concept of a vulnerability index that would identify those countries that, owing to their high economic exposure, remoteness, isolation, and proneness to natural disasters, are vulnerable despite their relatively high per capita incomes.

Definitions of Vulnerability

The Commonwealth Secretariat's 1997 report on vulnerability argues that "vulnerability is the consequence of two sets of factors: (a) the incidence and intensity of risk and threat and (b) the ability to withstand risks and threats (resistance) and to 'bounce back' from their consequences (resilience)." First, the United Nations has distinguished two important considerations in the notion of vulnerability: economic vulnerability and ecological fragility, noting the interconnection of these two factors. Second, the U.N. makes a distinction "between structural vulnerability, which results from factors that are durably independent from the political will of countries, and the vulnerability deriving from economic policy, which results from choices made in a recent past, and is therefore conjectural."

This is another example of the necessity for the international financial institutions to more closely define their understanding of "developing countries." There is no doubt that the World Trade Organization (WTO) has noted the needs of developing countries and Paragraph 8 of the Draft Ministerial Text of December 3, 1999, on Small Economies states that

> We undertake to take positive and concrete measures to ensure that developing countries, particularly the least developed countries and small, vulnerable economies, and transition economies, secure a share in the growth of international trade commensurate with their economic development needs. Reduction and elimination of protection on products and sector of export interest to developing countries would contribute to this goal. Recognizing that developing countries may need flexibility in the implementation of multilateral trade agreements and commitments, we are committed to making all areas of special and differential treatment effective and operational. We also recognize the problems and concerns facing economies in transition and instruct that these be given continuing importance in the WTO work program.

However, are these statements of intention sufficient? Constantine Michalapoulos[4] states, "Yet, WTO rules regarding the treatment of developing countries by developed is in most cases identical (except for the least developed countries). Singapore and Korea are supposed to be treated the same way as Ghana and Saint Lucia; Argentina and Brazil the same as the Maldives and Senegal."

Conclusion

Mauritius is a multicultural, pluri-ethnic country, and this is its strength. The WTO, while constantly referring to S&D Treatment, has failed to deal successfully with this question, since it has not been willing to accept the basic concept that there is not just one but many S&D groups of developing countries that need positive and proactive programs adapted to their specific needs. It is not by exempting countries from specific rules of the WTO that a clear policy on S&D Treatment is being created.

Again, to quote Constantine Michalopoulos, "Without a gradation policy which would permit a narrower definition of which countries should be eligible for special and differential, developed countries would: (a) continue to make commitments to developing countries in general which are not concrete; (b) make concrete commitments only to least developed nations which have a small share of world trade; (c) rely on their own criteria—frequently nontransparent and politically motivated—in the determination of which countries to provide more favorable treatment or market access."

Under the AGOA, there is such a gradation. Six or seven Sub-Saharan African countries, owing to their higher development, have fewer benefits than the majority that are still at a poorer level of development. Mauritius is one of those countries with fewer benefits. Mauritius is not always happy about this, but if this is the cost to pay so that the African region as a whole can move forward and upward, then of course we accept this gradation. However, there must be a clear understanding of those economies that are vulnerable. This is why Mauritius also supports Paragraph 56 of the Draft Ministerial Text, which states, "We initiate a work program, involving all relevant WTO bodies, to identify concrete trade-related measures for the fuller integration of small, vulnerable economies into the multilateral trading system."

This is why it is essential for the international financial institutions to revisit the concept of S&D Treatment not as an exception to WTO rules but as a right. This is why the specificities of each country should be studied closely to seek the most appropriate way forward for their economic development in the globalization process. Small economies, landlocked countries, remoteness, economically and ecologically vulnerable states, small islands, resource-challenged countries, and faster developing countries that have their specific problems not only can but must be addressed individually and in groups and not through passive exemptions but by active programs.

Notes

1. In 1963, the original six signatories (France, Germany, Italy, and the Benelux countries) signed a trade and aid agreement with the Associated African States and Madagascar in Yaoundé, Cameroon. It remained in effect until the Lomé Convention in 1975.

2. The Lomé Convention is an international aid and trade agreement between the Africa, Caribbean, and Pacific (ACP) group and the European Union aimed at supporting the "ACP States' efforts to achieve comprehensive, self reliant and self-sustained development." Four such conventions have been signed to date. The first convention (Lomé I) was signed on February 28, 1975. Lomé II and III were signed in 1979 and 1985, respectively. The current convention, Lomé IV, covers the period from 1990 to 2000 and is the most extensive development cooperation agreement between northern and southern countries both in terms of scope (aid and trade) and the number of signatories. The convention states that ACP cooperation is to be based on partnership, equality, solidarity, and mutual interest. The convention also recognizes the principle of sovereignty and the right of each ACP state to define its own development strategies and policies, affirming development centered on people, respect, and promotion of human, political, social, and economic rights. Lomé IV covers a broad range of sectors eligible for support under the development finance cooperation chapters of the convention. These include the environment, agriculture, food security and rural development, fisheries, commodities, industry, mining and energy, enterprise (private sector) development, services, trade, cultural and social cooperation, and regional cooperation. Lomé also has extensive provisions for trade cooperation that provide preferential treatment for ACP exports to the European Union.

3. The Cotonou Convention is the new partnership agreement between the 77-member ACP group of states and the 15-member European Union. The Cotonou Convention replaces the four previous Lomé conventions, which structured ACP–European Union trade, development, and broader relations since 1975. Lomé IV expired at the end of February 2000, while the year and a half–long negotiations for a successor arrangement between the ACP and the European Union was reaching finality. The convention is geared to tackle poverty within the ACP states by establishing effective ACP–European Union political dialogue, development support, and trade and broader economic cooperation. It is particularly concerned to reverse the trend toward economic, technological, and social marginalization of the ACP states, specifically endeavoring to stimulate regional integration among the ACP states and their better involvement in globalization trends. The convention strives to enhance ACP–European Union adherence to the accepted international principles of respect for human rights, the rule of law, good governance, and democratic processes and practices.

4. See Michalopoulos, Constantine. 2000. "The Role of Special and Differential Treatment for Developing Countries in GATT and the World Trade Organization." Working Paper 2388. World Bank, Washington, D.C.

9

Leveraging Trade and Global Market Integration for Poverty Reduction

Krisda Piampongsant

The Association of Southeast Asian Nations (ASEAN) was established in 1967 to promote the economic, social, and cultural development of the region through cooperative programs; to safeguard the political and economic stability of the region against big-power rivalry; and to serve as a forum for the resolution of intraregional differences. The current members are Brunei Darussalam, Cambodia, Indonesia, the Lao People's Democratic Republic, Malaysia, Myanmar, the Philippines, Singapore, Thailand, and Vietnam. The ASEAN Free Trade Area (AFTA) was established in 1992. A Common Effective Preferential Tariff was signed in 1992 and stipulated that the tariff rates levied on a wide range of products traded within the region was to be reduced to 0–5 percent. Moreover, quantitative restrictions and other nontariff barriers would be eliminated. The target date for AFTA's full establishment is 2002.

Not a Level Playing Field

The economic world is not a level playing field. There are differences among nations in size, economic growth, and political power. The Special and Differential (S&D) Treatment was designed to take account of such differences.

The need for S&D Treatment is imperative in agriculture, given the recent financial crisis in Southeast Asia and Latin America. Furthermore, the world economic slump continues unabated and further drives down agricultural production and output and commodity prices. A number of developing countries find it difficult to implement some of the agreements of the Uruguay Round (UR) Agreement on Agriculture (AoA). The economic crisis resulted in considerable pressure on their exports and balance of payments.

Relevant S&D Elements in Agriculture for Developing Countries

The ASEAN nations have stipulated a few key issues in the AoA in regard to agriculture: (a) direct or indirect measures that include input subsidies and investment as identified in Article 6.2 of the AoA must remain exempt from reduction commitments, (b) measures intended to promote agricultural diversification must be exempt from reduction commitments, (c) the existing *de minimis* concept and threshold must continue to be applied to developing countries, (d) developing countries must be given an effective and meaningful degree of autonomy on policy instruments to address food security concerns, and (e) developing countries must have differential commitments and modalities and must be allowed the flexibility to continue the application of special safeguards.

Initiatives for ASEAN Integration

ASEAN has made commitments to further integrate itself into the world trade system. By 2002 the average tariff rate among ASEAN countries will be 3.54 percent, a drastic drop from 1993, when the average tariff was 12.76 percent. In 2003 the rate will drop further, and by the end of the decade will be 0 percent for the original six members (Indonesia, Malaysia, the Philippines, Singapore, Brunei, and Thailand). However, for newer members, the S&D Treatment will come into effect, and the target dates have been more lenient: new members must phase in their products before 2015 and must achieve 0 percent tariff by 2018 or earlier.

During the Fourth Informal ASEAN Summit held in Singapore on November 24, 2000, the ASEAN leaders launched an Initiative for ASEAN Integration to narrow the divide within ASEAN and to provide a framework on law. More developed ASEAN members could help the newer members. To date, all new members have submitted their Training Needs Assessment. Also, the six original members have agreed to provide a bilateral Generalized System of Preferences (GSP) to the new members. The implementation of the ASEAN-GSP scheme to new members is anticipated to start in 2002.

Regional Integration Initiatives

Australia and New Zealand

In keeping with the principle of open regionalism, ASEAN is now engaged in establishing further integration with Australia and New Zealand and their Closer Economic Relations (CER) Agreement. ASEAN, Australia, and New Zealand have begun discussions to identify the five fields of co-operation that will fall under trade facilitation, capacity building, trade and investment promotion, and the new economy.

ASEAN-China

With ASEAN Plus Three, ASEAN met with China and agreed in March 2001 to establish the ASEAN-China Expert Group on Economic Cooperation. The first meeting was held in Beijing on April 26–27, 2001. Under the theme of "Forging Closer ASEAN-China Economic Relations in the Twenty-First Century," both have started work on the enhancement of economic relations between them, including a possibility of a free trade area. A deeper and broader cooperation has been identified in all economic fields to promote greater trade and investment flows regionally and globally, and will cover trade and investment facilitation, capacity building, minimization of trade impediments and the cost associated with it, and a narrowing of the development gap.

ASEAN-Japan

ASEAN-Japan Expert Group is also focusing its future task on the possibility of establishing a free trade area between ASEAN and Japan. The areas of cooperation would include, among others, trade and investment, information technology, environment, small and medium enterprises, industrial standards, and intellectual property rights.

ASEAN and the WTO

Currently, three ASEAN members, Cambodia, the Lao People's Democratic Republic, and Vietnam, are applying for WTO membership. Speaking at the East Asia Economic Summit of the World Economic Forum in Singapore in October 1998, General-Secretary Severino said that ASEAN welcomes, in principle, the further liberalization of world trade, especially at this time of Southeast Asia's developing economic recovery. He predicted that ASEAN would benefit particularly from a significant liberalization of world trade in food and agricultural products, the freer movement of persons, and the lowering of tariffs on labor-intensive manufactured products.

The Secretary-General added that several ASEAN countries are major exporters of agricultural products and of commercial services. Exports of professional services would increase if the movement of persons was made freer. He also said that ASEAN had recently announced its e-ASEAN initiative, under which a comprehensive action plan is to be worked out for developing information technology in the region and launching it into the information age.

The Secretary-General observed that ASEAN had generally low tariffs on industrial goods and would therefore benefit from the lowering of such tariffs by other countries. The Secretary-General said that ASEAN had responded to the financial crisis and paved the way for its economic recovery in four ways: undertaking domestic financial and economic reform, proposing ideas for the reform of the international financial system, accelerating the ASEAN Free Trade Area and regional economic integration in general, and remaining open to the global economy.

It is in this spirit, the Secretary-General said, that ASEAN welcomed a new round of global trade negotiations. In September 1999, the ASEAN economic ministers called for the effective implementation of special and differential treatment provisions of the WTO AoA and greater attention to capacity building and technical assistance to facilitate their ability to participate fully in the WTO.

Conclusion

As the WTO Ministerial Meeting draws near, developing countries have been voicing their concerns over the lack of a "development box" or a "development round" as an integral element in the negotiations. There has been a further disintegration and erosion of their economies less than two years after Seattle. Developing countries have reiterated the need to pay more attention to the real sectors of the economy that would sustain and survive through the cycles of the present economic downturn. It is a pity that their economies are now in tatters after having benefited from three or four decades of hard work financed by the development community. It is imperative that the World Bank and industrialized countries refrain from imposing sanctions and penalizing further the "Love's Labor" that has almost been lost since 1997.

More important, in spite of the implementation under all the colorful boxes, an additional "enabling box," encompassing and cutting across sectors, should be established. With the help of the World Bank and other international organizations, including nongovernmental organizations, this so-called enabling box will facilitate, as it were, the least developed countries and the developing countries in implementing their trade-related development activities as a key element of the Development Round.

Part III

The World Trade Organization, the New Trade Round, Development, and Poverty Reduction

10
Options for Agricultural Policy Reform in the World Trade Organization Negotiations

Mary E. Burfisher

The Uruguay Round (UR) Agreement on Agriculture (AoA), signed in 1994, was a first step in a long-term process of global agricultural policy reform. The agreement provided the starting point for further reform by including a provision that member countries resume negotiations on agriculture by December 31, 1999, one year before the end of the AoA implementation period for developed countries. Although efforts failed to begin a full round of negotiations in Seattle, in November 1999, the negotiations on the agriculture sector were initiated in Geneva in March 2000. They are being conducted as special sessions of the WTO Committee on Agriculture.

The new negotiations are expected to address three areas of national agricultural policies. These areas, which are sometimes called the three pillars of the agreement, are market access (tariffs, tariff rate quotas, and other trade barriers), domestic support, and export subsidies. Article 20 of the AoA also provided for other topics to be considered in further negotiations. These "built-in" agenda items include discussion of members' experiences with the implementation of the UR commitments; the effects of the reduction commitments on world trade in agriculture; nontrade issues such as environmental concerns, rural development, and food security; and provisions for Special and Differential (S&D) Treatment of less developed countries.

Although the new negotiations are mandated to continue a process of reform, analyzing a hypothetical scenario in which all agricultural tariffs and subsidies are fully eliminated can help to define what is at stake in global agricultural negotiations, and to prioritize negotiating objectives. Global agricultural policy distortions impose substantial costs on the world economy. Over the long term (of about 15 years), their full elimination would lead to an increase in world welfare, or consumer purchasing power, of US$56 billion annually, which represents about two-tenths per-

**Figure 10.1 Many Countries Would Share Consumer
Purchasing Power Gains from Elimination of Agricultural
Tariffs and Subsidies**

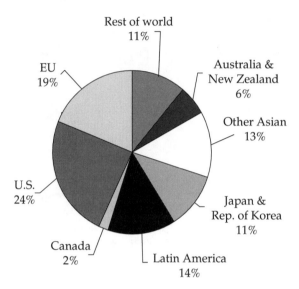

Source: Diao, Somwaru, and Roe (2001).

cent of projected global gross domestic product (GDP) in 15 years. Benefits to the United States from the elimination of world agricultural policy
distortions would be US$13 billion annually (figure 10.1). Because U.S.
tariffs, domestic support, and export subsidies are relatively low, most of
the benefits for the United States would come from policy reforms in our
trade partners.

Eliminating agricultural policy distortions would help raise world
agricultural prices in several ways. A country's removal of tariffs and
other import barriers will lower its production and increase its demand
for products from exporting countries, and raise world prices. Eliminating domestic support removes the motivation for farmers to overpro-
duce, which depresses the price of subsidized commodities. Eliminating
export subsidies prevents the dumping onto world markets of excess supplies, which are often the result of domestic subsidies. In total, eliminating
all agricultural policy distortions (tariffs, tariff-rate quotas, domestic support, and export subsidies) could raise world agricultural prices to about
12 percent higher than they would otherwise be. Elimination of only tariffs and tariff-rate quotas (TRQs) would account for most (52 percent) of
the potential price increase. Eliminating only domestic support or only

export subsidies would have comparatively smaller roles in the price effect, of 31 percent and 13 percent, respectively. (The remaining 4 percent reflects the interactions when removing all policies simultaneously.) Eliminating all of the agricultural policies of the European Union alone would account for 38 percent of the potential agricultural price effects of global policy reforms. Japanese and Korean policies combined would account for 13 percent of the global price increase, and U.S. policies would account for about 16 percent. Despite higher world food prices, consumers in most countries would still benefit because the removal of tariffs lowers domestic food prices, and because of the overall economic gains from a more efficient allocation of global agricultural resources.

Options for Reforming Agricultural Policies

Planning a process of reform is more complicated than assuming a full elimination of tariffs and subsidies. Partial reform requires a choice among targets or strategies, and the alternatives are likely to imply different distributions of costs and benefits from reform. In this project we analyzed broad, generic reforms that framed the likely outcomes of the negotiations. We did not analyze any specific country proposals. Also, some farm subsidies are operationally linked with trade policies, and reforms of one policy can have an impact on the costs and benefits of interrelated policies. For example, price support programs that attempt to support a domestic price level for commodities at levels above the world price can only be cost effective if there are insulating trade policies in place. Where possible, our analysis took this policy interdependence into account.

Options for Reducing Tariffs and Making Them More Uniform

Despite the progress made in the UR, global agricultural tariffs remain high: The average (simple, unweighted) global agricultural tariff of industrial countries is 62 percent, compared with about 4 percent for manufactures. The average U.S. agricultural tariff is relatively low (12 percent) compared with the average rates of the European Union (21 percent), Canada (24 percent), Japan (33 percent), and Norway (152 percent).

There is also substantial variation, or dispersion, in tariff rates across commodities. Tariff dispersion refers to differences in a country's rates of protection across commodities. Dispersion can increase the distorting effects of tariffs. An example of dispersion is the escalation of tariffs with the degree of product processing. Tariff escalation can result in the effective protection exceeding the nominal rate if tariffs are relatively low on imported intermediate inputs. Imposing higher tariffs on processed goods also impedes trade in high-value products, the fastest growing segment of world agricultural trade, which tends to be highly sensitive to price. Another issue related to dispersion is the problem of the occasional very high tariffs, or "mega-tariffs," which are sometimes called tariff peaks.

One way to measure and compare tariff dispersion is to analyze the frequency with which countries' tariff lines fall within ranges of tariff rates. The United States differs from other industrial countries in that most of its tariffs are extremely low, at 5 percent or less, while only a very small share are extremely high, at over 100 percent. All other industrial countries have a much larger proportion of relatively high tariffs.

Historically, trade negotiations have taken two broad approaches to tariff reform: formula and request-and-offer. The formula approach defines a general rule that applies to all tariffs; for example, "reduce all tariffs by 10 percent." In request-and-offer negotiations, countries draw up lists of the tariffs they want other countries to reduce and the tariffs they are willing to reduce in exchange. Request-and-offer negotiations can be effective in achieving greater market access for specific commodities than might be achieved by formulas. However, they can leave protection in place for the least competitive industries, and they may be unable to achieve deep enough cuts in the very high tariffs that abound in industrial countries' tariff schedules.

A third alternative—potentially complementary to either of the first two—is to attempt to solve sectoral tariff problems on a multilateral basis. Sectoral negotiations might seek to harmonize tariffs for a commodity or commodity group. One example of this that has been used with some success is "zero-for-zero," in which all countries agree upon a zero tariff on specific commodities. During the UR, a zero-for-zero agreement was reached for beer.

While a formula approach has some distinct advantages, there can be very different outcomes depending on the type that is adopted. There are two generic types of formulas, and they target the level and the dispersion of tariffs. A linear reduction formula reduces tariff levels by reducing all tariffs proportionately. As an example, consider the case of a country with a uniform tariff, which means there is no tariff dispersion. A linear reduction of 10 percent would reduce the country's average tariff by 10 percent, but would not affect the dispersion, because its tariffs are already uniform. In contrast, harmonization formulas directly target the problem of tariff dispersion. Conceivably, a harmonization formula could require that countries make all of their tariffs a uniform rate. This would leave the average tariff unchanged, but would reduce the dispersion to zero. In practice, many of the tariff reduction formulas proposed in past trade negotiations have included variants that address both tariff levels and tariff dispersion. Many combine some overall reduction of the average rate with harmonization, based on the progressively larger reduction of higher rates, or at least a requirement that all tariffs be reduced so that the problem of tariff dispersion is not significantly worsened.

Given the tariff rates that countries currently have in place, what is likely to be the most effective formula in terms of achieving greater market access? From a global perspective, harmonization formulas that target higher tariffs are more likely to be effective than a linear approach in lowering both the average tariff and the dispersion because of the many, very high tariff lines in the current structure of global tariffs (table 10.1). Harmonization formulas that focus on eliminating low, or "nuisance," tariffs would have a relatively large affect on the average U.S. tariff, because most U.S. tariffs are low. Formulas such as the "Swiss" formula applied to manufactures in the Tokyo Round, which mandates proportionately larger cuts in high tariffs and have a relatively greater impact on other industrial countries' tariffs than on the United States. This is because most other industrial countries have a larger number of higher tariff rates.

Options for Reforming Domestic Support

One of the most important aspects of the AoA was the distinction made between domestic agricultural support that significantly distorts production and trade (amber box subsidies) and those subsidies that were agreed to have minimal or no distorting impacts (green box subsidies). Only the former was made subject to reduction commitments. (The AoA also exempted blue box policies, which are subsidies offset by supply constraints.) These commitments were implemented by defining an aggregate subsidy measure, the aggregate measurement of support (AMS), as a means to quantify and compare countries' overall annual levels of domestic support that are subject to AoA disciplines. WTO members were required to reduce their amber box domestic support during the implementation period relative to a base level of support in the 1986–88 period. (See table 10.2.)

The AoA left in place an uneven playing field of domestic support across countries and commodities. Countries with relatively high support levels in the base period have AMS limits, or ceilings, that allow continued relatively high support, while countries with no support in the base period are constrained in their ability to introduce it. In addition to the disparity among countries in their total levels of support, there is dispersion in the level of support provided to individual commodities. Many countries provide most of their commodity-specific AMS support to a small number of commodities, especially rice, sugar, and dairy.

As in the case of tariffs, there are two general approaches to domestic policy reform: lower the aggregate levels and lower the dispersion of

Table 10.1. Effects of Alternative Tariff Reduction Formulas on Average and Dispersion of Tariffs
(Percentage rates)

Formula name	Formula	United States		Industrial country total	
		Average	*Dispersion*	*Average*	*Dispersion*
Base Linear	— 50 percent reduction in all tariffs	11.9 6.0	55.0 27.5	45.0 22.5	130.0 65.0
Sliding scale	Eliminate tariffs under 5 percent, 50 percent reduction in other tariffs, with a cap of 50 percent	4.2	8.9	11.3	16.6
Swiss	Progressively larger cuts on high tariffs, with a cap of 45 percent	7.4	11.0	12.3	

Notes: Dispersion is measured as one standard deviation, the average distance of all tariffs from the mean tariff.
Source: Wainio, Gibson, and Whitley (2001).

Table 10.2. Reduction Commitments if Uruguay Round Base Is Lowered an Additional 20 Percent

Country	Percent of WTO ceiling met in 1998	Required percent cut in AMS
Australia	23.4	0.0
Canada	8.6	0.0
European Union	74.5	–7.1
Japan	77.2	–10.4
Korea, Rep. of	80.1	–13.5
Mexico	6.6	0.0
Norway	87.8	–21.1
New Zealand	0.0	0.0
Poland	8.3	0.0
Switzerland	71.0	–2.5
United States	44.7	0.0

Source: Young et al. (2001). Calculations based on data from the Organisation for Economic Co-operation and Development and WTO.

domestic support. A reduction in countries' overall levels of domestic support, without affecting the distribution of its support across commodities, could be achieved by extending the AoA commitment for industrialized countries with a further 20 percent reduction in the AMS ceilings (40 percent below the 1986–88 base AMS). This would affect countries differently because many countries' aggregate domestic support is already below the ceilings they committed to in the AoA, based on 1998 program levels. As an example, an additional 20 percent reduction in the AMS ceilings would leave many countries unaffected, including the United States, Canada, Mexico, Australia, and New Zealand.[1]

An alternative approach to reforming domestic support is to level the playing field across countries and commodities. Variation in levels of support can be reduced by setting limits on commodity-specific support, expressed as a percentage of value of production. (Non-commodity-specific support is assumed to be distributed to commodities based on shares in total farm production or historical program benefits.) If commodity support is leveled across countries and commodities, more countries and a different mix of commodities will be affected by reform. Most countries, including the United States, would now be required to reduce support for at least one commodity, especially for livestock, dairy, rice, and sugar (table 10.3).

Most of the value of domestic farm support is provided through price support programs, and most price support programs are implemented

Table 10.3. Commodity-Specific AMS: Reduction Needed to Keep Commodity-Specific AMS Less than 30 Percent

Country		Percent change from base AMS										
	Total	Wheat	Rice	Coarse grains	Oilseeds	Sugar	Milk	Beef and sheep	Other meat	Wool	Horti-culture	Miscel-laneous
Australia	0	0	0	0	0	0	0	0	0	0	0	0
Canada	0	0	0	0	0	0	-48	0	0	0	0	0
European Union	0	0	0	0	0	0	-44	-15	0	0	-16	-28
Iceland	-38	0	0	0	0	0	-63	0	-70	0	0	0
Japan	-19	-65	-64	-56	-17	-51	-62	-6	-11	0	0	0
Korea, Rep. of	0	0.00	-57	-57	-61	0	0	-27	0	0	0	0
Mexico	0	0.00	0	0	0	-9	0	0	0	0	0	0
Norway	0	-37	0	-31	0	0	-10	0	-20	0	0	0
New Zealand	0	0	0	0	0	0	0	0	0	0	0	0
Poland	0	0	0	0	0	0	0	0	0	0	0	0
Switzerland	-41	-35	0	36	-52	-47	-43	-36	-40	0	0	-40
United States	0	0	0	0	0	-19	-49	0	0	0	0	0

Source: Young et al. (2001), based on WTO notifications, Organisation for Economic Co-operation and Development producer subsidy equivalent data, and calculations from the U.S. Department of Agriculture Economic Research Service.

through trade restraints and export subsidies rather than through stock holding. The dependence of domestic support on trade policies has led some to argue for a strategic approach to negotiations: focus on reducing tariffs and export subsidies and let tighter trade policy rules force reforms on domestic farm programs. Assuming that countries respond to constraints on domestic support by dismantling related import barriers and export subsidies, the trade policy component of both the AMS scenarios considered here accounts for 83 percent of their global trade effects. This provides a measure of the dependence of domestic support on trade policies.

Reforming Export Subsidies

Export subsidies are usually used when relatively high domestic support prices create an excess supply, and subsidies are needed to sell export products at lower world prices. The AoA approached the reform of export subsidies by placing restrictions on both the volume and the value of subsidized exports. Targeting both the value and the volume creates effective constraints in times of both high and low prices. When world prices are low, the value constraint is more effective, because the subsidy (the wedge between the internal domestic support price and the competitive export price) becomes larger. When world prices are high, the value constraint becomes less binding, but the volume constraint can still set some limit on export subsidies. Value limits also help to weaken the link between export subsidies and fixed internal price supports, since constrained export subsidies can now only partially offset the effects of declining world prices.

Options for reforming export subsidies are mainly related to the effects on European Union trade policy, since the European Union accounts for more than 90 percent of global export subsidy expenditures. In 1995–96, when world prices were high, the European Union came closer to filling its volume commitments than its value commitments. As world prices fell beginning in 1997, the value of the European Union's export subsidies has increased. Through 1998, the volume commitments have still been more binding on European Union exports than value commitments, with the exceptions of sugar, processed fruits and vegetables, tobacco, and alcohol. Even if it fully eliminates export subsidies, the European Union will be able to competitively export grains and oilseeds, and some pork and poultry, but will continue to be uncompetitive in exports of beef.

Global Policy Reform Facilitates Trade

The movement toward a more market-oriented and orderly global agricultural trading system is important for the United States because of the large and increasing role of trade in U.S. agricultural production and food consumption. Expanding export markets provide an outlet for U.S. agricultural producers as technological advances and increased productivity lead to higher levels of production. For consumers, trade rules help to ensure access to a safe, varied, and abundant, year-round supply of food.

Global agricultural policy distortions impose substantial long-term costs on U.S. producers, consumers, and the world economy. U.S. agricultural tariffs and subsidies are relatively low, suggesting that U.S. domestic adjustments to its own reform are likely to be small, relative to the potentially large benefits to the United States from global reform. Furthermore, U.S. reforms of our own policies within a global framework can help to ensure the overall, long-term competitiveness of the U.S. farm sector in world markets.

Notes

1. This article synthesizes the findings from an Economic Research Service team research project. Team members' articles are published in Burfisher (2001).

References

Burfisher, Mary E., ed. 2001. *Agricultural Policy Reform in the WTO: The Road Ahead.* AER 802. Washington, D.C.: U.S. Department of Agriculture.

Diao, X., A. Somwaru, and T. Roe. 2001. In Mary E. Burfisher, ed., *Agricultural Policy Reform in the WTO: The Road Ahead.* AER 802. Washington, D.C.: U.S. Department of Agriculture.

Wainio, J., P. Gibson, and D. Whitley. 2001. In Mary E. Burfisher, ed., *Agricultural Policy Reform in the WTO: The Road Ahead.* AER 802. Washington, D.C.: U.S. Department of Agriculture.

Young, C., M. Gehlhar, F. Nelson, M. Burfisher, and L. Mitchell. 2001. In Mary E. Burfisher, ed., *Agricultural Policy Reform in the WTO: The Road Ahead.* AER 802. Washington, D.C.: U.S. Department of Agriculture.

11
Policies for Price Risk under Trade Liberalization

Bruce L. Gardner

No feasible World Trade Organization (WTO) agreement on agriculture will achieve fully liberalized markets, but one that followed up and made effective the provisions of the Uruguay Round (UR) Agriculture Agreement (AoA) can result in significant market integration even if trade protection were to remain substantial. The AoA envisions "tariffication" to replace quantitative trade barriers, and as the tariffs get low enough to permit trade above the levels of tariff-rate quotas (TRQs), then domestic prices will move together with international prices even if the remaining tariffs are substantial. Therefore, it is possible, although unlikely, that further trade liberalization, even if incomplete, can increase the variability of domestic prices in commodity-importing countries.

There are three basic points to make. First, although increased price variability is possible with trade liberalization, in most cases it is unlikely to be a serious problem; second, in those cases where it is likely to be a serious problem, relatively efficient price insurance mechanisms are available; and third, attempts to go beyond private sector mechanisms to stabilize price through domestic policy instruments have achieved very mixed results.

Effects of Liberalization on Prices

The possibility of increased domestic price risk under liberalization arises for countries whose current regimes isolate their domestic markets from international markets and which are successful in stabilizing domestic prices within that restricted market. The European Union is an example. But where are the examples in developing countries, especially the poorest ones? The real price risk problems in those countries tend to arise from domestic market crop failures, wars, exchange rate crises, macroeconomic fluctuations, or other internal sources and not from exposure to international commodity markets.[1]

Moreover, international prices facing developing countries are made more unstable by the attempts of industrial countries to insulate their domestic markets. The basic reason is simple: When a global production shortfall or demand surge occurs, buyers and sellers somewhere must adjust their purchases or sales, and it is their resistance to doing so (inelasticity of demand and supply) that causes prices to rise. When some countries insulate their domestic markets, their buyers and sellers do not have to adjust; but the effect is that now people in noninsulating markets—most notably in developing countries—must take on a greater burden of adjustment, and this implies greater price changes in those countries than would occur if markets were fully integrated rather than insulated. Evidence on these points was well summarized in the World Bank's 1986 *World Development Report*, which among other findings reports estimates that global market liberalization would reduce the volatility of all major traded commodities by one-half or more (pp. 131–32).

Nonetheless, more direct evidence that liberalization is beneficial or at least not harmful to stability would be welcomed, especially in countries that prior to liberalization have some degree of policy-induced price stability even if not full insulation from price movements. An example of an episode of liberalization that has occurred since the AoA has gone into effect is the abandonment of annual acreage controls, the government grain stock management, and the grain export subsidies in the United States under the "Freedom to Farm" provisions of the 1996 Farm Act (notwithstanding that significant market distortions remain, notably under the "marketing loan" programs).

Pre-1996 programs placed floors under market prices through the Commodity Credit Corporation loan support and stockholding, at least until the late 1980s. The programs stabilized farmers' receipts through deficiency payments that rose as market prices fell, reduced acreage through annual set-asides when markets were weak, and targeted export subsidies to stimulate foreign demand (in the 1980s). The years since 1996, when these mechanisms were eliminated, have been seen as an unstable period so far, but the question is, how different would recent history have been if pre-1996 programs had been maintained?

Figure 11.1 shows price data for corn and soybeans before and after the Federal Agriculture Improvement and Reform (FAIR) Act of 1996. It is difficult to know when to place the date at which the FAIR Act regime replaced the pre-1996 program as the policy environment for commodity prices. The 1996 crops were the first ones produced and marketed under the FAIR Act, but the influence of the act (and the absence of the pre-1996 programs) should have been felt before the 1996 crop year began, in September 1996. However, the failure of the 1995 version of Freedom to Farm to be enacted suggests that before January 1996, the old regime should be

Figure 11.1 Corn and Soybean Prices Received by Farmers, Monthly, September 1973 to May 2001

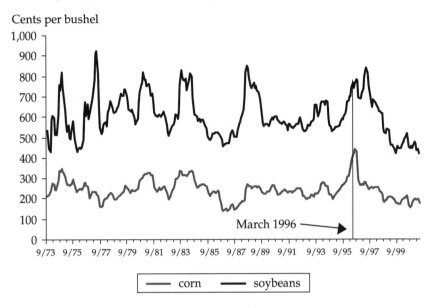

Cents per bushel

March 1996 →

corn — soybeans

regarded as still in place. For purposes of the following analysis, the inception of the FAIR Act, in farmers' and traders' expectations and actions, is assumed to have occurred at the time of the key votes in Congress that ensured passage of the FAIR Act, which is March 1996 and after as the FAIR Act period. February 1996 and earlier will be considered as belonging to the prior regime.

March 1996 was three months before the mid-1990s peak in corn prices and almost a year before the peak in soybean prices, so that peak and the subsequent price declines are part of the FAIR Act experience. As a result, there have been claims that the FAIR Act has been insufficient as a stabilization policy. However, as figure 11.1 indicates, there was plenty of price variability before 1996 (even omitting the early 1970s price runups).

The average farm-level price was slightly lower under the first five years of the FAIR Act than during the preceding 20 years in nominal terms, but real (deflated by the gross domestic product [GDP] deflator) prices averaged much lower in 1996–2001 than in 1975–95. Several measures of price variability are shown. The standard deviation of price within each subperiod around the mean price for that subperiod was much greater in nominal terms under the FAIR Act but in real terms increased only from 62 cents (1996 US$) before FAIR to 66.8 cents after, and the standard deviation of real soybean prices was lower under FAIR. A

Table 11.1. Some Evidence for Corn and Soybeans

Indicator	Pre-FAIR (270 months)		FAIR (63 months)	
	Corn	Beans	Corn	Beans
Mean price (cents/bushel)				
Nominal	244.0	611.0	235.0	583.0
Real (1996 US$)	349.0	872.0	228.0	566.0
Standard deviation of price (cents/bushel)				
Nominal	43.4	95.2	68.9	131.8
Real	62.0	136.0	66.8	128.0
Volatility (standard deviation of price changes)				
Cents/bushel	9.1	24.8	10.8	19.8
Relative (percent change)	3.8	4.0	4.4	3.4

closely related but distinct measure of instability is volatility (using the jargon of finance), the standard deviation of month-to-month prices. Volatility is much lower than the standard deviation of prices themselves because high and low prices tend to be grouped together as figure 11.1 shows. Volatility, measured in terms of either changes in cents or in percentage changes, increased during the FAIR Act period for corn but decreased for soybeans. (See table 11.1.)

Time series regressions were carried out on several measures of volatility as related to commodity stock levels and changes in the U.S. Department of Agriculture's (USDA) supply-demand estimates as well as a dummy for months before and after March 1996. In addition to monthly changes in farm prices received, the analysis also considered monthly changes in prices on the day just after USDA's crop production estimates were announced. The results were similar to those of the raw data above in that the coefficients for the FAIR Act period showed slightly higher volatility for corn and lower volatility for soybeans. But in neither case is the effect statistically significant. Therefore, despite the assertions of uncertainty created by the FAIR Act as compared to prior "countercyclical" policies, in fact there has been no significant increase in price instability in the corn and soybean markets.

Price Risk Management

One means of diffusing the costs to various groups of moving from insulated commodity sectors to a regime of world market price signals is to make use of international forward and futures contracts.[2] Indeed, the use of futures and derivatives markets to offset the ill effects of international price volatility in immature market economies has generated a degree of enthusiasm among economists, analysts, and other experts in international organizations (for example, Claessens and Duncan 1993; Faruqee, Colman, and Scott 1997; and Tsetsekos and Varangis 1998).

The World Bank has taken a lead role in ongoing attempts to make market-based risk management tools available to producers in developing countries that sell into highly volatile world markets (for example, cocoa and coffee). The idea is to work with financial intermediaries, producer cooperatives in the producing countries, and international trading companies to offer price insurance—essentially put options—to producers, perhaps with an international intermediary guaranteeing some of the risk if necessary. Questions remain as to whether this scheme will be able to overcome obstacles, such as sovereign risk and needed producer education, that have prevented private market intermediaries from arising to fulfill this function.

Although likely useful in some contexts, reliance on forward markets as the focus of policy proposals for reform-minded governments is of limited value in light of conditions in world commodity markets and many underdeveloped economies. Forward markets can aid in the reduction of short-term variation, but they would contribute little to avoiding the worst effects of those occasional prolonged periods during which persistently low prices might hurt a developing country's otherwise promising agricultural sector. Moreover, the important food commodities in several developing countries are also often those for which either no forward markets exist, the market is thinly traded (for example, white maize in East Africa), or prices on local commodity markets are sufficiently isolated from futures prices that basic risk renders hedging ineffective. This raises an important question that needs to be addressed: If risk management institutions are as yet missing, and forward markets are inadequate for hedging against several periods of low prices, can a country nevertheless implement policies that would both calm political fears of world commodity price instability and at the same time minimize the distortionary effects usually associated with intervention?

Domestic Policies to Counter Increased International Price Pressures

Governments may attempt to smooth farm income fluctuations by implementing a variety of compensatory income supplements, crop and revenue insurance programs, and debt and tax rescheduling. This approach emphasizes farm income stabilization and is, besides being fiscally expensive, hard to implement efficiently because of the inherent moral hazard and asymmetric information that characterizes such schemes. Various approaches are being tested in developing countries to overcome the element of moral hazard and information problems of crop insurance, but these approaches have substantial fiscal costs and are unlikely priorities from a developing country perspective.

In cases where import pressure is deemed excessive, or trading practices by exporters are alleged to be unfair, the net importing country can take antidumping action or implement "safeguards." Antidumping actions may be taken against a foreign country through import duties when products are priced less than the normal value and thereby threatening or causing damage to a domestic industry. However, it is widely accepted that antidumping has itself developed into an instrument of protection. But there are those who believe that antidumping and other similar mechanisms are an essential safety valve needed to deal with the adjustment costs of trade liberalization.

A safeguard is designed to provide temporary relief for domestic activities when imports are entering a country in such increased quantities deemed large enough to cause or threaten serious injury to domestic producers. Under the AoA, safeguard measures must be nondiscriminatory, may not be introduced without a proper investigation by the competent authorities, and must include public notice and hearing requirements. A time limit has been placed on safeguard measures that may be maintained for four years, renewable for another four years.

Turning to internal market policies, price stabilization can be achieved through storage of commodities from one harvest to the next. The theory of storage denotes that profit-seeking agents will add commodities to carryover stocks if the expected price gain is greater than the marginal cost of storage, so that the competitive equilibrium is reached when the expected price gain just equals the marginal cost of storage, and this equilibrium condition is the criterion for socially optimal as well as privately profitable storage. If expected price at the time of the next harvest exceeds the current price by less than the cost of storage, then it is optimal to have carryover stocks of zero (beyond pipeline stocks that, as discussed above, the private trade holds even when an inverse price relationship exists—that is, expected future price below current price).

Arguments have been advanced against the optimality of private stockholding. Some rely on risk aversion by farmers and others who hold stocks. Some point to imperfect information under which private traders fail to see prospects for future crop shortfalls until it is too late. These arguments are dubious, but one that is solid is the following: when a shortfall occurs, those who suffer most are the poor who do not have sufficient income to buy staple commodities when their prices are extremely high (especially if they are producers whose incomes are low precisely because it is the failure of their crops that made prices high). Private storage responds to expected market demand and not to the potential purchases of people who cannot pay; that is, socially optimal storage should respond to the potential demand of poor people.

The first-best policy response to the situation of the poor is to provide contingent income transfers that would offset the loss of real income when the prices of staple commodities rise. This would effectively monetize the potential demand of poor people and the optimality of private storage would be restored. But in the absence of such income transfers, which most developing countries lack the capacity to implement (although such transfers are more likely to be possible in transition economies), a public buffer stock is a plausible policy remedy in theory.

In fact, such stockpiling has been abandoned almost everywhere it has been tried. Why? First, there are large technical and informational requirements in formulating and implementing an optimal stockpiling policy. The shortcut typically used is a buffer stock with fixed floor (buying) and ceiling (selling) prices. The choice of price band is crucial, and even if chosen to center on the mean expected price, is suboptimal compared to a policy that would lower the buying price as stocks accumulate (see Gustafson 1958; Williams and Wright 1991).

Second, the high storage costs mentioned earlier are a major obstacle for public as well as private stockholding. Not only is there an expected monetary loss on public stocks that are carried beyond the level at which expected price gains exceed storage costs, but these losses are magnified because the existence of the public stock causes some private stocks that would otherwise be carried for commercial reasons no longer to be profitable, so what begins as a small storage effort has to expand (see Williams and Wright 1991, ch. 15).

Finally, the political pressures placed upon storage agencies make it difficult to dispose of stocks when they become too large (because producers object to further downward pressure on market prices). The inherent difficulties of designing and operating a storage regime, the budgetary costs, and the political pressures have conspired to cause the failure of practically every buffer stock policy that has been tried in both industrial and developing countries. A further chastening story in practical policy history is the demise of all international commodity stock arrangements (see Gilbert 1996).

Johnson and Sumner (1976) show that optimal carryover levels of grains for several Asian countries are reduced by factors of 5–10 when free international trade is permitted as compared with each country covering its own shortfalls from its own stocks.

Provision of information can be helpful because producers may have only limited knowledge of prices at other locations, and for internationally traded goods, prices on futures markets or world production prospects may be related to the longer term gains expected from storage. Also, such provision of information as a public good is likely to yield benefits over and above the contributions to rational storage decisions (for example, choice of crop to grow or whether to expand or contract crop acreage). Investments in marketing infrastructure—roads, central market facilities, and legal structure for contracts and trade—similarly provide good prospects for reducing marketing margins as well as seasonal price variability.

Moreover, information and infrastructure are key elements in the viability of the risk management tools discussed earlier that are a substitute for commodity storage as a means of reducing producers' exposure to price fluctuations. Technical assistance is a key part of the World Bank's efforts in its Commodity Risk Management Group, necessary if price insurance via put options or other derivatives is to succeed.

Notes

1. The current problem of low commodity prices facing many developing country exporters is not attributable to liberalization so much as to distortions of markets in industrial countries that liberalization would eliminate.

2. This section and most of the next are excerpts from Valdes, Gardner, and Gordon (2001), which discusses these and related topics in much more detail.

References

Claessens, S., and R. Duncan. 1993. *Managing Commodity Price Risk in Developing Countries*. Baltimore: Johns Hopkins University Press.

Faruqee, R., J. Coleman, and T. Scott. 1997. "Managing Price Risk in the Pakistan Wheat Market." *The World Bank Economic Review* 11(2):263–92.

Gilbert, Christopher. 1996. "International Commodity Agreements: An Obituary Notice." *World Development* 24(January):1–19.

Gustafson, Robert. 1958. "Optimal Carryover Levels for Grains." Technical Bulletin 1178. U.S. Department of Agriculture, Washington, D.C.

Johnson, D. Gale, and Dan Sumner. 1976. "An Optimization Approach to Grain Reserves for Developing Countries." In D. Eaton and W. Steele, eds., *Analyses of Grain Reserves*. Washington, D.C.: U.S. Department of Agriculture.

Tsetsekos, G., and P. Varangis. 1998. "The Structure of Derivatives Exchanges: Lessons from Developed and Emerging Markets." Working Paper 1887. Development Research Group, World Bank, Washington, D.C.

Valdes, Alberto, Bruce Gardner, and Henry Gordon. 2001. "Toolkit Paper on Food Price Stabilization Policy." World Bank, Washington, D.C. Processed.

Williams, Jeffrey, and Brian Wright. 1991. *Storage and Commodity Markets*. New York: Cambridge University Press.

World Bank. 1986. *World Development Report, 1986*. New York: Oxford University Press.

Part IV

New Trade Issues and Challenges: The Way Forward

12

Time for Coherence among the World Trade Organization Escape Clauses

Gary Horlick

Governments could not secure the support of domestic producer interests for the trade-liberalizing agreements they negotiate with other countries without provisions in the agreements that permit a degree of flexibility in implementing the core obligations they undertake in the event of unforeseeable or even foreseeable problems.[1] Thus, in the General Agreement on Tariffs and Trade (GATT), there are escape clauses that allow as exceptions for members to exceed their tariff bindings and impose import restrictions that would otherwise violate the GATT articles.

The result is a constant tension between the rules drawn to permit limited exceptions to the general GATT obligations (including Articles I, II, III, and XI) and constant pressures within World Trade Organization (WTO) members to expand the escape clauses to provide protection to politically powerful constituencies (often without much regard for the limits within the GATT) in the other direction. Politics dictate the pressures that predominate, but to ensure that protectionist pressures do not gain excessively, the different escape clauses in the WTO must be narrowly defined. They are justified in various ways. Little or no coordination or consistency, however, is left between the terms under which they are applicable, given the changes that have taken place with the rapid integration of the world economy since the GATT came into force in 1947.

Range of Safeguard Provisions

Escape clauses might all be viewed as safeguard measures, some for *unforeseeable* difficulties and some for *foreseeable* ones. Those in the GATT can include the provisions in Article XII and Article XVIII:B for general trade restrictions for balance of payments purposes. At a microeconomic level, they include the provisions in Article VI and Article XVI for antidumping actions and subsidy-countervailing measures, and they include the provision in Article XIX for emergency protection against a sudden surge of imports of a particular product, which in the United States is often called the escape clause and in the WTO forum, and more widely, is called the safeguard clause or the safeguard provision. Escape clauses include the provision in Article XXVIII for bound tariffs to be renegotiated and the provision in Article XXV for rules to be waived, enabling unanticipated problems to be addressed.

The GATT also provides for departures from the principle of nondiscrimination to form customs unions or free trade areas (Article XXIV), an example of the exception overwhelming the rule. In another departure from the principle, the GATT allows developing countries Special and Differential (S&D) Treatment, including preferential tariffs in their favor and among themselves (Part IV, added in 1965, and the Enabling Clause). The GATT also allows developing countries to protect for infant industry purposes (Article XVIII:C).

The GATT 1947 permitted quantitative restrictions on *imports* of agricultural products (Article XI) and contained special rules on *exports* of agricultural products (Article XVI), but these provisions have been superseded by the WTO Uruguay Round (UR) Agreement on Agriculture (AoA). The GATT admits measures to defend national security (Article XXI) and, more generally, to safeguard public morals, national treasures, and public health and to secure compliance with laws that are not inconsistent with GATT rules, including the protection of patents, trademarks, and copyrights (Article XX).[2]

There was also the grandfather clause, the Protocol of Provisional Application, which provided that the rules in the GATT's Part II, covering nontariff measures, must be applied only "to the fullest extent not inconsistent with existing legislation." Because of it, many nontariff measures were able to stay in force for years, long past their expiration dates. The grandfather clause finally lapsed when the WTO became effective.

Importance of Coordination

It is important for the terms and conditions of escape clauses to be coordinated. Countries wanting to restrain imports may be able to choose from several GATT-consistent methods. Often several methods are used at the same time, providing layer on layer of protection, and for many observers that is the main problem. The aim of liberalizing international trade by increasing "discipline" over the use of one method of restricting imports, by making it more difficult to invoke, will not reduce the overall level of protection if there are other GATT-consistent measures that can be used in its place.

When the AoA was being concluded, it was anticipated that prohibiting the use of "voluntary" export restraints (VERs) involving governments, and requiring governments "not to encourage industry-by-industry VERs," would probably lead to increased use of the antidumping provision because tightened disciplines were not likely to be translated effectively into national laws. Where antidumping laws are used, it remains easier to invoke them than to invoke the provision for emergency action, under the GATT Article XIX, in the face of a sudden surge of imports of a particular product that is too competitive for the corresponding domestic suppliers.

Moreover, by requiring developing countries to improve access to their markets and to bind more of their tariffs at lower levels, it was anticipated that many more of them would introduce antidumping laws. By then, several had already done so, among them Argentina, the Republic of Korea, and Mexico. Thus, it is important to consider how GATT escape clauses have operated in the past, how they were modified in the UR negotiations, the extent to which they overlap, and whether further improvements are needed to achieve a coherent framework of safeguard measures.

Perhaps there is already a degree of coherence in the GATT repertoire of escape clauses. They deal with allegedly unfair trade practices, trade-inflicted injuries to a specific industry and an economy, health-and-safety and national security concerns, and unanticipated problems. The list appears to be comprehensive. Any trade problem that a country might face would probably fall within one of those categories, and the relatively infrequent use of the provisions for waivers and renegotiations suggests that there have been relatively few unanticipated problems.

Review of the GATT Escape Clauses

Only the escape clauses related to antidumping actions, subsidy-countervailing duties, and safeguard measures are considered here.[3]

Antidumping and Countervailing Actions

The GATT permits member countries to impose antidumping and subsidy-countervailing duties, in excess of bound tariffs, to offset dumping and subsidization *if* dumping or subsidization materially injures, or threatens material injury to, domestic producers. Essentially, the justification for this escape clause in Article VI is that dumped or subsidized imports are unfairly traded and therefore ought to be subject to control, at least if they cause material injury. Investigations of dumping and subsidization have become more frequent.

Hundreds have been initiated in recent years. From 1995 to mid-1999, 40 subsidy-countervailing investigations were initiated, including 16 by the European Union and 16 by the United States, and there were 291 antidumping investigations begun, including 41 by the European Union and

43 by the United States. The number is likely to increase as more countries adopt antidumping and subsidy-countervailing laws, supplementing emergency protection laws already on the books or introduced at the same time.[4] By 1997, at least 27 countries were applying antidumping laws, while many more had such laws on their books.

Until the early 1990s, the main users of antidumping laws were Australia, Canada, the European Community (as it was then), New Zealand, and the United States. They have been joined by many others, including such developing countries as Argentina, Brazil, the Republic of Korea, Mexico, and South Africa. In the late 1980s, developing countries accounted for one-fifth of antidumping actions, but by the late 1990s, they accounted for one-half. Developing countries have become the target of antidumping actions at about the same rate as developed countries. By the turn of the decade, the *World Development Report 1999/2000* (World Bank 2000) noted that antidumping actions were becoming a widespread phenomenon, "diluting market access and the gains from trade liberalization." Whether behavior covered by the antidumping and subsidy-countervailing laws is really unfair is a controversial question.

Even so, the criteria for applying antidumping laws are well defined, even if they are often ignored in national laws or practices. More precision was added to the criteria during the UR negotiations, in the Antidumping Agreement (ADA), and the Agreement on Subsidies and Countervailing Measures (ASCM). If dumping or subsidization is found, then the remedy permitted is limited to (a) imposing duties that offset the margin of dumping or subsidization or (b) accepting an undertaking from the exporters to adjust their prices to achieve that result (assuming the amount of dumping or subsidy is calculated correctly). No WTO review is required prior or subsequent to the imposition of duties, or to the acceptance of price undertakings, although their use must be reported to the WTO Secretariat.

Furthermore, no compensation is due to affected countries, even though duties are raised above bound levels. In essence, the problem is viewed as the fault of the exporting country, either directly through its subsidy policies or indirectly by failing to regulate the prices charged by its exporters. If the exporting country believes that antidumping or subsidy-countervailing duties have been imposed in violation of Article VI and the ADA/ASCM, the matter may be examined by a dispute settlement panel, where, in the past, challenged measures have been found to violate GATT/WTO rules (and in past GATT cases, illegally imposed duties have been refunded).[5]

Antidumping Controversies

Antidumping laws are widely perceived to be misused and abused, and there are problems with their implementation. They have been heavily criticized by economists and legal scholars not only in the United States and the European Union but all around the world. So there is considerable potential for disputes over antidumping laws.

The main problem with antidumping actions is that the actions have been expanded far beyond the language of Article VI (and contemporary practice in 1947). Article VI took aim primarily at sales in export markets that are below the price in the home market on a theory of cross-subsidization. Even if a company would not have been found to be dumping in 1947, the rules have been stretched so that the same company would today be found to be dumping under Article VI, even if it (a) charges identical prices in both markets, (b) sells through an affiliate (normal practice in a modern business), or (c) fails to make a profit on at least 80 percent of the individual sales.

In principle, an escape clause allowing the imposition of trade restrictions to offset the use of unfair trade practices entailing predatory behavior makes sense. Predatory behavior is easy to speculate about, but in practice it is rare, for the opportunities are severely limited by intense competition. The issue is whether dumping and subsidization *as defined in the WTO* are really unfair trade practices. Many argue that WTO rules are too broad and alleged unfair trade practices could be more appropriately dealt with by applying existing antitrust and competition laws, as some have argued.[6]

To evaluate the coherence of WTO escape clauses, it is necessary to consider the extent to which antidumping actions or subsidy-countervailing duties may be used, or are being used, instead of other WTO escape clauses. The requirements for invoking the antidumping or subsidy-countervailing provisions are threefold: (a) the existence of dumping/subsidization, (b) material injury, and (c) a causal connection.

Compared with the safeguard provision in GATT Article XIX, Article VI contains a lesser injury standard, for it is easier to show "material" than "serious" injury, but there is a similar causation standard since in each case the injury must be caused by the imports in question. So the question of whether Article VI actions could substitute for Article XIX actions turns on how the first criterion—dumping or subsidization—is applied.

Almost all scholarly writing on this subject concludes that the definition of dumping is too broad and far more often than not encompasses normal competitive behavior. Moreover, the calculation of antidumping duties is biased in a way that further expands the coverage of antidumping rules.[7] The results are demonstrated by an examination of practices in the United States, where the U.S. Department of Commerce makes negative final dumping determinations in fewer than 5 percent of all cases, while the U.S. International Trade Commission makes negative injury determinations in about 50 percent of all cases. If an industry seeking relief from imports can show material injury, then it would appear that a finding of dumping is almost automatic. This suggests that the criteria for invoking a dumping or subsidy remedy may be too loose by comparison with other WTO escape clauses and, in particular, with the safeguard provision.

In short, while the WTO may need a mechanism to deal with unfair trade practices, more restrained devices than the antidumping and subsidy-countervailing laws are necessary.[8] Even though (a) the criteria are precisely defined, (b) the range of possible responses is suitably circumscribed, and (c) the lack of compensation is (theoretically) appropriate (if the trade is proven to be predatory) if the supervision of the WTO is inadequate simply because the two escape clauses can cover a great deal of conduct that is not really unfair. They overlap too much with the provisions of Article XIX.

The most logical approach to achieving coherence would be a nondiscriminatory application of competition (antitrust) law against unfair practices within an economy and a discriminatory border measure against imports from other economies that benefit in those economies from unfair practices. The first reaction in the United States is usually, "Congress won't buy it," but attitudes in the U.S. Congress may be changing.

Traditionally, antidumping laws have been most used in Australia, Canada, the European Union, and the United States. Since the Agreement on Safeguards came into force, however, antidumping laws have been increasingly used as surrogates for selective (that is, discriminatory) safeguard or gray area measures that have been prohibited. In the United States the law makes it much more difficult to invoke a safeguard measure than an antidumping action. As a result, Japan, as well as Brazil, Chile, and several other developing countries, have put a high priority on antidumping law reform in spite of the U.S. government attitude that it is an untouchable subject. The European position has shifted to support the United States.

As anticipated, since the Agreement on Safeguards came into force, more developing countries have introduced antidumping laws modeled on U.S. or European practices. They reason that as their tariffs are reduced and bound, they may need to have such an easy-to-use and selective escape clause in their arsenal. The trend may gradually result in pressure for change as more U.S. firms come to understand what is happening.

At the same time, it is realized in trade policy communities around the world (even in the United States) that the explosion in antidumping activity in both developed and developing countries poses a danger that may already be outweighing the value of antidumping laws as a political escape valve. The danger is a discriminatory, selective, and semipermanent unbinding of tariffs, so some change will be necessary. The longer it is put off, the greater the added danger that vested interests in the maintenance of antidumping laws in developing countries, as well as in developed countries, will become entrenched and hard to budge.

If the logical course, reforming antidumping laws to conform to antitrust or competition laws, is too much for legislatures, bureaucracies, and industries heavily addicted to public assistance to bear, then what else could be considered? One possibility would be to apply antidumping action only to the behavior that is claimed to be the rationale for antidumping activity. Importing countries could be required to prove that the market of the exporting countries is, indeed, closed to foreign competition by government action and that the proposed duty is proportional to the degree of cross-subsidization caused by closure. Some of the more blatant abuses could perhaps be limited by a requirement of prior WTO review (at least as much as occurs in Article XIX cases under the Agreement on Safeguards).

Emergency Safeguard Actions

Article XIX of the GATT, the safeguard provision, permits the use of emergency protection—including quotas and tariffs above bound rates—for such time as may be necessary to remedy serious injury to a domestic industry caused (or threatened) by a sudden surge of imports of a particular product. It generally requires prior consultations with the WTO and those member countries that have a substantial trade interest in the product in question.

The Agreement on Safeguards has added further obligations by requiring investigations of possible injury to meet certain procedural requirements (including prior WTO reviews) by specifying factors that must be considered in assessing injury and by putting time limits (a maximum of eight years) on measures taken under Article XIX. If the country taking a safeguard action and those adversely affected cannot reach agreement on compensation, Article XIX permits the affected member countries to retaliate by suspending concessions made to that country.

The Agreement on Safeguards provides, though, that no compensation is due for the first three years of a safeguard action if it is imposed in accordance with the agreement, including the requirement to consult the countries likely to be affected. Compensation is viewed as appropriate under Article XIX actions because the imports were fairly traded.

Nowadays, the safeguard provision is not often invoked. Until the end of 1993, the safeguard provision was invoked only about three times a year. This was probably because of the widespread use in the 1970s and 1980s of VERs in major industries. If the Agreement on Safeguards succeeds in its goal of eliminating the use of VERs, it is likely that, in due course, Article XIX will be used more often. In the five years 1995–99, 34 safeguard measures were initiated, or about seven a year.

In the early years of the GATT (and through the first few years of the 1960s), trade compensation was typically agreed when a country invoked Article XIX and retaliatory measures were only occasionally imposed. Over the last 30-odd years, however, compensation and retaliation have been quite rare. This may be explained by the fact that greater scope for compensation was afforded by "water" in tariff levels in the 1950s and 1960s. Later, when safeguard action was taken via VERs, compensation was achieved by letting quota rents accrue to the exporters. Today, high tariffs are jealously guarded by the industry they benefit.

A coherent framework of escape clauses in an international trade agreement needs a clause like the safeguard provision. There will be occasions when imports cause significant dislocation to an industry, and it has long been accepted that in such cases it is appropriate to allow such an industry time to adjust to increased imports. The problem is to set conditions for invoking the provision at a level that is appropriate, given the general free trade orientation of the WTO system.

The UR reforms go a long way in that direction. The concept of serious injury is defined more precisely, and there is considerably more surveillance over the use of the safeguard provision than previously. Moreover, with the discouragement of informal safeguards—the prohibition of VERs involving governments and the stipulation that member countries "shall not encourage or support" industry-to-industry VERs—the reforms have suggested that more rigorous control will be exercised over safeguards than in the past, particularly since the GATT had no influence over VERs at all.

The problem is that if the requirements for the safeguard provision are too strict, and when those for antidumping and subsidy-countervailing actions are not, countries seeking to restrain imports may avoid the greater discipline on the use of safeguard measures and continue to resort instead to Article VI measures. That would be unfortunate because the remedy afforded by antidumping and subsidy-countervailing laws has little to do with the remedy traditionally afforded to injured industries under the safeguard provision.

Antidumping and subsidy-countervailing duties are based at least to some extent on the degree of dumping or subsidization, an amount that is not necessarily related to the degree of injury (even in some countries that claim to base the duty on injury). Accordingly, antidumping and subsidy-countervailing duties tend to overprotect a domestic industry in light of its injury, perhaps underprotecting on occasions. Such measures, moreover, tend to remain in place for a long time, even where there are (in theory) provisions calling for expiration after a specified period.

A switch to the use of antidumping or subsidy-countervailing actions instead of safeguard actions could mean that the increased discipline of the Agreement on Safeguards would be easily evaded. Is this concern a legitimate one? Looking at experience in the United States, one would think so, for petitioners for safeguard relief until recently have generally not been successful under current rules.

Even if such relief is not made more difficult to obtain in the United States as a result of the UR reforms, U.S. industries interested in import relief will probably prefer to initiate antidumping or subsidy-countervailing actions, since they are more likely to obtain relief. There is evidence that they already do. The steel industry, for instance, initiated numerous antidumping cases when the various steel VERs expired in 1992. It did not seek safeguard relief. Much the same happened with a spate of cases in 1999, when only one safeguard action was taken. The textile industry has brought several antidumping cases in recent years as well.

While the safeguard provision is a necessary component of an international trade agreement, the disciplining of safeguard actions needs to be coordinated with the disciplining of other provisions that allow for the imposition of import restraints, particularly the antidumping and subsidy-countervailing laws. It is evident that, as currently structured, the relationship is not properly balanced.

Notes

1. This was originally prepared as a contribution to a study group of the Cordell Hull Institute, Washington, D.C., on preparations for a new round of multilateral trade negotiations under the auspices of the WTO. It has benefited from an unpublished paper by William J. Davey, of the College of Law, University of Illinois, Urbana-Champaign. On the role of escape clauses in international agreements, see Kravis (1975).

2. As for the analogous provisions in the General Agreement on Trade in Services (GATS), there is little in them (and some wonder whether they are necessary, but the safeguard clause is found in Article X, the balance of payments provision in Article XII, and the renegotiation provision in Article XXI). There is no waiver provision in the GATS, but its obligations can be waived under the AoA. There are no provisions analogous to GATT Article VI. The health-and-safety exception is in Article XIV, and the national security exception in Article XIV *bis*.

3. These provisions and the related AoA have been extensively analyzed in other places, so the discussion here is relatively brief and will address their relationships with one another and other GATT provisions. Of the remaining escape clauses, the two balance of payments provisions were once significant, but have been subjected to tighter discipline. The waiver and renegotiation provisions are touched upon only briefly.

4. For a discussion of the trend, see Miranda, Torres, and Rutz (1998).

5. See, for example, Committee on Antidumping Practices (1993) and Committee on Subsidies and Countervailing Measures (1993).

6. See Davey (1988, pp. 8–11).

7. See Dale (1981), Hindley (1988), Boltuck and Litan (1991), and Lindsey (1998).

8. The more direct discipline on subsidies provided in the ASCM has worked well on export-contingent subsidies, but not on all the other subsidies, as argued in Horlick (1999).

References

Boltuck, Richard, and Robert E. Litan, eds. 1991. *Down in the Dumps: Administration of the Unfair Trade Laws.* Washington, D.C.: Brookings Institution.

Committee on Antidumping Practices. 1993. "Korea: Antidumping Duties on Imports of Polyacetal Resins from the United States." Document ADP/92. Geneva: GATT Secretariat.

Committee on Subsidies and Countervailing Measures. 1993. "Canadian Countervailing Duties on Grain Corn from the United States." In *Basic Instruments and Selected Documents*, 39th Supplement. Geneva: GATT Secretariat.

Dale, Richard. 1981. *Anitdumping Law in a Liberal Trade Order.* London: Macmillan.

Davey, William, J. 1988. "Antidumping Laws: A Time for Restriction." In Barry Hawk, ed., *North America and Common Market Antitrust and Trade Laws.* New York: Matthew Bender.

Hindley, Brian. 1988. "Dumping and the Far East Trade of the European Community." *The World Economy* 11:445–63.

Horlick, Gary N. 1999. *Subsidies Discipline under WTO and U.S. Rules.* Florence: European University Institute.

Kravis, Irving. 1975. *Domestic Interests and International Obligations: Safeguards in International Trade Organizations.* Westport, Conn.: Greenwood Press.

Lindsey, Brink. 1998. *The U.S. Antidumping Law.* Washington, D.C.: Cato Institute.

Miranda, Jorge, Raul A. Torres, and Mario Rutz. 1998. "The International Use of Antidumping: 1987–1997." *Journal of World Trade* 32:5–71.

World Bank. 2000. *World Development Report 1999/2000.* New York: Oxford University Press.

13

Multifunctionality and Optimal Environmental Policies for Agriculture in an Open Economy

Jeffrey M. Peterson, Richard N. Boisvert,
and Harry de Gorter

Though agriculture has long been recognized as a polluter, it has also more recently been noted as a provider of nonmarket benefits. Examples of these public goods that are by-products of agriculture include landscape amenities, a habitat for wildlife, and the preservation of agrarian cultural heritage (Bohman et al. 1999; OECD 1997a, 1997b). Though many of these benefits are difficult to define and measure, nonmarket valuation studies have found substantial nonmarket values for farmland in different regions around the world (Beasley, Workman, and Williams 1986; Hackl and Pruckner 1997; Lopez, Shah, and Altobello 1994).

The notion of agriculture providing a set of nonmarket goods and bads as joint products with market goods has given rise to the term "multifunctionality" (Runge 1998; Lindland 1998; and Nersten and Prestegard 1998). Conceptually, a multifunctional agriculture means that the agricultural production process is a multioutput technology, where some outputs are privately traded commodities and others are public goods. This case differs from standard environmental models, where some activity in the economy generates a single externality.

The realization that agriculture is multifunctional has important implications for policymaking at both the domestic and international levels. In the domestic sphere, policies aimed at the various externalities from agriculture are typically legislated and administered independently. Likewise, the economics literature almost always examines externalities in isolation, either implicitly or explicitly assuming that other (potentially related) externalities are fixed or unimportant. If agriculture is multifunctional, then the interrelationships among externalities imply that "compartmentalized" government programs may work at cross purposes (Poe 1997). For example, many governments use price supports in combination with acreage subsidies in an effort to internalize the positive externalities from agricultural production, but it has been shown that the level of these policies must affect the amount of agricultural pollution generated and vice versa (Ollikainen 1999). Jointness among externalities implies that policies to correct them must also be selected jointly, but the proper design of such a set of agro-environmental policies remains largely unexplored.

In the international arena, as evidenced by the recent controversy surrounding the agenda for the next round of World Trade Organization (WTO) negotiations, the complexity of agricultural externalities will also make new trade agreements difficult to achieve (Blandford and Fulponi 1999; Anderson and Hoekman 1999; Runge 1999). Many countries have made known their fear that, without adequate safeguards, free trade will jeopardize the public good functions of agriculture. Trading partners who seek access to those markets, however, question whether so-called environmental safeguards may be trade-distorting protectionism in disguise (ABARE 1999; Bohman et al. 1999).

High-cost agricultural producing countries with high levels of support, notably the European Union, Norway, Switzerland, Japan, and the Republic of Korea, insist that subsidies on farm commodities are the most efficient way to secure public goods that are by-products of farm output. National food security and an authentic agricultural landscape, for example, cannot be produced separately from farm commodities (WTO 1999a, 1999b, 1999c; Norwegian Royal Ministry of Agriculture 1998). Furthermore, reduced subsidies and freer trade would generate additional production in low-income and low-support countries; high-support countries have argued that such an expansion in those countries could damage the environment (because of deforestation and the lack of environmental regulations).

Lower-cost producers would stand to gain considerably from reduced support in protected countries. These governments have argued that price supports as a way of obtaining agricultural public goods are neither optimal nor desirable. Such policies distort market incentives toward the intense use of polluting inputs, and there exist less distorting policy instruments to achieve the same goal (WTO 1998; Bohman et al. 1999). Moreover, they argue, the weight of empirical evidence suggests that freer trade would improve environmental quality in both industrialized and developing nations, although even more could be gained if free trade were combined with environmental protection policies (for example, Anderson 1992a; Whalley 1999). Yet the most fundamental concern is that, however high-minded the purpose of public good–providing policies may be, those policies may be manipulated to distort terms of trade.

For the case of a single externality, the relationship between environmental policy and trade has been a subject of much recent study (Anderson 1992b; Copeland 1994; Krutilla 1991; Beghin et al. 1995; Schamel and de Gorter 1997). This literature has revealed the potential for using an environmental policy as a tool to distort trade: A large importer, for example, may select lax environmental regulations in order to encourage domestic production, reduce the demand for imports, and lower prices to domestic consumers. However, the relationship between trade and a set of joint policies aimed at multiple externalities (that is, the multifunctional case) has not yet been studied.

This chapter develops a general equilibrium framework to determine the optimal set of internalizing policies under multifunctionality and relates these policies to trade. The model is based on an aggregate multi-output technology, where two basic factors (land and nonland inputs) produce two private commodities (agricultural and industrial goods) and two public goods (the positive and negative externalities from agriculture). Because the focus is on the agricultural sector, the model abstracts from marginal changes in industrial externalities. Production in the economy is cast in a modified Hecksher-Ohlin framework where agriculture generates two externalities.

The analysis identifies the interdependence among optimal environmental policies. In principle, a welfare maximum can be achieved through a combination of a subsidy on agricultural land and a tax on agricultural nonland inputs, but the levels of these policies must be selected jointly. In particular, if the pollution function for each acre is convex, a marginal acre of land reduces total pollution, and the optimal subsidy on an acre of farmland therefore exceeds the amenity value of that acre. Based on a set of stylized policy simulations of the aggregate U.S. agricultural sector, this interaction between policies appears to be empirically important; the estimated optimal subsidy for farmland is about 50 percent larger than its amenity value.

The relationship between these joint environmental policies and trade is also characterized. Small economies have no incentive to distort environmental policies away from their internalizing levels, but large economies will manipulate domestic policies in order to exploit terms of trade. Consistent with observation, large importers such as Japan can improve domestic welfare by oversubsidizing public goods, while large exporters like the United States prefer strict regulations to limit pollution. Empirical simulations of U.S. agriculture suggest that environmental policies can be effective at distorting trade. If these policies were used to exploit terms of trade, then the United States alone could increase world agricultural prices by an estimated 9 percent over a base case of no environmental policy.

The Model Economy

Let x and y represent agricultural and nonagricultural goods, respectively. These two commodities can be produced from two basic factors, land L

and nonland inputs Z. In addition, the agricultural production process generates nonmarket amenities a and emissions of pollution e. The technology set for aggregate production in this economy is

$$T = \{(x, y, a, e, L, Z) \in \mathfrak{R}_+^6 : (L, Z) \text{ can produce } (x, y, a, e)\}.$$

If there are no direct links between the agricultural and nonagricultural production processes, then a tradeoff between the output of the two commodities occurs only because inputs must be diverted away from one industry in order to increase production in the other. Assume the two technologies can be represented by the production functions

$$F_x(L_x, Z_x) \text{ and } F_y(L_y, Z_y)$$

where L_i and Z_i are the amount of land and other inputs allocated to the production of good i, respectively.

Let L and Z represent the endowment of land and nonland inputs, respectively, and assume the entire endowment of each factor is homogeneous in quality. Presuming nonwasteful allocations, production is subject to the feasibility conditions

$$L_x + L_y = L$$
$$Z_x + Z_y = Z.$$

Each $F_i(\cdot)$ is strictly increasing, strictly concave, and exhibits constant returns to scale. By homogeneity, $F_i(L_i, Z_i) = L_i F_i(1, Z_i/L_i) \equiv L_i f_i(z_i)$, where z_i represents the Z_i/L_i ratio (per acre input) and $f_i(\cdot)$ is the per acre production function.

Without loss of generality, aggregate emissions of agricultural pollution can be expressed as a function of the agricultural inputs L_x and Z_x: $e = G(L_x, Z_x)$.[1] If L_x and Z_x both double (thus keeping z_x constant), total emissions must also double when land is of undifferentiated quality. Hence, $G(\cdot)$ is homogeneous of degree one. By the same argument as above, emissions may be equivalently expressed as $e = L_x g(z_x)$, where $g(\cdot)$ represents the amount of pollution generated per acre. Assume that g is strictly increasing, strictly convex, and that $g(0) = 0$. Under these conditions, pollution falls with marginal increases in the agricultural land base; that is, $\partial e / \partial L_x < 0$.[2]

The nonmarket amenities from agriculture, such as open space and a habitat for wildlife, depend only on the quantity of agricultural land. The extent to which pollution detracts from any of these amenities can be captured in consumers' preferences with respect to e. As above, homogeneous land implies that the amenity function is homogeneous of degree one, or that each acre of land provides a fixed amount of amenity services. If we choose to measure these services so that each acre of farmland provides one unit of amenities, then $a = L_x$.[3]

Consumers' preferences are represented by the aggregate utility function $u(x, y, a, e)$, where $u(\cdot)$ is strictly quasi-concave; strictly increasing in x, y, and a; and strictly decreasing in e. National income I is the total payments received on the factors used in the two industries. Consumers use income to purchase x and y, but cannot influence the levels of a and e. Taking y to be the numeraire and letting p be the price of x, indirect utility is

$$v(p, I, a, e) = \max u(x, y, a, e)$$

$$\text{subject to } px + y \leq I, (x, y) \in \Re^2_+.$$

The function $v(\cdot)$ can be interpreted as social welfare for a given combination of price, income, and externalities. The solutions to the maximization problem $x(p, I, \cdot)$ and $y(p, I, \cdot)$ are the demands for agricultural and manufactured goods, respectively.

Optimal Policies in a Closed Economy

Because a and e are public goods, the market price system cannot internalize the marginal amenity benefits of agricultural land and the marginal cost of pollution, and producers will not choose the socially optimal factor allocation unless there is some policy intervention. Below, the optimal policies are determined using the following procedure: First, social welfare is derived as a function of the factors L_x and z_x, and the welfare maximization problem is solved to determine the optimal allocation of the two factors. Second, the free market allocations of L_x and z_x are derived under an arbitrary policy scheme, and the optimal scheme is then chosen so that the free market and welfare maximizing allocations coincide.

Social welfare in this economy $v(\cdot)$ can be written as a function of L_x and z_x, provided the utility function is properly restricted so that $x(\cdot)$ is monotonic in p. To verify this, note that monotonicity of demand implies a unique market clearing price p for any amount of agricultural production. Further, profits are always zero due to constant returns to scale, and factor payments to households (national income I) must therefore equal total revenue from the two industries. Thus, p and I can be regarded as functions of L_x and z_x that are implicitly defined by the equations

$$x(p(L_x, z_x), I(L_x, z_x), \cdot) = L_x f_x(z_x) \tag{13.1}$$

$$I(L_x, z_x) = p(L_x, z_x) L_x f_x(z_x) + (L - L_x) f_y(z_y) \tag{13.2}$$

where $z_y \equiv Z_y/L_y = (Z - z_x L_x)/(L - L_x)$. The problem of maximizing social welfare in a closed economy can therefore be written

$$\max \quad v(p(L_x, z_x), I(L_x, z_x), L_x, L_x g(z_x))$$
$$L_x \in [0, L], \quad z_x \in [0, Z/L_x]. \tag{13.3}$$

Under appropriate assumptions on $u(\cdot)$ and $F_i(\cdot)$, a solution to this problem cannot occur on the boundary of the constraint set.[4] If a solution exists, then it must satisfy the first-order conditions for an interior maximum:

$$v_p p_L + v_I I_L + v_a + v_e g(z_x) = 0 \tag{13.4}$$

$$v_p p_z + v_I I_z + v_e L_x g'(z_x) = 0 \tag{13.5}$$

where subscripts denote derivatives. The Envelope Theorem applied to the consumer's utility maximization problem implies that $v_I = u_y$, $v_a = u_a$, and $v_e = u_e$; $v_p = - x(p, I)v_I$ by Roy's Identity; and the first-order conditions for utility maximization require that $p = u_x/u_y$. Substituting these conditions, the derivatives of I from equation (13.2), and the market clearing condition (13.1) into (13.4) and (13.5), we obtain the following equivalent conditions expressed in terms of the utility and production functions (demonstration in appendix):

$$\frac{u_x}{u_y} f_x(z_x) - [f_y(z_y) - f_y'(z_y)(z_y - z_x)] + \frac{u_a}{u_y} + \frac{u_e}{u_y} g(z_x) = 0 \tag{13.6}$$

$$\frac{u_x}{u_y} f_x'(z_x) - f_y'(z_y) + \frac{u_e}{u_y} g'(z_x) = 0. \tag{13.7}$$

Each of these conditions requires the net marginal benefits of each factor to be zero. Equation (13.6) defines the optimal allocation of L_x. The first term is the marginal benefit of using land to produce x, the term in brackets is the marginal opportunity value of using land to produce y, u_a/u_y is the marginal amenity benefit of land in agriculture, and the last term (note that u_e < 0) is the marginal cost of pollution. Because each term has been divided by u_y, the benefits and costs are compared in terms of the numeraire. In equation (13.7), the optimal choice of z_x is determined by setting to zero the sum of the marginal benefits of producing x, the marginal opportunity value in terms of y production forgone, and marginal environmental cost.

Although each of the preceding equations describes the optimal allocation of one factor, they are collectively a simultaneous system in both variables (L_x appears in both equations through the expression for z_x). Letting (L_x^0, z_x^0) represent the socially optimal allocation, simultaneity implies any shift in preferences that changes either u_a or u_e will induce a change in both L_x^o and z_x^o.

Several types of policies have been proposed to internalize the environmental effects of agriculture. Consider four policy instruments that may be imposed jointly: a subsidy on agricultural output (s_x), a subsidy on agricultural land (s_L), a tax on agricultural input (t_z), and a direct tax on pollution (t_e).[5] The policy problem is therefore to determine a policy scheme $s = (s_x, s_L, t_z, t_e)$ that allows the socially optimal outcome to be decentralized through free markets. Given a set of policies s, a price p, and factor endowments (L, Z), the "invisible hand" of competition will solve the revenue maximization problem (Dixit and Norman 1980):

$$\max \quad (p + s_x)L_x f_x(z_x) + s_L L_x - t_z L_x z_x - t_e L_x g(z_x) + (L - L_x)f_y(z_y)$$

$$L_x \in [0, L], \quad z_x \in [0, Z/L_x].$$

Because the maximization is strictly concave, the unique solution must satisfy the first order conditions:

$$(p + s_x)f_x(z_x) + s_L - t_z z_x - t_e g(z_x) - [f_y(z_y) + f_y'(z_y)(z_y - z_x)] = 0 \tag{13.8}$$

$$(p + s_x)f_x'(z_x) - t_z - t_e g'(z_x) - f_y'(z_y) = 0. \tag{13.9}$$

Using the fact that $u_x/u_y = p$ and comparing equations (13.6) and (13.7) to (13.8) and (13.9), the welfare-maximizing policies s_x, s_L, t_z, and t_e must satisfy

$$s_x f_x(z_x^0) + s_L - t_z z_x^0 - t_e g(z_x^0) = \frac{u_a}{u_y} + \frac{u_e}{u_y} g(z_x^0) \tag{13.10}$$

$$s_x f_x'(z_x^0) - t_z + t_e g'(z_x^0) = -\frac{u_e}{u_y} g'(z_x^0) \tag{13.11}$$

where the derivatives of $u(\cdot)$ are evaluated at the socially optimal levels L_x^o and z_x^o. If pollution can be observed and measured, then the simplest choice of policies is to set $(s_x, s_L, t_z, t_e) = (0, u_a/u_y, 0, -u_e/u_y)$. This policy scheme is the Pigouvian outcome, where each externality is rewarded by its marginal social value. Thus, if the effluent can be taxed directly, neither an output subsidy nor an input tax is necessary.

A major difficulty in regulating agricultural pollution is that damages cannot be observed and policies must instead regulate outputs and inputs directly.[6] If the effluent tax t_e is eliminated, then equations (13.10) and (13.11) are a system of two equations in the three unknowns s_x, s_L, and t_z.

This arrangement allows a degree of freedom in selecting policies and suggests that a social optimum can be obtained by combining commodity policy with input taxes and subsidies. However, this result depends on the simplification of only two factors and does not hold in general. Indeed, the possibility of using *any* commodity policy disappears if there exist other factors of production that are unregulated and do not affect the externalities a and e.[7]

Among the four policies in s, only s_L and t_z are both feasible (because they act on observable transactions) and remain valid in more general cases (because they do not act on other factors of production). If the policy set is limited to these two instruments, equations (13.10) and (13.11) imply they must satisfy

$$t_z = -\frac{u_e}{u_y} g'(z_x^0) \qquad (13.12)$$

$$s_L = \frac{u_a}{u_y} + t_z z_x^0 + \frac{u_e}{u_y} g(z_x^0). \qquad (13.13)$$

In other words, the optimal tax is the marginal social cost of applying agricultural inputs at z_x^o. The optimal subsidy in equation (13.13) is made up of two components. First, farmers are rewarded for the amenity benefit per acre of farmland u_a/u_y. Substituting the expression for the tax into (13.13), the second and third terms of the subsidy are equal to (u_e/u_y) $[g(z_x^o) - g'(z_x^o)z_x^o] = (u_e/u_y)(\partial e/\partial L_x)$ (see endnote 2). Thus, the subsidy rewards farmers by the combined social value of amenity benefits and the marginal change in pollution. This is a generalization of Holtermann's (1976) result for a single externality; a welfare maximum can be achieved through taxes/subsidies on inputs that penalize or reward each input by its marginal contribution to the externality. Here, the social value of pollution u_e/u_y and the change in pollution with respect to L_x are both negative, and the optimal subsidy therefore exceeds the amenity value of farmland.

Therefore, even if agricultural land provides no landscape amenities (that is, $u_a \equiv 0$), then it should still be subsidized in conjunction with the input tax t_z. Further, subsidizing land by the "net" value of amenities per acre will not achieve an efficient allocation of resources. Landscape amenity value net of pollution cost is $[u_a/u_y + (u_e/u_y)g(z_x^o)]$, but a subsidy of this amount falls short of the optimal subsidy in (13.13) by the amount $t_z z_x^o$. Thus, an empirical study of the willingness to pay for farmland amenities will not estimate the appropriate land subsidy, even if it accounts for the cost of agricultural pollution. Determining whether this difference is likely to be empirically significant is an important goal of the empirical analysis below.

The optimal levels of s_L and t_z are based on the welfare-maximizing allocations L_x^o and z_x^o, which are in turn determined in a simultaneous system; see equations (13.6) and (13.7). Consequently, any change in the value of either externality (that is, a shift in u_a/u_y or u_e/u_y) would induce an adjustment in both the optimal allocation (L_x^*, z_x^o) and policy choice (s_L, t_z). For example, suppose the value of agricultural land amenities increases by $b per acre. In general, this change would lead to some (nonzero) adjustment in the optimal input tax even if u_e/u_y remains fixed, while the optimal land subsidy would change by some amount other than $b.

Open Economies

Suppose the economy described above is opened to international trade. For simplicity, assume that (a) foreign and domestic production technologies are identical, (b) foreign agriculture does not generate any externalities, and (c) foreign utility does not depend on domestic allocations. Under these assumptions, the allocations that maximize global welfare are the solution to the following combined Pareto problem:

$$\text{max} \quad u(x, y, L_x, L_x g(z_x)) + \alpha u^*(x^*, y^*)$$

$$\text{subject to:} \quad x + x^* = L_x f_x(z_x) + L_x^* f_x(z_x^*)$$

$$y + y^* = (L - L_x)f_y(z_y) + (L^* - L_x^*)f_y(z_y^*)$$

$$L_x \in [0, L], \quad z_x \in [0, Z/L_x],$$

$$L_x^* \in [0, L^*], \quad z_x^* \in [0, Z^*/L_x^*]$$

where α is the relative welfare weight of foreign consumers and asterisks denote foreign variables. The first-order necessary conditions for allocations of land and other inputs (assuming an interior solution) simplify to

$$u_x f_x(z_x) - u_y[f_y(z_y) - f_y'(z_y)(zy - zx)] + ua + ueg(zx) = 0 \quad \text{(13.14a)}$$

$$uxfx'(zx) - uyfy'(zy) + ueg'(zx) = 0 \quad \text{(13.14b)}$$

$$ux^*fx(zx^*) - uy^*[fy(zy^*) - fy'(zy^*)(zy^* - zx^*)] = 0 \quad \text{(13.14c)}$$

$$ux^*fx'(zx^*) - u\,y^*fy'(zy^*) = 0. \quad \text{(13.14d)}$$

Equations (13.14a) and (13.14b) describe the optimal levels of L_x and z_x, respectively, while equations (13.14c) and (13.14d) correspond to the optimal allocations in the foreign economy. In the foreign country, each factor is employed in agriculture until the marginal benefits of agricultural pro-

duction equal the opportunity value of manufactured production. The domestic allocation equations include terms for the externalities, and are
equivalent to the closed economy conditions in equations (13.6) and (13.7).

Though a global perspective is of theoretical interest, it is reasonable to
assume that the home government wishes only to maximize domestic
welfare. The remainder of this section determines the allocations that are
optimal from this domestic viewpoint and compares each outcome with
those that maximize global welfare. The small country and large country
cases are analyzed in turn.

A small open economy views the world price of agricultural goods as an
exogenous variable. Now regarding p as a parameter, national income is

$$I(L_x, z_x) = pL_x f_x(z_x) + (L - L_x)f_y(z_y).$$

The social welfare maximization problem becomes

$$\max \quad v(p, I(L_x, z_x), L_x, L_x g(z_x))$$
$$L_x \in [0, L], z_x \in [0, Z/L_x]$$

with first order conditions

$$v_I I_L + v_a + v_e g(z_x) = 0 \text{ and } v_I I_z + v_e L_x g'(z_x) = 0.$$

Substituting the derivatives of I from the definition above and the envelope conditions $v_I = u_y$, $v_a = u_a$, and $v_e = u_e$, these conditions reduce to
(see appendix)

$$pf_x(z_x) - [f_y(z_y) - f_y'(z_y)(z_y - z_x)] + \frac{u_a}{u_y} + \frac{u_e}{u_y} g(z_x) = 0$$

$$pf_x'(z_x) - f_y'(z_y) + \frac{u_e}{u_y} g'(z_x) = 0.$$

Because $p = u_x/u_y$, these conditions imply exactly the same factor allocation that maximizes world welfare in conditions (13.14a) and (13.14b).
Therefore, the optimal domestic policy for a small open economy is also
optimal from a global point of view.

If the home economy is large enough so that changes in domestic production and consumption affect the world price, then the price must be
regarded as endogenous. The policy problem becomes

$$\max \quad v(\widetilde{p}(L_x, z_x), \widetilde{I}(L_x, z_x), L_x, L_x g(z_x))$$
$$L_x \in [0, L], \quad z_x \in [0, Z/L_x].$$

The price and income relations $\widetilde{p}$ and $\widetilde{I}$ satisfy

$$x^*(\widetilde{p}, \widetilde{I}, \cdot) + x^*(\widetilde{p}) = L_x f_x(z_x) \tag{13.15}$$

$$\widetilde{I} = \widetilde{p} L_x f_x(z_x) + (L - L_x) f_y(z_y) \tag{13.16}$$

where the arguments of $\widetilde{p}$ and $\widetilde{I}$ have been suppressed to simplify notation, and $x^*(\cdot)$ is the demand for exports. The first order conditions are

$$v_p \widetilde{p}_L + v_I \widetilde{I}_L + v_a + v_e g(z_x) = 0 \text{ and } v_p \widetilde{p}_z + v_I \widetilde{I}_z + v_e L_x g'(z_x) = 0.$$

Substituting the derivatives of v ($v_I = u_y$, $v_a = u_a$, $v_e = u_e$) and $\widetilde{I}$, the condition $\widetilde{p} = u_x / u_y$, Roy's Identity $v_p = -x v_I$, and market clearing, these conditions become (demonstration in appendix):

$$\frac{u_x}{u_y} f_x(z_x) + x^*(\widetilde{p}) \widetilde{p}_L - [f_y(z_y) - f_y'(z_y)(z_y - z_x)] + \frac{u_a}{u_y} + \frac{u_e}{u_y} g(z_x) = 0 \tag{13.17}$$

$$\frac{u_x}{u_y} f_x'(z_x) + x^*(\widetilde{p}) \widetilde{p}_z - f_y'(z_y) + \frac{u_e}{u_y} g'(z_x) = 0. \tag{13.18}$$

Compared to those that maximize world welfare—equations (13.14a) and (13.14b)—each of these conditions contains the extra term $x^*(\cdot)\widetilde{p}_j$, or the product of exports and the change in price with respect to factor j. Assuming that $x_p < 0$ and $x_p^* < 0$, the derivatives of the market clearing condition (13.15) with respect to L_x and z_x imply that $\widetilde{p}_L < 0$ and $\widetilde{p}_z < 0$. Thus, a domestic planner could decrease the world price by increasing either of the factor allocations to agriculture. If the domestic economy is an agricultural importer, then $x^* < 0$ and the extra terms in each condition are positive. This implies that the marginal benefits of L_x and z_x are higher in relation to the small economy case, and the optimal allocations are therefore higher as well. If the home economy is an exporter ($x^* > 0$), then the extra terms are negative, implying a smaller allocation of factors to agriculture.

These results are intuitively consistent with the use of subsidies and taxes to regulate a single externality (Krutilla 1991); importers gain from policies that increase production and decrease the world price, while the reverse is true for exporters. If policy interventions must be justified on the basis external benefits and costs, then the model predicts that importers' policies will emphasize the benefits of agricultural land and undervalue the environmental costs of agricultural inputs, while exporters are likely to do the opposite.

These predictions generally coincide with observed differences in policies and negotiating tactics across nations. Importers, such as Japan, Norway, and Switzerland, all have significant policy schemes aimed at protecting farmland, and argue for the importance of the extra-market benefits from agriculture in trade negotiations. If these countries retain domestic farmland against free market pressures, and succeed in convincing their trading partners to do the same, then the resulting high level of agricultural production will lower world prices and benefit consumers in importing nations. Large exporters like the United States, on the other hand, have sought to protect the environment from agricultural pollution by "harmonizing up" environmental regulations across all trading partners. If this strategy is successful, then world supply will contract owing to the extra cost of environmental regulations, and producers in exporting countries will receive a higher price.

A Stylized Empirical Application to U.S. Agriculture

To illustrate the relationships between policies and their quantitative significance, this section simulates the model developed above for agricultural environmental policies in the United States. In the international trade arena, the United States is a net agricultural exporter and has a significant market share of several major commodities. Thus, it is generally believed the United States is a "large" country because its trade volume is significant enough to have a measurable effect on world prices. Conversely, agriculture makes up only a small part of the U.S. economy. In 1994, the aggregate value added from agricultural production was US$104 billion, or 1.5 percent of the US$6.9 trillion economy, and the cost of food items (which includes processing costs and the value of food retail services) makes up only about 10 percent of household expenditure.

U.S. agriculture has been cited as the source of numerous forms of pollution, such as soil erosion, nutrient runoff into streams and lakes, offensive odors, and contamination of water supplies. Here, the focus is on the harmful effects of agricultural chemicals on human health. This form of pollution was selected because its link to agriculture is well documented, the problem is widespread, and to date a limited (though growing) set of regulations have been imposed to control chemical use at the farm level. On the positive side, the agricultural landscape has been found to provide a significant amenity value to residents on the suburban fringes of major cities (Halstead 1984; Krieger 1999; Beasley, Workman, and Williams 1986.) These values have led to a significant policy interest in the preservation of open space, even at the national level of government (for example, Office of Management and Budget 2000).

Simulation Model

Based on the observations made above, several simplifying assumptions can be made in modeling the U.S agricultural sector. First, the small share of agriculture in gross domestic product implies that changes in the farm sector have almost no effect on prices or production in the rest of the economy. Second, the income effect on the demand for food items is likely to be negligible because it is a necessity item that makes up a small share of consumption expenditures. Third, although pollution and landscape amenities enter the utility function and therefore influence food demand, their effects are not thought to be empirically important.

Given these simplifications, the agricultural sector can be described by the following model:

$$x = B_x p^{-\eta_x} \tag{13.19}$$

$$x^* = B_x^* p^{-\eta_x^*} \tag{13.20}$$

$$x + x^* = F_x(L_x, Z_x) \tag{13.21}$$

$$p \frac{\partial F_x}{\partial L_x} = p_L - s_L \tag{13.22}$$

$$p \frac{\partial F_x}{\partial Z_x} = p_Z + t_Z \tag{13.23}$$

$$L_x = B_L p_L^{\eta_L} \tag{13.24}$$

$$Z_x = B_z p_z^{\eta_z} \tag{13.25}$$

$$a = L_x \tag{13.26}$$

$$e = L_x g(Z_x / L_x) \tag{13.27}$$

where η_x and η_x^* are the elasticities of domestic and export demand, respectively; η_L and η_z are the supply elasticities of the land and nonland inputs facing agriculture; p_L and p_z are the equilibrium prices of land and nonland inputs; and the B_i's are demand and supply constants. This system of nine equations uniquely determines the nine unknowns: x, x^*, L_x, Z_x, p, p_L, p_z, a, and e, which must be solved simultaneously with the land subsidy s_L and input tax t_z.

Equations (13.19) and (13.20) specify the domestic and export demands to be of the constant elasticity form. Equation (13.21) is the market clearing condition for agricultural goods. The profit-maximizing conditions for land and nonland inputs are represented in equations (13.22) and (13.23), which state that the marginal value product of each factor must equal its (post-policy) market price. Equations (13.24) and (13.25) are the market clearing conditions for land and nonland inputs, respectively, where the supplies of both factors are assumed to follow constant elasticity functions. Equations (13.26) and (13.27) are restatements from the conceptual model, relating the externalities a and e to the production factors L_x and Z_x.

This model is based on a framework that has been widely used to simulate the aggregate effects of several different policies in agriculture (Floyd 1965; Gardner 1987). Though it describes the agricultural sector in isolation, the model preserves the relevant general equilibrium effects of nonfixed factor prices through the supply functions for L_x and Z_x. In order to implement the model empirically, it is necessary to specify several functional relationships and parameter values. First, an aggregate utility function must be specified to calculate the welfare-maximizing levels of s_L and t_z. In addition, functional forms for F_x and g must be selected and parameterized, and parameter values for the supply and demand equations must also be chosen. These elements of the empirical model are discussed in turn below.

Aggregate utility is assumed to follow the money metric, quasi-linear form (Mas-Collel, Whinston, and Green 1995):

$$u(x, y, a, e) = \phi(x) + y + \gamma a - \delta e \qquad (13.28)$$

where $\phi(\cdot)$ is the utility of food, y is the dollar value of nonfood consumption, γ is the marginal value of landscape amenities, and δ is the marginal health cost of chemical pollution. $\phi(\cdot)$ represents the function that produces constant elasticity demands. Thus, maximizing equation (13.28) subject to the budget constraint $px + y \leq I$ results in the demand function (13.19), which is independent of income and the environmental measures a and e. To parameterize utility, values must be selected for the elasticity of demand η_x (which appears in ϕ), and the environmental parameters γ and δ. Based on a substantial body of empirical evidence that supports a highly inelastic demand for food, the parameter η_x is varied over the range 0.2–0.5.

Poe (1999) summarizes several nonmarket valuation studies that have attempted to estimate the external benefits of farmland. Halstead (1984), Bergstrom, Dillman, and Stoll (1985), and Krieger (1999) have converted estimates of household willingness to pay to amenity values per acre by aggregating over households to obtain social willingness to pay and dividing by the number of acres in the study region. Applying the estimates from these studies to a similar conversion procedure for aggregate data, estimated amenity values of farmland range from less than US$1 per acre to US$11 per acre. Since the base values are from study regions where farmland is considered scarce, these per acre values may be overestimated. The parameter γ is thus varied from US$0 to US$10.

Because there is no standardized measure of agricultural pollution, δ is normalized to unity and e is measured in dollars of health costs that are attributable to agricultural chemicals. The two primary categories of chemicals that pose health risks to humans are pesticides and nitrates that occur in drinking water from the use of nitrogen fertilizer. Because the health costs of these pollutants cannot be directly observed, we must rely on estimates from the environmental literature.

Poe (1998) has estimated a damage function that relates household willingness to pay for improved water quality to observed contamination levels. Households whose water supply exceeds the European health standard of 4.4 ppm are willing to pay about US$170 per year for safer drinking water, while households that exceed the U.S. Environmental Protection Agency standard of 10 ppm are willing to pay an average of US$380. Based on population data compiled by the Environmental Working Group (1996), these estimates imply aggregate nitrate damages of approximately US$2.3 billion. Other studies have estimated household willingness to pay for general improvements in water quality, including the removal of all agricultural and industrial contaminants (Schultz and Lindsay 1990; Powell 1990). These estimates imply aggregate damages from all water pollutants in the range of US$3.8–6.2 billion per year.

Pimentel et al. (1982) estimate that the direct health cost of pesticides (including treatment of poisonings and pesticide-induced cancers as well as accidental fatalities) total US$780 million per year, and that the indirect costs through drinking water contamination are US$1.8 billion per year. Combining the direct and indirect health costs of all agricultural chemicals, the body of evidence suggests aggregate damages in the range of US$3–7 billion, although these may be overestimates because they potentially account for nonagricultural contaminants. The base value of e is thus varied from US$2 billion to US$5 billion.

The functional relationship between chemical application rates and damage to human health is not yet completely understood. Because yield is a concave function of polluting inputs, physical properties imply the pollution function must be convex (Siebert et al. 1980). Thus, convexity is a natural property to impose on the health costs of pollutants as well, but there is little scientific justification for any particular functional form. Here, health costs are assumed to follow a quadratic form: $e = B_e Z_x^2 / L_x = L_x B_e z_x^2$. This function has linear derivatives in Z_x and z_x and therefore imposes constant marginal health costs. Thus, the specification is a linear approximation to the underlying marginal health cost function; and this simplification seemed reasonable, given the stylized focus of the application and the approximate nature of the data.

Data on aggregate agricultural production are available from the U.S. Department of Agriculture Economic Research Service (Ahearn et al. 1998; Ball et al. 1997). This data series includes indexes of aggregate output as well as inputs in several categories for the years 1948–94. For purposes here, agricultural technology was assumed to be separable so that input categories can be further grouped into a "land aggregate" (L_x), which is made up of land and other factors that are combined with it, and a "nonland aggregate" (Z_x). In particular, the land aggregate includes indexes of land itself, capital equipment, and labor; and the nonland aggregate is made up of chemicals, fuel and electricity, and other purchased inputs. When technology is separable, the production decision can be divided into two stages, where inputs are combined in a least-cost way within each aggregate in the first stage and the profit maximizing levels of the aggregates are chosen in the second stage (Chambers 1988).

To be able to compute quantity and price series for L_x and Z_x, it is necessary to employ an indexing procedure that combines the inputs within each aggregate factor. Because the underlying functional form of the technology is unknown, any index must be regarded as an approximation that reflects the productive capacity of the various inputs. Here, it is assumed that the inputs within each aggregate are combined in Leontief fixed proportions. Though this procedure abstracts from substitution of the inputs within the aggregates, it greatly simplifies the analysis because the implicit price of each aggregate becomes a linear expression of the category prices. Consequently, a subsidy on land alone is equivalent to a subsidy on the entire land aggregate L_x, and a tax on chemicals is equivalent to a tax on the nonland aggregate Z_x.[8]

To solve the second-stage problem, it is necessary to specify a functional form that relates L_x and Z_x to agricultural output. Here, a Cobb-Douglas form is assumed: $F_x(L_x, Z_x) = B_x L_x^{\beta_L} Z_x^{\beta_L}$, where $\beta_L + \beta_Z = 1$ by constant returns to scale. Under profit maximization, β_L and β_Z are the cost shares of the land and nonland aggregates, respectively. Calculating the average shares over the years 1948–94 resulted in point estimates of $\beta_L = 0.71$ and $\beta_Z = 0.29$, and the parameters are varied over the ranges [0.5, 0.9] for β_L and [0.1, 0.5] for β_Z.

The remaining parameters to be chosen are the elasticity of export demand and the supply elasticities for the aggregate factors L_x and Z_x. Export demand is probably quite elastic, but may not be perfectly elastic because the United States is a large country. To explore the consequences of market power in international trade, the export demand elasticity was varied between 2 and ∞. The extreme values represent the polar cases of a very large economy with substantial market power and a small economy with no market power. Because land makes up a significant part of the aggregate L_x, we would expect its supply elasticity to be quite small. However, the inputs in Z_x can be produced at very nearly constant cost, implying a relatively high supply elasticity. Thus, the parameters η_L and η_Z are varied over the ranges [0.1, 0.3] and [5, 15], respectively. Table 13.1 summarizes the range of parameter values, along with a set of "pri-

Table 13.1. Parameter Values

Parameter	Symbol	Range	Primary value
Elasticity of domestic demand	η_x	0.2–0.5	0.3
Elasticity of export demand	η_x^*	2–∞	5.0
Supply elasticity of L_x	η_L	0.1–0.3	0.2
Supply elasticity of Z_x	η_Z	5–15	10.0
Production elasticity of L_x	L	0.5–0.9	0.71
Production elasticity of Z_x	Z	0.1–0.5	0.29
Marginal value of amenities (US$/acre)	γ	0–10	5.0
Aggregate external health costs (US$billion)	e	2–5	3.5

mary" values that are used in the simulations reported below. The constants B_i are determined by calibrating the model relationships to base data for 1994; and these base values are reported in the second column of table 13.2.

Results

To explore the relationships among domestic environmental policies, the model is initially solved under three policy experiments for the small economy case. The assumption of a small economy precludes the possibility of distorting trade and ensures that the simulated policies include only externality-correcting components. In the first policy scenario, chemicals are taxed at their marginal external cost with no land policy, while the second scenario subsidizes land at its amenity value but does not tax nonland inputs. These two experiments thus correspond to policy schemes that target each externality independently. The third experiment is based on the relationships derived in the theoretical section and includes both a land subsidy and a chemical tax that simultaneously correct both externalities.

The results of these experiments are reported in table 13.2. When the tax is imposed in isolation (scenario 1), farmers pay a US$0.13 tax per pound of chemicals.[9] Even though estimated chemical use and health costs fall in this scenario (by about 14 and 27 percent, respectively), the increased cost of farming drives land out of agriculture and reduces total production. Thus, in an independent effort to improve water quality, the tax policy has damaged the public-good function of agriculture and has reduced the aggregate value of farm production. If instead a subsidy is introduced to protect farmland without any regulations on chemical use (scenario 2), the stock of farmland and the value of production increase from their base values, but so do aggregate chemical use and estimated health costs. In sum, a policy to independently improve one externality leads to an adverse change in the other.

Table 13.2. Base Data and Simulation Results

Variable	Base data (1994)	Small economy			Large economy[a]
		Tax only (scenario 1)	Subsidy only (scenario 2)	Joint policy (scenario 3)	
Land subsidy (US$/acre)	0.00	0.00	5.00	7.67	−7.38
Chemical tax (US$/pound)	0.00	0.13	0.00	0.13	0.29
Food price[b]	1.00	1.00	1.00	1.00	1.09
					8.7
Production (US$ billion)	166.61	158.32	167.91	160.29	170.04
		−5.0	*0.8*	*−3.8*	*2.1*
Net exports (US$ billion)	19.17	10.88	20.46	12.85	13.3
		−43.2	*6.7*	*−33.0*	*−28.4*
Consumption (US$ billion)	147.44	147.44	147.44	147.44	156.31
					6.0
Agricultural land (million acres)	975	967	983	979	968
		−0.8	*0.8*	*0.4*	*−0.7*
Rent on land (US$/acre)	121.35	116.30	126.32	123.93	117.31
		−4.2	*4.1*	*2.1*	*−3.3*
Chemical use (billion pounds)	44.8	38.3	45.1	38.8	36.6
		−14.4	*0.7*	*−13.4*	*−18.2*
Price of chemicals (US$/pound)	1.08	1.06	1.08	1.06	1.06
		−1.5	*0.1*	*−1.4*	*−2.0*
Input intensity (pound/acre)	46.0	39.7	45.9	39.6	37.8
		−13.6	*−0.1*	*−13.7*	*−17.6*
Health costs (US$ billion)	3.50	2.56	3.52	2.61	2.36
		−27.0	*0.6*	*−25.3*	*−33.4*
Land amenity value (US$ billion)[c]	4.87	4.83	4.91	4.89	4.84
		−0.8	*0.8*	*0.4*	*−0.7*

Note: Numbers in italics are percentage changes from base values.
a. Assumes an export demand elasticity of 5.
b. Index of all agricultural prices, 1994 = 1.
c. Assumes an amenity value of US$5 per acre.

Only if the subsidy and tax are imposed jointly can there be an improvement in both externalities (scenario 3). The tax on chemicals of US$0.13 per pound, if imposed jointly with the land subsidy of US$7.67 per acre, will achieve an efficient allocation of both factors. Farmland rises from its base value by 4 million acres, and external health costs fall by an estimated US$900 million (25 percent). The optimal subsidy on an acre of farmland includes the US$5 it contributes to amenity value as well as its marginal effect on pollution; an extra acre of agricultural land, *ceteris paribus*, reduces external health costs by US$2.67. Thus, the optimal subsidy differs from the amenity value of farmland by more than 50 percent.

In the joint policy case, the fall in nonland inputs outweighs the effect of the increase in farmland, and domestic production decreases by US$6.6 billion. Net exports contract by a matching amount, but the international price is not affected because of the small economy assumption. If the economy is large enough so that export quantities influence the world price, then optimal environmental policies include components that improve domestic welfare through trade distortion. Thus, the resulting tax and subsidy may differ substantially from the external cost of chemicals and amenity benefits of farmland.

The last column in table 13.2 corresponds to this large economy case, where the tax and subsidy are imposed jointly and the elasticity of export demand is set at 5. Since the United States is an exporter, it will have an incentive to select policies that restrict production and in turn raise the international price. Therefore, the chemical tax of US$0.29 is more than twice as high as the small economy case, while the subsidy becomes negative (–US$7.38) so that land is taxed as well. These policies do result in some environmental improvements because external health costs are reduced by over 30 percent, but these gains are partially offset by a 0.7 percent decrease in the stock of farmland.

The "environmental" policies provide additional welfare benefits through trade distortion. They have succeeded in raising international prices by 9 percent and expanding U.S. production by 2 percent. Net exports decrease compared to base values where environmental consequences are ignored completely, but are about US$900 million larger than the small economy case where trade-distorting effects are precluded.

Though the cases of alternative parameter values are not reported, the results in table 13.2 are generally quite robust as market and production parameters are varied. With environmental parameters set at their primary values and the other domestic parameters (η_x, η_L, η_Z, β_L, and β_Z) individually varied across their ranges, the small economy tax ranges from US$0.12 to US$0.14 per pound, while the subsidy is between US$7.04 and US$7.81 per acre. These parameters have a somewhat greater impact on the policies for a large economy; with the export elasticity set at 5, the tax and subsidy range from US$0.18 to US$0.39 per pound and from –US$12.79 to –US$2.40 per acre, respectively. The environmental and trade parameters naturally have a more direct effect on the environmental policies. The different environmental values would imply small economy input taxes from US$0.08 to US$0.18 per pound and small economy land subsidies between US$2.68 and US$12.67 per acre. With environmental parameters at their primary values, the extreme case of an export demand elasticity of 2 implies an optimal tax and subsidy of US$0.37 per pound and –US$14.28 per acre, respectively.

Policy Implications

This chapter has determined the optimal policy rules when agricultural production generates both landscape amenities and pollution from chemical inputs. The optimal subsidy on land and tax on nonland inputs depend on the size of both externalities, and a change in the social value of either land amenities or pollution therefore implies a change in both policies. It has been shown empirically that independent policies are likely to work at cross purposes; that is, a single policy directed at one externality leads to an adverse change in the other externality.

One important implication of empirical research is that an optimal subsidy on agricultural land does not equal the net value of land amenities. Numerous studies have estimated the social amenity benefits from land in agriculture using nonmarket valuation techniques, but these estimates cannot be interpreted as the appropriate farmland subsidy, even if the values are "corrected" to account for the value of pollution generated per acre. A simulation of U.S. agriculture suggests the interaction between policies is empirically important, and if the incentive to use environmental policy as a trade-distorting tool is ignored, then the estimated optimal land subsidy is about 50 percent larger than the amenity value of farmland. In the large economy case, the policies include components that improve domestic welfare through terms of trade, and the optimal tax and subsidy differ even more from the social values of the two external effects.

The model here abstracts from the site-specific factors that cause environmental values to be spatially heterogeneous. As a practical matter, proposed policies differ by location and tend to focus on areas that are known to be environmentally sensitive or farming regions in close proximity to large population centers. Yet our findings are even more important for policymaking in these areas, because the interaction among joint policies is more pronounced if the social values placed on the external effects from agricultural production are large.

In the international arena, small economies will choose the same policies that maximize world welfare, but large economies have an incentive to set policies at noninternalizing levels to exploit terms of trade effects. In particular, large importers will choose policies that increase agricultural factors beyond globally efficient allocations, while large exporters prefer to restrict factor allocations (and hence agricultural production) to raise the international price. For large economies, production policies that are ostensibly justified on environmental grounds can become instruments to distort international prices. Indeed, based on empirical policy simulations, we estimate the United States alone could manipulate its domestic environmental policies to change the world price by about 9 percent.

Even for small countries with environmental concerns, there are additional policy goals such as supporting farm incomes or enhancing food security. In the WTO negotiations over environmental issues, therefore, it may be impossible to determine whether so-called environmental policies are really vehicles to help achieve some other goal. The key to making domestic policies compatible with free trade lies in the types of policies used. The less the policy instruments distort trade, the more autonomy nations can have in selecting and executing domestic policy goals.

Appendix
Derivation of Optimal Factor Allocation

Conditions: Closed Economy

From equation (13.2), the derivatives of national income I are

$$I_L = p_L L_x f_x(z_x) + p(\cdot) f_x(z_x) - [f_y(z_y) - f_y'(z_y)(z_y - z_x)]$$
$$I_z = p_z L_x f_x(z_x) + p(\cdot) L_x f_x'(z_x) - L_x f_y'(z_y).$$

Substituting these derivatives and Roy's Identity ($v_p = -x(p, I)v_I$) into equations (13.4) and (13.5):

$$-x(p, I)v_I p_L + v_I p_L L_x f_x(z_x) + v_I p(\cdot) f_x(z_x) - v_I [f_y(z_y) - f_y'(z_y)(z_y - z_x)]$$
$$+ v_a + v_e g(z_x) = 0$$

$$-x(p, I)v_I p_z + v_I p_z L_x f_x(z_x) + v_I p(\cdot) L_x f_x'(z_x) - v_I L_x f_y'(z_y) + v_e L_x g'(z_x) = 0.$$

The market clearing condition—(equation (13.1)—implies that the sum of the first and second terms in each of the above equations is zero. The Envelope Theorem implies that $v_I = u_y$, $v_a = u_a$, and $v_e = u_e$; and $p(\cdot) = u_x/u_y$ by the first-order conditions of utility maximization. Substituting these relationships into the remaining nonzero terms and dividing the second equation by L_x:

$$u_x f_x(z_x) - u_y [f_y(z_y) - f_y'(z_y)(z_y - z_x)] + u_a + u_e g(z_x) = 0$$
$$u_y fx'(z_x) - u_y f_y'(z_y) + u_e g'(z_x) = 0.$$

Dividing each of these equations by u_y reveals equations (13.6) and (13.7) in the chapter.

Derivation of Optimal Factor Allocation Conditions: Small Open Economy

Because the price p is a parameter for small economies, the derivatives of national income I are:

$$I_L = pf_x(z_x) - [f_y(z_y) - f_y'(z_y)(z_y - z_x)]$$
$$I_z = pL_x f_x'(z_x) - L_x f_y'(z_y).$$

Substituting these derivatives and the envelope conditions ($v_I = u_y$, $v_a = u_a$, and $v_e = u_e$) into the welfare maximizing conditions:

$$u_y pf_x(z_x) - u_y[f_y(z_y) - f_y'(z_y)(z_y - z_x)] + u_a + u_e g(z_x) = 0$$
$$u_y pL_x f_x'(z_x) - u_y L_x f_y'(z_y)_z + u_e L_x g'(z_x) = 0.$$

The small economy conditions are obtained by dividing the first of these equations by u_y and the second by $u_y L_x$.

Derivation of Optimal Factor Allocation Conditions: Large Open Economy

From equation (13.16), the derivatives of the large economy national income function $\tilde{I}$ are

$$\tilde{I}_L = \tilde{p}_L L_x f_x(z_x) + \tilde{p}_L(\cdot) f_x(z_x) - [f_y(z_y) - f_y'(z_y)(z_y - z_x)]$$
$$\tilde{I}_z = \tilde{p}_z L_x f_x(z_x) + \tilde{p}(\cdot) L_x f_x'(z_x) - L_x f_y'(z_y).$$

Substituting these derivatives and Roy's Identity ($v_p = -xv_I$) into the conditions for a welfare maximum:

$$-x(\tilde{p}, \tilde{I}) v_I \tilde{p}_L + v_I \tilde{p}_L L_x f_x(z_x) + v_I \tilde{p}(\cdot) f_x(z_x)$$
$$-v_I[f_y(z_y) - f_y'(z_y)(z_y - z_x)] + v_a + v_e g(z_x) = 0$$

$$-x(\tilde{p}, \tilde{I}) v_I \tilde{p}_z + v_I \tilde{p}_z L_x f_x(z_x) + v_I \tilde{p}(\cdot) f_x'(z_x) - v_I L_x f_y'(z_y) + v_e L_x g'(z_x) = 0.$$

By the market clearing condition—(equation (13.15)—the sum of the first and second terms in the first of the foregoing equations is $x^*(\tilde{p}) \tilde{p}_L v_I$. Similarly, the first and second terms in the second equation sum to $x^*(\tilde{p}) \tilde{p}_z v_I$. Proceeding as above, substitute these relationships along with the envelope and utility maximization conditions ($v_I = u_y$, $v_a = u_a$, and $v_e = u_e$; and $\tilde{p} = u_x/u_y$) into the preceding conditions and divide the second condition by L_x:

$$x^*(\tilde{p})\tilde{p}_L\,u_y + u_x f_x(z_x) - u_y[f_y(z_y) - f_y'(z_y)(z_y - z_x)] + u_a + u_e g(z_x) = 0$$

$$\frac{x^*(\tilde{p})\tilde{p}_z\,u_y}{L_x} + u_y f_x'(z_x) - u_y f_y'(z_y) + u_e g'(z_x) = 0.$$

Dividing each of these equations by u_y reveals equations (13.17) and (13.18).

For exporters (importers), the term $x^*(\tilde{p})\tilde{p}_j$ ($j = L, z$) in equations (13.17) and (13.18) will be negative (positive), as claimed in the text, provided that the derivatives of $\tilde{p}(\cdot)$ are negative. To determine the signs of $\tilde{p}_L$ and $\tilde{p}_z$, differentiate the market clearing condition (13.15) to obtain

$$x_p\tilde{p}_L + x_I\tilde{I}_L + x_p^*\tilde{p}_L = f_x(z_z) \tag{13.15a}$$

$$x_p\tilde{p}_z + x_I\tilde{I}_z + x_p^*\tilde{p}_z = L_x f_x'(z_z). \tag{13.15b}$$

Solving condition (13.17) for $(u_x/u_y)f_x(z_x) = \tilde{p}(\cdot)f_x(z_x)$ and substituting the resulting expression into $\tilde{I}_L$ above:

$$\tilde{I}_L = \tilde{p}_L L_x f_x(z_x) - x^*(\tilde{p})\tilde{p}_L - \frac{u_a}{u_y} - \frac{u_e}{u_y}g(z_x) = x(\cdot)\tilde{p}_L - \frac{u_a}{u_y} - \frac{u_e}{u_y}g(z_x)$$

where the second equality follows from market clearing. Similarly, equation (13.18) and the expression for $\tilde{I}_z$ above imply

$$\tilde{I}_z = x(\cdot)\tilde{p}_z - L_x \frac{u_e}{u_y}g'(z_x).$$

Substituting the foregoing expressions for $\tilde{I}_L$ and $\tilde{I}_z$ into equations (13.15a) and (13.15b) and rearranging:

$$\tilde{p}_L = \frac{f_x(\cdot) + x_I\dfrac{u_a}{u_y} + x_I\dfrac{u_e}{u_y}g(z_z)}{x_p + x_I x(\cdot) + x_p^*}$$

$$\tilde{p}_z = \frac{L_x\left[f_x'(\cdot) + x_I\dfrac{u_e}{u_y}g'(z_z)\right]}{x_p + x_I x(\cdot) + x_p^*}.$$

The Slutsky equation and the assumption that $x_p^* < 0$ ensure that the denominator of both of these expressions is negative. Assuming that food is a normal good, the numerator of $\widetilde{p}_L$ is always positive when $(u_a/u_y) + (u_e/u_y)g(z_x) > 0$ (that is, when net externalities are positive). A sufficient set of conditions for both numerators to be positive is

$$\widetilde{p}f_x(\cdot) + \frac{u_a}{u_y} + \frac{u_e}{u_y}g(z_x) > (\,$$

$$\widetilde{p}f_x'(\cdot) + \frac{u_e}{u_y}g'(z_x) > 0$$

Thus, as long as the net marginal benefit of each factor in agriculture is positive (that is, the sum of marginal private and external benefits outweighs marginal costs), the price function must be decreasing in both arguments. Alternative cases (for example, when the cost of pollution on each acre is larger than the combined value of farm production and amenity benefits) are ruled out by assumption.

Notes

1. If emissions are some function of agricultural output (that is, $e = h(x)$), then pollution can also be expressed as $e = h(Fx(Lx, Zx)) = G(Lx, Zx)$.

2. To verify, $\partial e/\partial Lx = g(zx) + Lxg'(zx)(-Zx/Lx2) = g(zx) - g'(zx)zx$. The last expression has the same sign as $g(zx)/zx - g'(zx) < 0$, where the inequality follows from the Mean Value Theorem. Intuitively, an acre increase in Lx produces two effects on e: the extra pollution on the acre added and the decrease in pollution on the acres previously in production that follows from a change in the input ratio Zx/Lx. If pollution satisfies constant returns to scale (CRS), then the change in the input ratio decreases pollution by $g'(\cdot)zx$; the net effect is always negative because "average pollution" g/zx must be less than "marginal pollution" g' if g is convex (the opposite of the analogous relationships for a concave production function). More generally, if pollution is not necessarily CRS, then the effect on total pollution from an increase in farmland depends on the heterogeneity of land; and bringing an environmentally sensitive acre of land into production may increase total pollution. However, provided that the pollution function on every parcel of land is convex, the extra pollution from an extra acre is likely to be outweighed by the combined decrease in pollution on the acres already in production.

3. Conceptually, there is a more general amenity function that relates the quantity of agricultural land to the amount of amenity services produced. Because of the obvious difficulties in measuring and observing amenity services per se, the valuation literature assumes that amenities are produced in proportion to the agricultural land base and attempts to estimate the value of amenities per acre (Poe 1999).

4. More precisely, if marginal utilities and marginal products become infinite as their respective arguments approach zero, then there must be a positive allocation of both factors to both industries.

5. Because amenities are proportional to Lx, the subsidy on agricultural land is equivalent to a direct subsidy on amenities. All these policies that operate on prices are meant to represent a broader class of policy tools. Because there is an equivalent restriction on factor quantities for every tax, the input tax can also represent regulations that limit input use. Similarly, when land is initially taxed (as it is in most countries), the land subsidy is equivalent to policies that reduce property tax burdens or place controls on land use conversion.

6. In principle, pollution could be inferred from observations on inputs if the pollution function is known or estimable. In this case, farmers would be charged from predicted levels of pollution based on their input use. Administratively, such a scheme would be inferior to one with an equivalent outcome that acts on inputs directly.

7. To see this, suppose there were a third factor W that is neither taxed nor subsidized and does not influence a or e. The socially optimal allocation of W must satisfy $(ux/uy)(\partial Fx/\partial W) - \partial Fy/\partial W = 0$, while the free market allocation can be described by $(p + sx)(\partial Fx/\partial W) - \partial Fy/\partial W = 0$. Because $p = ux/uy$, social optimality requires that $sx = 0$.

8. In particular, the aggregate factor index functions are

$$Lx(l, K, N) = \min\{l, K/bK, N/bN\} \text{ and } Zx(C, E, M) = \min\{C, E/bE, M/bM\}$$

where l represents land, K is capital, N is labor, C is chemicals, E is fuel and electricity, and M is purchased materials. The coefficients bK and bN are the quantities of capital and labor that must be combined with each acre of land, respectively, and bE and bM are the amounts of energy and materials used with each unit of chemicals. The implicit price of the land aggregate is the cost function of Lx, or $pL = \min\{pll + pKK + pNN : Lx(l, K, N) = 1\} = pl + bKpK + bNpN$. By a parallel argument, the price of the nonland aggregate is $pZ = pC + bEpE = bMpM$. Thus, an addition or subtraction to pl or pC implies the same change in pL and pZ. If there are substitution possibilities within the aggregate factors, the linear price relation is a first-order approximation to a concave function. Since this concave function rises more slowly for price increases and falls more quickly for price decreases, the linear approximation will estimate a lower bound on the subsidy and an upper bound on the tax.

9. Note that chemicals include all nutrients and the active ingredients of pesticides.

References

ABARE (Australian Bureau of Agricultural and Resource Economics). 1999. "'Multifunctionality': A Pretext for Protection?" *ABARE Current Issues* 99 (3):1–6. http://www.abare.gov.au/pubcat/trade.htm.

Ahearn, M., J. Yee, V. E. Ball, R. Nehring, A. Somwaru, and R. Evans. 1998. *Agricultural Productivity in the United States.* Economic Research Service, Agriculture Information Bulletin 740. Washington, D.C.: U.S. Department of Agriculture.

Anderson, K. 1992a. "Agricultural Trade Liberalization and the Environment: A Global Perspective." *The World Economy* 15:153–72.

———. 1992b. "The Standard Welfare Economics of Policies Affecting Trade and the Environment." In K. Anderson and R. Black, eds., *The Greening of World Trade Issues*. Ann Arbor: University of Michigan Press.

Anderson, K., and B. Hoekman. 1999. "Agriculture and the New Trade Agenda." Paper presented at the American Economic Association Annual Meeting, New York, January 3–5.

Ball, V. E., J. Bureau, R. Nehring, and A. Somwaru. 1997. "Agricultural Productivity Revisited." *American Journal of Agricultural Economics* 79:1045–63.

Beasley, S. D., W. C. Workman, and N. A. Williams. 1986. "Estimating Amenity Values on Urban Fringe Farmland: A Contingent Valuation Approach." *Growth and Change* 17:70–78.

Beghin, J., S. Dessus, D. Roland-Holst, and D. van der Mensbrugghe. 1995. "The Trade and Environment Nexus in Mexican Agriculture. A General Equilibrium Analysis." *Agricultural Economics* 17(2–3):115–32.

Bergstrom, J. C., B. L. Dillman, and J. R. Stoll. 1985. "Public Environmental Amenity Benefits of Private Land: The Case of Prime Agricultural Land." *Southern Journal of Agricultural Economics* 17:139–49.

Blandford, D., and L. Fulponi. 1999. "Emerging Public Concerns in Agriculture: Domestic Policies and International Trade Commitments." *European Review of Agricultural Economics* 26:409–24.

Bohman, M., J. Cooper, D. Mullarkey, M. A. Normile, D. Skully, S. Vogel, and E. Young. 1999. *The Use and Abuse of Multifunctionality*. Washington, D.C.: U.S. Department of Agriculture, Economic Research Service. http://www.econ.ag.gov/briefing/wto/.

Chambers, R. G. 1988. *Applied Production Analysis: A Dual Approach*. New York: Cambridge University Press.

Copeland, B. R. 1994. "International Trade and the Environment: Policy Reform in a Polluted Small Open Economy." *Journal of Environmental Economics and Management* 26:44–65.

Dixit, A. and V. Norman. 1980. *Theory of International Trade: A Dual, General Equilibrium Approach*. New York: Cambridge University Press.

Environmental Working Group. 1996. "Pouring It On: Nitrate Contamination of Drinking Water." Processed. Washington, D.C.

Floyd, J. E. 1965. "The Effects of Farm Price Supports on the Return to Land and Labor in Agriculture." *Journal of Political Economy* 73:148–58.

Gardner, B. L. 1987. *The Economics of Agricultural Policies*. New York: Macmillan.

Hackl, F., and G. J. Pruckner. 1997. "Towards More Efficient Compensation Programmes for Tourists' Benefits from Agriculture in Europe." *Environmental and Resource Economics* 10:189–205.

Halstead, J. M. 1984. "Measuring the Nonmarket Value of Massachusetts Agricultural Land: A Case Study." *Journal of the Northeastern Agricultural Economics Council* 13:12–9.

Holtermann, S. 1976. "Alternative Tax Systems to Correct for Externalities and the Efficiency of Paying Compensation." *Economica* 43:1–16.

Krieger, D. J. 1999. "Saving Open Spaces: Public Support for Farmland Protection." Working Paper CAE/WP99-1. American Farmland Trust Center for Agriculture in the Environment, DeKalb, Ill.

Krutilla, K. 1991. "Environmental Regulation in an Open Economy." *Journal of Environmental Economics and Management* 20:127–42.

Lindland, J. 1998. "Non-Trade Concerns in a Multifunctional Agriculture." Paper presented at the OECD Workshop on Emerging Trade Issues in Agriculture, Paris, October 26–27. http://www. oecd.org/agr/trade/.

Lopez, R. A., F. A. Shah, and M. A. Altobello. 1994. "Amenity Benefits and the Optimal Allocation of Land." *Land Economics* 70:53–62.

Mas-Collel, A., M. D. Whinston, and J. R. Green. 1995. *Microeconomic Theory.* New York: Oxford University Press.

Nersten, N. K., and S. S. Prestegard. 1998. "Non-Trade Concerns in the WTO Negotiations." Paper presented at the International Agricultural Trade Research Consortium Annual Meeting, Florida. December.

Norwegian Royal Ministry of Agriculture. 1998. *Non-Trade Concerns in a Multifunctional Agriculture: Implications for Agricultural Policy and the Multilateral Trading System.* Oslo.

OECD (Organisation for Economic Co-operation and Development). 1997a. *Environmental Benefits from Agriculture: Issues and Policies. The Helsinki Seminar.* Paris.

———. 1997b. *Helsinki Seminar on Environmental Benefits from Agriculture: Country Case Studies.* GD(97)110. Paris.

Office of Management and Budget. 2000. *Budget of the United States Government, Fiscal Year 2000.* Washington, D.C.

Ollikainen, M. 1999. "On Optimal Agri-Environmental Policy: A Public Finance View." Paper presented at the Ninth European Association of Agricultural Economists Congress, Warsaw, Poland, August.

Pimentel, D., H. Acquay, M. Biltonen, P. Rice, M. Silva, J. Nelson, J. Lipner, S. Giordano, A. Horowitz, and M. D'Amore. 1982. "Environmental and Economic Costs of Pesticide Use." *Bioscience* 42:750–60.

Poe, G. L. 1997. "Extra-Market Values and Conflicting Agricultural Environmental Policies." *Choices*, 4–8.

———. 1998. "Valuation of Groundwater Quality Using a Contingent Valuation Damage Function Approach." *Water Resources Research* 34:3627–33.

———. 1999. "'Maximizing the Environmental Benefits per Dollar Expended': An Economic Interpretation and Review of Agricultural Environmental Benefits and Costs." *Society and Natural Resources* 12:571–98.

Powell, J. R. 1990. "The Value of Groundwater Protection: Measurement of Willingness-to-Pay Information and its Utilization by Local Government Decision-Makers." Ph.D. diss. Cornell University, Department of Agricultural Economics, Ithaca, N.Y.

Runge, C. F. 1998. "Emerging Issues in Agricultural Trade and the Environment." Paper presented at the OECD Workshop on Emerging Trade Issues in Agriculture, Paris, October 26–27.

————. 1999. "Beyond the Green Box: A Conceptual Framework for Agricultural Trade and the Environment." Working Paper WP99-1. Center for International Food and Agricultural Policy, University of Minnesota.

Schamel, G., and H. de Gorter. 1997. "Trade and the Environment: Domestic versus Global Perspectives." Working Paper 34/97. Humboldt-Universität zu Berlin, Wirtscafts und Sozialwissenschaften an der Landwirtschaftlich-Gartnerischen Fakultät.

Schultz, S. D., and B. E. Lindsay. 1990. "The Willingness to Pay for Groundwater Protection." *Water Resources Research* 26:1869–75.

Siebert, H., J. Eichberger, R. Gronych, and R. Pethig. 1980. *Trade and Environment: A Theoretical Enquiry.* Amsterdam: Elsevier.

Whalley, J. 1999. "Environmental Considerations in New Multilateral Agricultural Negotiations, and Associated Developing Country Concerns." Paper presented at the Conference on Agriculture and the New Trade Agenda in the WTO 2000 Negotiations, Geneva, October 1–2.

WTO (World Trade Organization). 1998. "Non-Trade Concerns in the Next Agricultural Negotiations." WTO/CTE/W/97. Submission by Argentina to the Committee on Trade and Environment. Geneva. http://www.wto.org/wto/ddf/ep/public.html.

————. 1999a. "Environmental Effects of Trade Liberalization in the Agricultural Sector." WTO/CTE/W/100. Submission by Norway to the Committee on Trade and the Environment. Geneva. http://www.wto.org/wto/ddf/ep/public.html.

————. 1999b. "Preparations for the 1999 Ministerial Conference: Negotiations on Agriculture." WTO/GC/W/220. Communication from Japan to the General Council. Geneva. http://www.wto.org/wto/ddf/ep/public.html.

————. 1999c. "Preparations for the 1999 Ministerial Conference: Negotiations on Agriculture." WTO/GC/W/261. Communication from Switzerland to the General Council. Geneva. http://www.wto.org/wto/ddf/ep/public.html.

14

Genetically Modified Foods, Trade, and Developing Countries

Chantal Pohl Nielsen, Karen Thierfelder, and Sherman Robinson

The current debate about the use of genetic engineering in agricultural production reveals substantial differences in perception of the risks and benefits associated with this new biotechnology. Farmers in North America and a few large developing countries such as Argentina, Mexico, and China are rapidly adopting the new genetically modified (GM) crop varieties as they become available, and citizens in these countries are generally accepting this development. Growing genetically modified crop varieties provides farmers with a range of agronomic benefits, mainly in terms of lower input requirements and hence lower costs to consumers. However, in other parts of the world, especially Western Europe, people are concerned about the environmental impact of widespread cultivation of GM crops and the safety of foods containing genetically modified organisms (GMOs). In response to the strong consumer reaction against GM foods in Western Europe, and to a certain extent also in Japan, separate production systems for GM and non-GM crops are emerging in the maize and soybean sectors.[1] To the extent that GM-critical consumers are willing to pay a price premium for non-GM varieties, there may be a viable market for these products alongside the new GM varieties.

Developing countries—regardless of whether they are exporters or importers of agricultural crops—will be affected by changing consumer attitudes toward genetic modification in the industrialized world. Some developing countries are highly dependent on exporting particular primary agricultural products to GM-critical regions. Depending on the strength of opposition toward GM products in such regions and the costs of segregating production, the developing countries may benefit from segregated agricultural markets, which will have different prices. In principle, these countries may choose to grow GM crops for the domestic market and for exports to countries that are indifferent as to GM content and to grow

GM-free products for exports to countries where consumers are willing to pay a premium for this characteristic. Such a market development would be analogous to the niche markets for organic foods. Other developing countries are net importers and can benefit from the widespread adoption of GM technology. Assuming consumers in those countries are not opposed to GM products, they will benefit from lower world market prices. If changing consumer preferences have an effect on world agricultural markets, this latter outcome may also be affected.

Here we offer a preliminary quantitative assessment of the impact that consumers' changing attitude toward genetic modification might have on world trade patterns, with emphasis on the developing countries. It extends earlier work described in Nielsen, Robinson, and Thierfelder (2001) and Nielsen, Thierfelder, and Robinson (2001). The analytical framework used is an empirical global general equilibrium model, in which the two primary GM crops, soybeans and maize (corn), are specified as either GM or non-GM. This GM and non-GM split is maintained throughout the entire processing chain: GM livestock and GM food processing industries use only GM intermediate inputs; likewise non-GM livestock and non-GM food processing industries use only non-GM intermediate inputs.

Genetic Engineering in Agriculture

The most recent research and development (R&D) advances in modern biotechnology have introduced an ever-widening range of genetically engineered products to agriculture.[2] While traditional biotechnology improves the quality and yields of plants and animals through, for example, selective breeding, genetic engineering is a new biotechnology that enables direct manipulation of genetic material (inserting, removing, or altering genes).[3] In this way, the new technology speeds up the development process, shaving years off research and development programs. Protagonists argue that genetic engineering entails a more controlled transfer of genes because the transfer is limited to a single gene, or just a few selected genes, whereas traditional breeding risks transferring unwanted genes together with the desired ones. Against that advantage, antagonists argue that the side effects in terms of potentially adverse impacts on the environment and human health are unknown.

Genetic engineering techniques and their applications have developed rapidly since the introduction of the first genetically modified plants in the 1980s. In 1999, genetically modified crops occupied 40 million hectares of land, making up 3.4 percent of the world's total agricultural area and representing a considerable expansion from fewer than 3 million hectares in 1996.[4] Cultivation of transgenic crops has so far been most widespread in the production of soybeans and maize, accounting for 54 percent and

28 percent of total commercial transgenic crop production in 1999, respectively. Cotton and rapeseed each made up 9 percent of transgenic crop production in 1999, with the remaining GM crops being tobacco, tomato, and potato (James 1997, 1998, 1999).

To date, genetic engineering in agriculture has mainly been used to modify crops so that they have improved *agronomic* traits such as tolerance to specific chemical herbicides and resistance to pests and diseases. Development of plants with enhanced agronomic traits aims at increasing farmer profitability, typically by reducing input requirements and hence costs. Genetic modification can also be used to improve the final *quality* characteristics of a product for the benefit of the consumer, food processing industry, or livestock producer. Such traits may include enhanced nutritional content, improved durability, and better processing characteristics.

The United States holds almost three-fourths of the total crop area devoted to genetically modified crops. Other major GM producers are Argentina, Canada, and China. At the national level, the largest shares of genetically engineered crops in 1999 were found in Argentina (approximately 90 percent of the soybean crop), Canada (62 percent of the rapeseed crop), and the United States (55 percent of cotton, 50 percent of soybean, and 33 percent of maize) (James 1999). The U.S. Department of Agriculture (2000b) figures for the United States are similar in magnitude: It is estimated that 40 percent of maize and 60 percent of soybean areas harvested in 1999 were genetically modified.

Continued expansion in the use of transgenic crops will depend in part on the benefits obtained by farmers cultivating transgenic instead of conventional crops relative to the higher cost for transgenic seeds.[5] So far, the improvements have been not so much in increased yields per hectare of the crops, but rather reduced costs of production (OECD 1999). Empirical data on the economic benefits of transgenic crops are still very limited, however. The effects vary from year to year and depend on a range of factors such as crop type, location, magnitude of pest attacks, disease occurrence, and weed intensity.

In developing countries, one of the main reasons for low crop yields is the prevalence of biotic stresses caused by weeds, pests, and diseases. The first generation of improved transgenic crops, into which a single trait such as herbicide tolerance or pesticide resistance has been introduced, can provide protection against several of these. The development of more complex traits such as drought resistance, which is a trait controlled by several genes, is under way and highly relevant for tropical crops that are often growing under harsh weather conditions and on poor-quality soils. There are not many estimates of the potential productivity impact that widespread cultivation of transgenic crops may have in developing countries, but according to James and Krattiger (1999, p. 1), "[a] World Bank panel has estimated that transgenic technology can increase rice production in Asia by 10 to 25 percent in the next decade."

The data used in the empirical analysis described below are from version 4 of the Global Trade Analysis Project (GTAP) database, which is estimated for 1995 (McDougall, Elbehri, and Truong 1998). As discussed, the main crops that have been genetically modified to date are soybeans and maize. The sectoral aggregation of this database therefore comprises a cereal grains sector (which includes maize but not wheat and rice) and an oilseeds sector (which includes soybeans) to reflect these two GM-potential crops. The livestock, meat and dairy, vegetable oils and fats, and other processed food sectors are also singled out, since they are important demanders of oilseeds and cereal grains as intermediate inputs to production.

The importance of trade in GM-potential crops varies across the regions. Table 14.1 shows that the value of oilseed exports relative to total value of production is significant for the Cairns Group, the United States, and the rest of South America. Cereal grain exports are also moderately large in value terms for the first two regions, but otherwise most of the production value of these two crops is captured on the domestic markets. For the Cairns Group, the rest of South America, the United States, and Sub-Saharan Africa, the impact of genetic engineering would be much larger if these techniques were applicable to the crops contained in the much larger aggregate "other crops" sector. On the import side, the value of oilseed imports into Western Europe amounts to almost 40 percent of the total value of oilseed absorption. High-income Asia is also heavily dependent on imports of oilseeds and, to a lesser extent, cereal grains.

In general, the trade dependencies for livestock and processed food products are lower than in the agricultural sectors described above. However, trade in these products is still important for developing regions. For example, Sub-Saharan Africa exports 16 percent of its processed food products and 11 percent of its meat and dairy products. Low-income Asia exports 10 percent of its processed food products and 13 percent of its meat and dairy products. South America exports 11 percent of its processed food products.

Table 14.2 shows data on export market shares. The United States is by far the dominant exporter of both cereal grains and oilseeds, and high-income Asia is the main importer of cereal grains and the second largest importer of oilseeds. In terms of processed food trade, countries in the Cairns Group and Western Europe are large exporters of meat and dairy products and other processed food products. High-income Asia is a major importer of other processed food products. Developing countries account for a small share of global trade in GM-potential crops and processed products.

Bilateral export patterns indicate that low-income Asia and South America depend on both Western Europe and high-income Asia as mar-

Table 14.1. Trade Dependence: Agricultural and Food Products, 1995

Product	Cairns Group[a]	High-income Asia	Low-income Asia	United States	Rest of South America	Western Europe	Sub-Saharan Africa	Rest of world
Value of exports in percent of total production value								
Cereal grains	9.7	0.2	0.7	16.0	0.7	3.7	4.3	0.7
Oilseeds	15.7	4.1	2.7	28.7	32.4	1.8	5.8	11.2
Wheat	28.5	0.0	0.3	39.2	6.6	6.8	0.1	1.5
Other crops	15.4	0.7	3.5	18.9	29.2	4.7	20.0	6.6
Livestock	7.3	0.2	1.5	2.4	2.9	1.2	2.4	1.7
Veg. oils and fats	32.8	4.8	3.2	7.2	4.0	4.3	10.3	6.7
Meat and dairy	10.2	0.4	12.6	4.9	1.5	3.1	11.3	1.7
Other prepared foods	12.6	0.7	10.3	5.2	10.9	6.2	15.7	4.1
Value of imports in percent of total absorption value								
Cereal grains	7.2	18.3	5.5	0.9	14.8	5.0	7.2	10.3
Oilseeds	6.5	71.1	0.9	2.4	55.2	38.2	0.4	10.6
Wheat	11.9	17.1	10.4	3.4	51.4	3.7	15.5	17.7
Other crops	5.5	6.5	2.3	17.8	5.7	18.3	1.4	8.0
Livestock	0.9	5.4	1.5	2.1	1.6	2.3	0.4	2.4
Veg. oils and fats	3.1	19.0	17.2	5.0	15.3	4.1	14.5	23.1
Meat and dairy	2.0	9.9	6.4	1.8	8.9	1.5	35.1	10.4
Other prepared foods	4.6	4.2	3.5	4.6	5.9	3.6	15.8	10.3

a. Argentina, Australia, Bolivia, Brazil, Canada, Chile, Colombia, Costa Rica, Fiji, Guatemala, Indonesia, Malaysia, New Zealand, Paraguay, Philippines, South Africa, Thailand, and Uruguay.

Source: Multiregion genetically modified organism model database derived from GTAP version 4 data.

Table 14.2. Composition of World Trade, 1995

Product	Cairns Group[a]	High-income Asia	Low-income Asia	United States	Rest of South America	Western Europe	Sub-Saharan Africa	Rest of world	Total
Value of exports in percent of value of world trade									
Cereal grains	11.29	0.10	1.06	75.88	0.55	9.29	0.71	1.13	100
Oilseeds	26.48	0.48	6.89	49.83	4.18	2.43	2.52	7.20	100
Wheat	31.88	0.01	0.64	48.20	0.86	15.68	0.03	2.69	100
Other crops	28.05	1.83	8.78	16.29	15.01	7.47	12.44	10.13	100
Livestock	40.41	1.27	8.95	17.73	4.06	15.57	1.59	10.41	100
Veg. oils and fats	55.86	2.16	3.50	11.37	1.30	18.22	1.67	5.91	100
Meat and dairy	34.65	1.05	4.68	24.33	1.01	29.84	0.45	3.98	100
Other prepared foods	27.44	3.70	8.90	16.39	6.54	27.83	2.30	6.89	100
Value of imports in percent of world trade									
Cereal grains	8.50	40.82	8.97	3.42	11.42	8.14	1.27	17.46	100
Oilseeds	9.65	29.88	2.20	2.85	9.54	38.99	0.19	6.71	100
Wheat	8.45	13.99	21.40	2.00	9.49	5.10	4.74	34.82	100
Other crops	9.48	17.94	5.88	15.43	2.20	35.47	0.75	12.86	100
Livestock	4.79	28.59	9.62	14.66	2.12	25.43	0.26	14.53	100
Veg. oils and fats	4.10	10.50	25.26	7.81	5.69	17.04	2.71	26.90	100
Meat and dairy	6.74	32.60	2.36	8.75	6.51	14.10	2.40	26.53	100
Other prepared foods	10.63	26.08	3.30	15.31	3.65	17.60	2.73	20.69	100

a. Argentina, Australia, Bolivia, Brazil, Canada, Chile, Colombia, Costa Rica, Fiji, Guatemala, Indonesia, Malaysia, New Zealand, Paraguay, Philippines, South Africa, Thailand, and Uruguay.

Source: Multiregion genetically modified organism model database derived from GTAP version 4 data.

kets for their exports (see tables 14.3 and 14.4). Sub-Saharan Africa depends primarily on Western Europe, sending 68 percent of its other crops, and 93 percent of its vegetable oils and fats to that region (see table 14.5).

Global Computable General Equilibrium Model and Scenarios

Global Computable General Equilibrium Model with Segregated Food Markets

The modeling framework used in this analysis is a multiregion computable general equilibrium (CGE) model consisting of eight regions, which are interconnected through bilateral trade flows: the Cairns Group, high-income Asia, low-income Asia, the United States, the rest of South America, Western Europe, Sub-Saharan Africa, and the rest of the world. We begin from a standard global model and segment the GM-potential sectors: cereal grains and oilseeds. We also segregate intermediate users of GM and non-GM crops.[6]

In order to operate with segregated GM and non-GM sectors in the extended model, the base data must also reflect this segregation. First of all, the base data are adjusted by splitting the cereal grain and oilseed sectors into GM and non-GM varieties.[7] It is assumed that all regions in the model initially produce some of both GM and non-GM varieties of cereal grains and oilseeds. The assumed shares are adapted from estimates provided in James (1999) and U.S. Department of Agriculture (2000a).[8] The Cairns Group, low-income Asia, the United States, and the rest of South America regions in the model are the extensive GM adopters.

The structures of production in terms of the composition of intermediate input and factor use in the GM and non-GM varieties are initially assumed to be identical. The destination structures of exports are also initially assumed to be the same, and this determines the resulting import composition by ensuring bilateral trade flow consistency.

The next step is to identify the sectors that use cereal grains and oilseeds as intermediate inputs as GM and non-GM sectors to reflect the concept of identity preservation. The GM/non-GM split is applied to the following sectors: livestock, vegetable oils and fats, meat and dairy, and other processed foods. In the base data, the GM/non-GM split for these four sectors is determined residually, based on the share of GM inputs of cereal grains and oilseeds in total (GM plus non-GM) inputs of cereal grains and oilseeds for each sector. These shares are then used to split the data into GM and non-GM varieties of the four processing sectors. At this stage, the described procedure leaves all agricultural and food sectors using some of both GM and non-GM inputs. The input-output table is

Table 14.3. Pattern of Exports from Low-Income Asia, 1995

Product	Cairns Group	High-income Asia	Low-income Asia	United States	Rest of South America	Western Europe	Sub-Saharan Africa	Rest of world	Total
Cereal grains	19.5	33.1	0.0	0.0	0.0	7.6	1.7	38.1	100
Oilseeds	31.5	34.5	0.0	1.8	0.0	17.8	0.4	13.9	100
Wheat	13.3	2.7	0.0	0.0	0.0	1.3	24.0	58.7	100
Other crops	11.2	28.4	0.0	10.7	1.2	21.5	1.4	25.7	100
Livestock	4.8	53.2	0.0	6.9	0.1	30.7	0.0	4.2	100
Veg. oils and fats	17.1	44.3	0.0	6.6	0.0	22.1	0.0	9.9	100
Meat and dairy	5.9	56.0	0.0	0.4	0.1	9.0	0.5	28.0	100
Other prepared foods	13.8	46.9	0.0	7.6	0.3	11.6	3.6	16.0	100

Table 14.4. Pattern of Exports from South America, 1995

Product	Cairns Group	High-income Asia	Low-income Asia	United States	South America	Western Europe	Sub-Saharan Africa	Rest of world	Total
Cereal grains	91.8	1.6	0.0	1.6	0.0	4.9	0.0	0.0	100
Oilseeds	49.6	10.6	0.0	13.1	0.0	25.2	0.5	1.0	100
Wheat	4.0	0.0	0.0	0.0	0.0	46.5	0.0	49.5	100
Other crops	7.3	5.7	2.9	44.3	0.0	33.4	0.1	6.4	100
Livestock	4.7	1.4	0.0	89.6	0.0	4.2	0.0	0.2	100
Veg. oils and fats	43.1	1.1	0.6	26.0	0.0	24.3	0.0	5.0	100
Meat and dairy	17.1	19.1	0.3	37.4	0.0	23.3	0.3	2.5	100
Other prepared foods	11.9	9.6	7.6	39.6	0.0	25.9	0.1	5.4	100

Table 14.5. Pattern of Exports from Sub-Saharan Africa, 1995

Product	Cairns Group[a]	High-income Asia	Low-income Asia	United States	South America	Western Europe	Sub-Saharan Africa	Rest of world	Total
Cereal grains	39.0	14.3	2.6	0.0	1.3	27.3	0.0	15.6	100
Oilseeds	8.2	29.1	0.0	4.5	0.0	31.1	0.0	27.0	100
Wheat	100.0	0.0	0.0	0.0	0.0	0.0	0.0	0.0	100
Other crops	7.7	4.0	5.9	5.5	0.2	68.0	0.0	8.7	100
Livestock	3.8	9.9	6.5	2.3	0.0	25.6	0.0	51.9	100
Veg. oils and fats	3.4	0.4	0.0	0.4	0.0	92.7	0.0	3.0	100
Meat and dairy	8.9	0.6	0.6	0.6	0.0	76.4	0.0	12.7	100
Other prepared foods	4.9	13.6	0.4	3.6	0.0	74.0	0.0	3.4	100

a. Argentina, Australia, Bolivia, Brazil, Canada, Chile, Colombia, Costa Rica, Fiji, Guatemala, Indonesia, Malaysia, New Zealand, Paraguay, Philippines, South Africa, Thailand, and Uruguay.

**Figure 14.1. Endogenous Choice between GM
and Non-GM Foods**

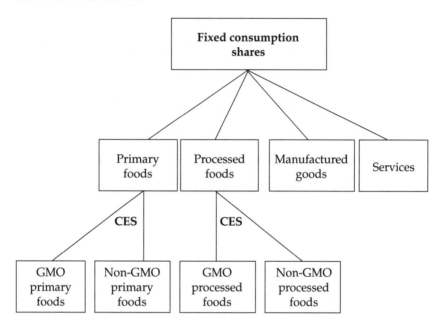

then adjusted so that GM sectors use only GM inputs and non-GM sectors use only non-GM inputs.[9]

In the model, the decision of consumers to place GM versus non-GM varieties in their consumption bundle is endogenized. Final demand for each composite good (that is, GM plus non-GM) is held fixed as a share of total demand, while introducing an endogenous choice between GM and non-GM varieties. In this way, all the initial expenditure shares remain fixed, but for six of the food product categories (oilseeds, cereal grains, livestock, vegetable oils and fats, meat and dairy, and other processed foods), a choice has been introduced between GM and non-GM varieties. All other expenditure shares remain fixed, as illustrated by figure 14.1.[10]

*Genetically Modified and Non–Genetically
Modified Production Technologies*

As mentioned, the distinguishing characteristic between the GM and non-GM maize and soybean sectors is the level of productivity. The GM cereal grain and oilseed sectors are assumed to benefit from increased productivity in terms of primary factor use as well as a reduction in chemical use.[11] The available estimates of agronomic and hence economic benefits to producers from cultivating GM crops are very scattered and highly diverse (see, for example, OECD [1999] for an overview of available estimates). Nelson et al. (1999), for example, suggest that glyphosate-resistant soybeans may generate a total production cost reduction of 5 percent, and their scenarios have genetically modified corn increasing yields by between 1.8 percent and 8.1 percent. For present purposes, the GM-adopting cereal grains and oilseed sectors are assumed to make more productive use of the primary factors of production as compared with the non-GM sectors. In other words, the same level of output can be obtained by using fewer primary factors of production, or a higher level of output can be obtained using the same level of production factors. In our scenarios, the GM oilseed and GM cereal grain sectors in all regions are assumed to have a 10 percent higher level of factor productivity as compared with their non-GM (conventional) counterparts. Furthermore, there seems to be evidence that cultivating GM varieties substantially reduces the use of chemical pesticides and herbicides (see, for example, Pray et al. 2000). Hence, the use of chemicals in the GM oilseed and GM cereal grain production is reduced by 30 percent to illustrate this cost-saving effect.

Consumer Preferences

There are many ways to formally model changes in consumer preferences. Here we illustrate how two such ways can be implemented in a computable general equilibrium model. This is done by shifting and altering the curvature of the indifference curve between GM and non-GM commodities. Each alternative has a different interpretation of what consumers might mean when they say they disapprove of GM foods.

The starting point for the consumer preference experiments is that food products come in two varieties distinguished by their method of production: GM and non-GM. The model has the representative consumer who views these two varieties as imperfect substitutes. Three different consumer response scenarios are examined. In the base case, consumers in all countries are relatively indifferent with respect to the introduction of GM techniques in food production, and so they find GM and non-GM food varieties highly substitutable.

The next two experiments then attempt to reflect the fact that citizens in Western Europe and high-income Asia dislike the idea of genetically modified foods. In the second experiment, this is illustrated by lowering the elasticities of substitution between the GM and non-GM varieties for consumers in these two regions. Consumers in these regions are assumed to be less sensitive to a given change in the ratio of prices between GM and non-GM varieties. They are seen as poor substitutes in consumption in these particular regions. Citizens in all other regions are basically in-

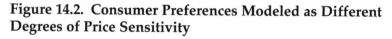

Figure 14.2. Consumer Preferences Modeled as Different Degrees of Price Sensitivity

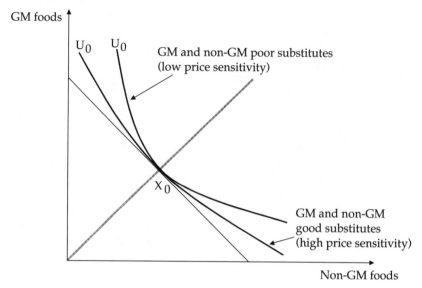

different, and hence the two varieties remain highly substitutable in consumption in those regions.

The change in consumer preferences described in experiments 1 and 2 corresponds to altering the curvature of the indifference curves of consumers in Western Europe and high-income Asia, as illustrated in figure 14.2. The two curves in the figure correspond to the same level of utility, U_0. When the relative prices of GM and non-GM foods change, consumers in Western Europe and high-income Asia are in the second experiment assumed to be less inclined to shift consumption toward GM varieties as they were in the base case, where substitutability was high. The representative consumer is on the same budget line (same expenditure on the composite food product [GM plus non-GM] and hence same level of utility).

It is not clear, however, whether reduced price sensitivity is an appropriate interpretation of consumers' critical approach to GM foods. In some rich countries, where consumers can indeed afford to be critical of these new techniques in food production, irrespective of how cheap these products may become (relative to non-GM foods), some consumers may simply not want to consume them. In this case, we are changing the ratio of GM to non-GM foods demanded at a given (constant) price ratio, holding utility constant. This is illustrated in figure 14.3, where the representative consumer in Western Europe and high-income Asia is as well off as

Figure 14.3. Consumer Preferences Modeled as a Structural Change

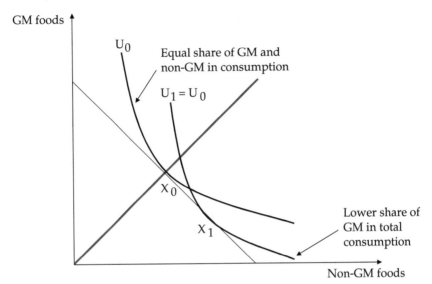

before but now with a lower share of GM foods in his/her consumption bundle. The total value of expenditure on each composite food item remains the same. In other words, consumers still spend the same amount on their consumption of food, but the composition is changed in favor of non-GM varieties. In the experiment, we reduce the GM share of foods in consumption in Western Europe and high-income Asia to 2 percent.

Results of Empirical Analysis: Price and Trade Results

Base case experiment. The increase in factor productivity and the reduced need for chemicals in the GM cereal grain and oilseed sectors causes the cost-driven prices of these crops to decline. The magnitude of this price decline in the different sectors and regions will differ, depending on the shares of primary production factors and chemicals in total production costs. In sectors and regions where these costs make up a large share of total costs, the impact of the productivity shock in terms of lower supply prices will be greater than in sectors and regions where the share is smaller. Intermediate users of GM inputs (the GM livestock and GM processed food producers) will benefit from lower input prices.

The non-GM product markets will be affected by the productivity gain in the GM sectors in three ways. First, there will be increased competition for primary factors of production and intermediate inputs because GM production will increase. Second, consumers domestically might change their consumption patterns in response to the new relative prices depending on their initial consumption pattern and substitution possibilities. Third, importers will change their import pattern depending on the relative world prices, their initial absorption structures, and the substitution possibilities between suppliers. In all three cases, the initial cost, consumption, and import structures on the one hand and the substitution possibilities between products for input use, final consumption, and imports on the other will determine the net impact of the productivity experiment. The net effects are theoretically ambiguous and hence must be determined empirically.

Figures 14.4a and 14.4b depict for developing and industrialized countries the price wedges that arise between the non-GM and GM varieties in the base case experiment, where GM and non-GM foods are considered to be good substitutes in consumption in all regions. Generally, the relative price of non-GM to GM commodities rises, and the percentage point differences between the prices of non-GM and GM varieties of cereal grains and oilseeds are between 6.3 and 9.4. As described, the price wedges vary across the regions in part because they have different shares of primary factor and chemical costs in total production costs. Hence, the extent to which the individual regions benefit from the productivity increase differs.

The lower GM crop prices in turn result in lower production costs for users of GM inputs, thereby reducing those product prices relative to the non-GM varieties as well. As can be seen in figures 14.4a and 14.4b, the price wedges that arise between the GM and non-GM livestock and processed food products are much smaller than the price wedges between GM and non-GM primary crops because the cost reduction concerns only a part of total production costs. Relatively speaking, oilseeds constitute a large share of production costs in vegetable oils and fats production (compared with oilseed and cereal grain use in other food production), and hence the spillover effect is largest.

The lower GM crop prices mean improved international competitiveness for exporters of these crops. Hence, as table 14.6 shows, the United States, a large exporter of cereal grains and oilseeds, increases its exports of GM crops in this base case by 9.0 percent. There are also large percentage increases in exports from the developing countries that are GM adopters, but the improvement is from a lower base. Owing to the reduced relative competitiveness of non-GM crops, exports of this variety decline somewhat. The large importers of these crops, high-income Asia and Western Europe, increase their imports of the cheaper GM varieties. This is particularly so in the case of oilseeds because these two regions are highly dependent on imported oilseeds from countries that are enthusi-

Figure 14.4. Base Case Experiment: Price Wedges between Non-GM and GM Products in Developing Countries

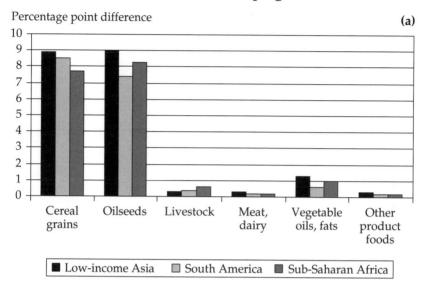

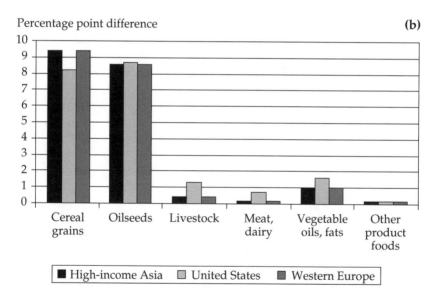

astic GM adopters. Imports of the non-GM varieties decline slightly owing to the reduced relative price competitiveness of non-GM products in an environment where consumers find GM and non-GM food varieties to be good substitutes.

Table 14.6. Selected Trade Results of Base Experiment, Percentage Changes

Product	Low-income Asia	South America	Sub-Saharan Africa	High-income Asia	United States	Western Europe
Exports						
Non-GM cereal grains	-8.0	-7.2	-4.1	-3.4	-2.4	-3.0
GM cereal grains	22.6	15.4	23.0	17.4	9.0	16.5
Non-GM oilseeds	-9.1	-5.4	-3.0	-3.0	-2.1	-2.9
GM oilseeds	16.7	12.8	20.7	13.5	8.6	17.6
Non-GM livestock	-0.4	-0.8	-0.3	-0.4	-0.4	-0.2
GM livestock	0.9	1.0	2.0	0.7	2.1	1.1
Non-GM meat and dairy	-0.4	-0.5	-0.1	-0.3	-0.5	-0.2
GM meat and dairy	0.8	1.0	1.2	0.8	1.6	1.0
Non-GM veg. oils and fats	-2.2	-1.4	-0.6	-1.9	-1.3	-1.0
GM veg. oils and fats	3.7	2.1	3.6	6.4	3.4	3.9
Non-GM other processed food	-0.4	-0.3	-0.1	-0.2	-0.3	-0.2
GM other processed food	0.9	0.8	1.1	0.8	0.7	0.8
Imports						
Non-GM cereal grains	-12.3	-8.7	-4.8	-0.2	-1.8	-0.3
GM cereal grains	19.7	14.4	32.8	1.7	2.7	0.8
Non-GM oilseeds	-14.8	-8.4	-5.5	-3.0	-4.3	-1.7
GM oilseeds	16.4	9.0	27.4	10.7	5.1	2.0
Non-GM livestock	-0.5	-0.6	-0.4	-0.2	-0.9	-0.1
GM livestock	0.9	1.6	2.6	1.2	0.8	1.1
Non-GM meat and dairy	-0.4	-0.5	-0.2	-0.3	-0.9	-0.1
GM meat and dairy	0.5	1.2	1.1	1.0	1.3	0.9
Non-GM veg. oils and fats	-2.6	-1.4	-0.8	-1.7	-1.3	-0.9
GM veg. oils and fats	3.6	2.4	4.7	4.7	1.9	3.9
Non-GM other processed food	-0.5	-0.3	-0.2	-0.2	-0.3	-0.1
GM other processed food	0.7	0.7	1.1	0.8	0.6	0.8

Figure 14.5. Price Sensitivity Case: Price Wedges between Non-GM and GM Products in Developing Countries

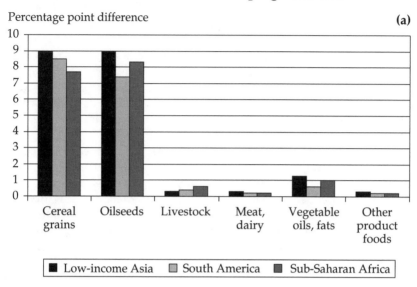

Percentage point difference **(a)**

Low-income Asia ■ South America ■ Sub-Saharan Africa

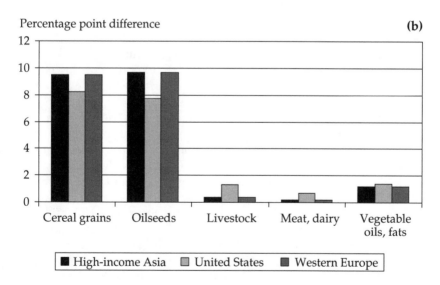

Percentage point difference **(b)**

■ High-income Asia ■ United States ■ Western Europe

Price sensitivity experiment. As can be seen in figures 14.5a and 14.5b, the price wedges resulting from the price sensitivity experiment are not markedly different from the ones reported in the base case experiment. However, the prices for GM cereal grains and especially oilseeds are slightly lower on the Western European and high-income Asian markets when consumers are critical (less price sensitive): Larger price reductions are required in order to sell GM varieties in GM organisms (GMOs)–critical markets. Conversely, demand for non-GM crops is relatively stronger, and hence the prices of non-GM oilseeds, for example, are higher. Hence, we find that the price wedges for especially oilseeds, but also cereal grains, are larger in high-income Asia and Western Europe in the price sensitivity experiment. In large oilseed-producing markets such as the United States, the price of the non-GM variety falls slightly more and the price of the GM variety falls less as compared with the base case; that is, the price wedges are smaller.

In comparison with the base case, the increase in GM oilseed and cereal grain exports from the United States is smaller when consumers in their important export markets are less responsive to the GM/non-GM price difference. Consequently, on the import side, the results show that the declines in imports of the more expensive non-GM oilseeds into high-income Asia and Western Europe are smaller. The decreases in non-GM cereal grain imports have even turned into minor increases. High-income Asia and Western Europe still increase their GM oilseed imports in this price sensitivity experiment (although at lower rates) because of their high dependence on importing from GM-enthusiastic regions. This result is because there is a symmetry in the trade dependence concerning oilseeds: U.S. oilseeds make up a large share of oilseed imports into high-income Asia and Western Europe, and exports for high-income Asia and Western Europe make up a large share of U.S. exports. For this reason, changes in consumer preferences in these countries will have an impact on the trading conditions for U.S. producers.

A similar pattern holds for the developing countries that are GM adopters. Exports of GM varieties do not expand as much, and exports of the non-GM varieties do not decline as much, in the price sensitivity experiment compared to the base case. In absolute terms, the changes in the United States are larger because that country is a larger exporter on world markets. Also, low-income Asia and the rest of South America are less dependent than is the United States on Western Europe and high-income Asia for sales of cereal grains and oilseeds. These developing countries are also dependent on the Cairns Group as a market for exports.

Structural change experiment. In this final experiment, consumers in Western Europe and high-income Asia simply turn against genetically modified foods (see figures 14.6a and 14.6b). Compared with the previous experiment, final demand in these regions is very insensitive to relative price differences between GM and non-GM food varieties. Consumers in Western Europe and high-income Asia are assumed simply to shift their consumption patterns away from GM varieties in favor of non-GM vari-

Figure 14.6. Structural Change Case: Price Wedges between Non-GM and GM Products in Developing Countries

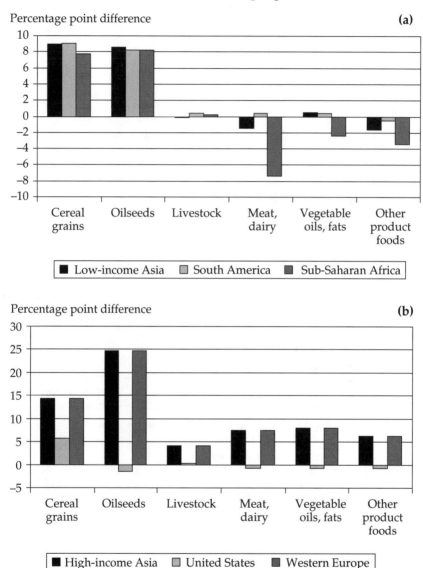

Percentage point difference (a)

Low-income Asia   South America   Sub-Saharan Africa

Percentage point difference (b)

High-income Asia   United States   Western Europe

eties, regardless of the relative price decline of GM foods. This shift is measured relative to the experiment in which price sensitivity in these regions is low to begin with. Hence, the effects of this structural shock are an addition to the second experiment.

The results show that this rejection is clearly a much more dramatic change compared with reduced price sensitivity (see table 14.7). Critical consumers simply do not want GM products. The price of GM varieties in the GMO-critical countries declines further because of the almost complete rejection of these products, whereas the price of non-GM foods increases. This leads to substantially larger price wedges in the GM critical regions as compared with the previous experiments, as is evident from figures 14.6a and 14.6b. The larger price wedges between GM and non-GM primary crops follow through the entire food processing chain. The price increase for non-GM foods is, however, moderated by the fact that there are markets for non-GM products in all regions in the model. All countries can produce both varieties and hence supply both GMO-indifferent and GMO-critical consumers.

Total U.S. GM cereal grain and oilseed exports fall by 17 percent and 33 percent, respectively (table 14.8), while exports of the non-GM varieties increase by 8 percent and 15 percent, respectively. These changes are a direct reaction to the relative prices obtainable on their key export markets, that is, high-income Asia and Western Europe. The prices of GM cereal grains and oilseeds on these markets plummet, and the prices of non-GM varieties increase slightly.

For low-income Asia and South America, exports of GM oilseeds decline, similar to the export response in the United States. However, exports of GM-cereal grains still expand. These countries are less dependent on GM-critical regions for cereal grains than is the U.S. For example, South America sends 92 percent of its cereal grain exports to the Cairns Group.

Changing consumer attitudes in Western Europe and high-income Asia also affect Sub-Saharan Africa's trade patterns. While that region is not a GM adopter, it does have strong trade ties to Western Europe. Its imports of GM processed products declines, despite the fact that it is not a GM-critical region. Instead, its major import source changes its production patterns and therefore the structure of its exports.

Table 14.8 shows that imports of GM cereal grain and oilseeds into Western Europe and high-income Asia decline substantially (between –57 and –71 percent). Conversely, imports of non-GM crops increase substantially, at slightly higher prices. The sourcing of these non-GM crop imports is spread across all regions, because in the model, all regions are assumed to be able to produce both varieties and to be able to credibly verify this characteristic to importers. Clearly, this is a simplification of reality, and we can easily imagine that for some regions, living up to the principles of identity preservation and verification would be very costly, thereby putting them at a cost disadvantage. Such effects are not captured in this model. The increases in non-GM cereal grain and oilseed imports are supplemented by increases in own production in both high-income Asia and Western Europe.[12]

Table 14.7. Selected Trade Results of Price Sensitivity Experiment, Percentage Changes

Product	Low-income Asia	South America	Sub-Saharan Africa	High-income Asia	United States	Western Europe
Exports						
Non-GM cereal grains	-7.9	-7.2	-4	-3.3	-2.2	-2.8
GM cereal grains	22.3	15.2	22.2	16.5	8.5	15
Non-GM oilseeds	-8.2	-4.6	-2.3	-1.5	-0.7	-2.4
GM oilseeds	14.7	10.7	18.9	8.7	4.9	13.8
Non-GM livestock	-0.3	-0.8	-0.3	-0.3	-0.3	-0.2
GM livestock	0.6	1	1.8	0.4	1.9	0.8
Non-GM meat and dairy	-0.3	-0.4	-0.1	-0.2	-0.4	-0.1
GM meat and dairy	0.6	0.8	0.8	0.6	1.4	0.7
Non-GM veg. oils and fats	-1.8	-1.4	-0.4	-1.2	-1	-0.7
GM veg. oils and fats	2.3	1.6	2.2	5.4	2.9	3
Non-GM other processed food	-0.3	0.3	0.1	-0.1	-0.2	-0.1
GM other processed food	0.7	0.7	0.7	0.6	0.5	0.6
Imports						
Non-GM cereal grains	-12.3	-8.7	-4.8	0.1	-1.8	0.1
GM cereal grains	19.7	14.5	32.8	0.3	2.8	-1.7
Non-GM oilseeds	-14.8	-8.5	-5.5	-0.7	-4.7	-0.8
GM oilseeds	17.3	9.5	28.4	5.1	6.6	2.8
Non-GM livestock	-0.5	-0.6	-0.4	-0.1	-0.9	0
GM livestock	1	1.6	2.6	0.9	0.8	0.5
Non-GM meat and dairy	-0.4	-0.5	-0.1	-0.1	-0.8	0
GM meat and dairy	0.5	1.2	0.9	0.6	1.2	0.4
Non-GM veg. oils and fats	-2.4	-1.3	-0.6	-0.4	-1.2	-0.5
GM veg. oils and fats	3.5	2.4	4.3	1.4	1.8	2.1
Non-GM other processed food	-0.4	-0.3	-0.2	-0.1	-0.3	-0.1
GM other processed food	0.7	0.7	1	0.4	0.6	0.4

Table 14.8. Selected Trade Results of Structural Shift Experiment, Percentage Changes

Product	Low-income Asia	South America	Sub-Saharan Africa	High-income Asia	United States	Western Europe
Exports						
Non-GM cereal grains	-1.7	-5.4	0.8	4	8.1	3.8
GM cereal grains	4.1	7.9	-2	-42.5	-17.4	-30.7
Non-GM oilseeds	1.6	4.3	5.1	12.9	14.5	2.2
GM oilseeds	-9.6	-12.1	-5.9	-45.8	-33.3	-33.7
Non-GM livestock	10.6	1.4	3.4	10.6	10.5	8.1
GM livestock	-4.3	-5.3	-19.1	-36.6	-36.1	-40.2
Non-GM meat and dairy	11.3	4.1	6.9	17.1	9.1	8.9
GM meat and dairy	-39.5	-23.6	-48.4	-39.3	-32.7	-38.4
Non-GM veg. oils and fats	6.5	1.6	6.4	11.3	3.7	6.5
GM veg. oils and fats	-35.6	-14.8	-50.2	-29.7	-10.6	-29.2
Non-GM other processed food	7.5	3.6	6.9	11.1	5.4	8
GM other processed food	-35.3	-19.8	-50.6	-39.6	-30.3	-37.4
Imports						
Non-GM cereal grains	-12.6	-10	-4	18.9	-0.1	9.8
GM cereal grains	21.2	19.4	34.8	-70.7	0.7	-59.1
Non-GM oilseeds	-14.1	-9.9	-4.2	23.5	-6	10.3
GM oilseeds	28.8	17.4	40.3	-56.8	22.7	-60.4
Non-GM livestock	-0.1	-1.9	1.8	19.5	1.4	9.4
GM livestock	5.6	10.5	-1.7	-56	1.4	-58.3
Non-GM meat and dairy	2.2	-0.8	6.2	23.3	1	8.6
GM meat and dairy	2.3	5	-28.7	-68.6	2.8	-62.8
Non-GM veg. oils and fats	0.8	0.4	5.4	24.8	2.6	9.5
GM veg. oils and fats	1.5	2.3	-11.2	-72.4	-1.7	-59.5
Non-GM other processed food	3.4	0.9	3.9	15.4	2.6	8.5
GM other processed food	-1	4.2	-10.5	-66.8	0.2	-60.2

Production Results

Being a major exporter of both crops, the increased demand for GM cereal grains and oilseeds in the base case experiment filters through to an increase in production of these crops in the United States. The effect is dampened, however, by the fact that its major destination regions (high-income Asia and Western Europe) have much larger non-GM sectors (relative to their GM sectors), which are required to use only non-GM inputs.[13] This also means, for example, that the production of non-GM crops does not fall as markedly in the United States as it does in low-income Asia, for example, a region that is not very heavily engaged in international trade in these particular crops. Figure 14.7 compares the impact on production in the United States of the different and changing assumptions made about consumer preferences in Western Europe and high-income Asia. Since exports make up a relatively large share of the total value of production in these sectors, particularly for oilseeds, we see that there is a marked effect on the composition of production. Production of GM crop varieties increases in the first two experiments, while production of non-GM varieties declines somewhat. The impact is slightly less when consumers in high-income Asia and Western Europe are less sensitive to the GM/non-GM price difference.

In the structural shift experiment, however, the production of GM oilseeds in the United States declines by 15 percent in spite of the factor

Figure 14.7. Production Effects in the United States

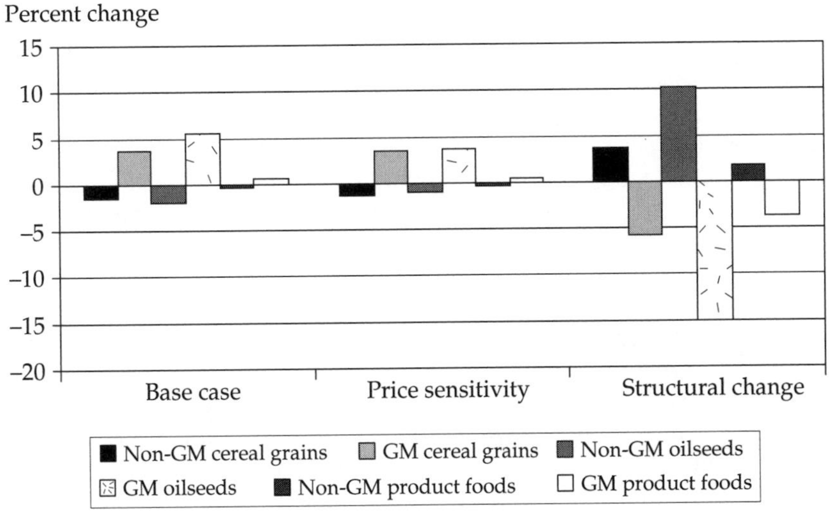

Figure 14.8. Production Effects in Low-Income Asia

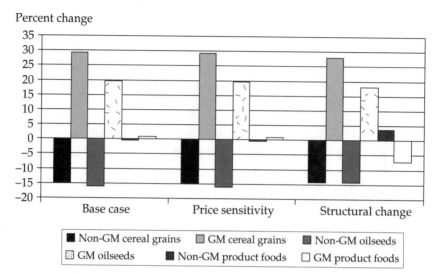

Percent change

| | Non-GM cereal grains | GM cereal grains | Non-GM oilseeds |
| GM oilseeds | Non-GM product foods | GM product foods |

productivity gain and the reduced chemical requirements. This is because the United States is so highly dependent on exporting especially oilseeds to the GM-critical markets and because a structural consumer preference change has much more of an impact on this region's trading opportunities compared with the reduced price sensitivity experiment. The production of non-GM oilseeds, however, increases by 10 percent, another direct reflection of the importance of the GMO-critical export markets is relatively less dependent on exports of these particular crops.

An interesting question is whether these changing preferences in Western Europe and high-income Asia can open opportunities for developing countries to export non-GM varieties of cereal grains and oilseeds to these regions. Sub-Saharan Africa has some production of oilseeds, for example, and although exports of these crops do not account for a significant share of total production value at present, they might if niche markets for non-GM crops develop in Western Europe. Similarly, low-income Asian countries might look into expanding their production of non-GM oilseeds if nearby niche markets in high-income Asian countries develop (see figure 14.8).

Although the differences are very small, comparing the trade and production results of the three experiments indicates that this might be a path to follow if the price premia obtainable for non-GM varieties are large enough to outweigh the relative decline in productivity and any identity preservation and labeling costs. But even more significant in value terms for these countries are exports of processed foods, that is, vegetable oils and fats, meat and dairy products, and other processed foods. Factors

Figure 14.9. Production Effects in South America

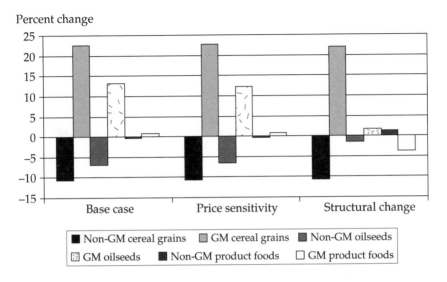

Percent change

such as existing trade patterns, proximity of markets, and historical ties will determine whether or not producers will choose to forgo productivity increases and lower costs in GM production in order to retain access to their traditional export markets by selling non-GM products. For a region like Sub-Saharan Africa, with strong ties to Western Europe, changing consumer attitudes toward genetically modified foods are expected to be an important determinant of future decisions regarding genetic engineering in food production (see figures 14.9 and 14.10). Production of GM processed food products expands in the first two experiments but declines in the structural shift case. Western Europe's increase in demand for non-GM–processed foods changes the pattern of production.

Absorption Results

In this modeling framework, where we are operating with a representative consumer, we are implicitly aggregating over two consumer types: those who are indifferent about GM products and those who are concerned about potential hazards of consuming GM products. We have considered two changes in preferences concerning GM-inclusive foods. First, attitudes harden. The size of the two groups does not change, but those who are concerned about GM products become more price sensitive. As described, this changes the curvature of the indifference curve, as shown in figure 14.2. Second, we have considered the effects of a structural pref-

Figure 14.10. Production Effects in Sub-Saharan Africa

Percent change

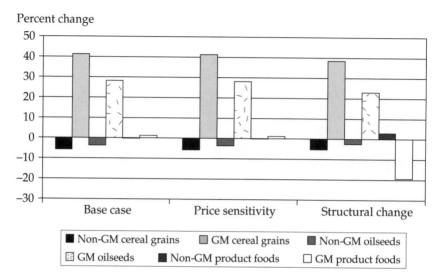

| | Non-GM cereal grains | | GM cereal grains | | Non-GM oilseeds |
| | GM oilseeds | | Non-GM product foods | | GM product foods |

erence shift; that is, more people believe that there are health hazards from consuming GM foods and choose to consume less, and the share of consumption of GM foods drops, regardless of relative price changes. In essence, the group of GM-sensitive consumers expands, which causes the indifference curve to shift, as depicted in figure 14.3.

The level of utility is assumed to stay the same when the indifference curve shifts. The representative consumer is on the same budget line with a different combination of GM and non-GM foods, and we do not assume that the consumer obtains additional utility from a decision to increase the share of non-GM products that is consumed. With this assumption, real absorption is an appropriate welfare measure. It indicates the change in the total amount of goods and services consumed following a change in preferences. The results of the experiments show that global absorption increases by US$7.4 billion in the base case, where consumers are assumed to find GM and non-GM foods to be good substitutes. Increasing the price sensitivity of GM-critical consumers in high-income Asia and Western Europe lowers this gain in total absorption marginally to US$7.2 billion. As the previous results have shown, the structural shift experiment represents a much more dramatic change in preferences, and hence we find that the global absorption gain is only US$0.02 billion in that experiment.

The absorption results are reported for selected regions in figure 14.11 for the three experiments. The changes are reported in US$ billions, and it should be noted that the percentage changes are very small. It is clear from this figure that low-income Asia, the United States, and the Cairns

Figure 14.11. Changes in Total Absorption

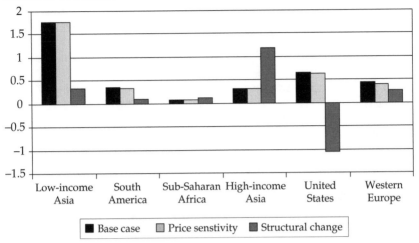

Billions of U.S. dollars

Legend: ■ Base case   ▨ Price senstivity   ▨ Structural change

Group (not shown in the figure) are the main beneficiaries of the productivity increase, given that these are the regions assumed to be intense adopters of the crop varieties. All other regions also experience an increase in total absorption, albeit at a lower absolute level. Reducing the price sensitivity of consumers in high-income Asia and Western Europe reduces the increase in global absorption only marginally and does not change the distribution of the gains across regions. Most important, all regions still gain in terms of aggregate absorption from the productivity increase and hence lower product prices in spite of the increased aversion toward GM foods in high-income Asia and Western Europe.

Interpreting consumer preference changes as a structural shift, however, alters the absorption results dramatically. Because our model has completely segregated GM and non-GM production systems, restricting input use to either GM or non-GM varieties, the structural preference shift has a strong effect on the demand for non-GM intermediates, and not all regions experience increases in total absorption in this experiment. Despite the productivity gain in the large GM crop sectors in the United States, these results reveal that aggregate absorption declines in these regions when consumers in important export markets turn against their main product and there is little diversion to other markets. Total absorption declines by US$0.9 billion in the United States. Although this decline amounts to a percentage change of only 0.007 percent, it illustrates how different types of preference changes will have very different impact on total absorption results.

It is particularly interesting that the increases in total absorption in *all* the developing country regions are *not* affected when GM-critical regions become more price sensitive (comparing the base case to the price sensitivity experiment). Low-income Asia is the major beneficiary in absolute terms, being both a net importer of the two crops and basically indifferent as to GM content. Hence, the region benefits from substantially lower import prices on GM crops. Despite the high dependence on the GM-critical regions for its exports of oilseeds, the increase in total absorption in South America is unaffected by the preference changes there because bilateral trade flows adjust well; that is, trade diversion offsets the effects of demand shifts in the GM-critical regions. In Sub-Saharan Africa, the gains are small in absolute terms, mainly owing to the small share of these particular crops in production and trade, but they are also unaffected by preference changes in GM-critical regions.

When consumers in Western Europe and high-income Asia reject GM varieties, the developing countries that are GM adopters (low-income Asia and South America) have less of an absorption gain. Interestingly, Sub-Saharan Africa has the biggest absorption gain in the structural shift scenario. In this case, the effective improvement in its international terms of trade leads to increased imports and a gain in absorption (and an appreciation of its real exchange rate).

Conclusions

The very different perceptions—particularly in North America and Western Europe—concerning the benefits and risks associated with the cultivation and consumption of GM foods are already leading to the segregation of soybean and maize markets and production systems into GM and non-GM lines. By using a global CGE model, this analysis has shown that such a segregation of markets may have substantial impacts on current trade patterns. The model distinguishes between GM and non-GM varieties in the oilseed and cereal grains sectors, as well as in the processing sectors that use these crops as inputs. GM crop production is assumed to have higher factor productivity as compared with conventional production methods. It is also assumed that the non-GM processing sectors can verify that they use only non-GM intermediate inputs.

The effects of a factor productivity increase in the GM sectors are then investigated in an environment where there are increasingly strong preferences *against* GM crops in Western Europe and high-income Asia. The change in preferences is modeled two ways. First, as a change in substitution elasticity; that is, consumers perceive GM and non-GM crops to be poor substitutes in these regions. Alternatively, as a reduction in the share of the GM variety consumed; that is, consumers reject GM varieties, regardless of the price differential.

The empirical results indicate that trade patterns adjust to changes in consumer attitudes when markets are segregated. Non-GM exports are diverted to the GM-critical regions, while GM exports are diverted to the indifferent regions. Historical trade patterns matter as well. We find that when consumers in Western Europe reject GM varieties, Western Europe produces and exports more non-GM varieties. This affects the non-GM composition of Sub-Saharan Africa's imports because that region depends strongly on Western Europe.

An important question for developing countries is whether genetic engineering in agriculture is an opportunity or a dilemma. The results of this empirical analysis offer some insights into the trade and welfare effects of adopting the new technology in a market with GM-critical regions. All of these results, it should be noted, are based on the heroic (and controversial) assumption that any environmental risks and hence externality costs associated with GM crops are manageable. To the extent that adopting genetically modified crops provides farmers with productivity benefits that outweigh the additional costs of GM seeds, the results seem to suggest that there are large welfare gains to be made for developing countries that adopt such a technology. Furthermore, changing GM preferences in Western Europe and high-income Asia do not affect these gains because markets adjust, and trade flows of GM and non-GM products are redirected according to preferences in the different markets.

The underlying assumption of this finding is, however, that production and marketing systems are indeed capable of dealing with the separation of GM and non-GM crop-handling systems, certainly a challenge for countries in the developing world. The difficulties and costs involved in separating GM and non-GM marketing and handling systems present the developing countries with a dilemma: They must decide whether or not to use their limited resources on developing such a capacity. For Sub-Saharan Africa, for example, current exports of GM-potential crops do not constitute a large share of total production, and so there may well be benefits to adopting GM crop varieties since consumers in the domestic market are indifferent, and this is the major market to be served.

However, to ensure future export markets, it may well make sense to establish identity preservation systems so that guaranteed non-GM products can serve GM-critical consumers in Western Europe, Africa's major export market for agricultural products. Indeed, a market for non-GM processed foods for exports can coexist with the production of GM processed foods for domestic consumption, allowing producers to exploit a niche market in GM-critical regions. Furthermore, GM technology may expand to other crops that are a large share of total production. The technology is evolving rapidly, and agricultural producers and policy makers in Sub-Saharan Africa and other developing countries must closely follow the development of the international debate on GMOs.

Notes

1. Another response to the growing concerns about GM products has been the agreement on the Cartagena Biosafety Protocol, which was concluded in January 2000, but is yet to be ratified. See Nielsen and Anderson (2000) for a discussion of the relationship between this protocol and the WTO rules, and an empirical analysis of the world trade and welfare effects of a Western European ban on GM imports.

2. The first part of this section draws on Nielsen and Anderson (2000).

3. Definitions of genetic engineering vary across countries and regulatory agencies. For our purposes, a broad definition is used, in which a genetically modified organism is one that has been modified through the use of modern biotechnology, such as recombinant DNA techniques. In the following, the terms "genetically engineered," "genetically modified," and "transgenic" will be used as synonyms.

4. Calculations are based on the FAOSTAT (Food and Agriculture Organization Statistical Database) accessible at www.fao.org.

5. As long as private companies uphold patents on their transgenic seeds, they will be able to extract monopoly rents through price premiums or technology fees.

6. The basic model is described in Lewis, Robinson, and Thierfelder (1999) and Nielsen, Thierfelder, and Robinson (2001).

7. As will be discussed, the distinguishing characteristic between these two varieties is the level of productivity. Furthermore, there may be environmental risks and hence externality costs associated with GM crops, and they are impossible to estimate at this time. Here we make no attempt to incorporate such effects in the empirical analysis.

8. See Nielsen, Thierfelder, and Robinson (2001) for the breakdown of GM shares by country and commodity.

9. Intermediate use in the GM sectors is restricted to only GM inputs and intermediate use in the non-GM sectors is restricted to only non-GM inputs. This is an important difference compared to the authors' earlier work (Nielsen, Robinson, and Thierfelder 2001) where intermediate users of oilseeds and cereal grains had a choice between GM and non-GM varieties.

10. See Nielsen, Thierfelder, and Robinson (2001) for details on how to calibrate the constant elasticity of substitution aggregate of the GM and non-GM varieties.

11. Note that this is an asymmetric shock and that it will therefore have different effects in different regions because of different cost structures: The shares of primary factor costs and chemical costs in total production costs are different.

12. Note that Western Europe might be restricted by the Blair House Agreement in terms of increasing acreage for oilseed production, and so the reported production increase may not be allowed.

13. Comparing these production effects with the results of our previous analysis, which did not have the identity preservation requirement in place (Nielsen, Robinson, and Thierfelder 2000), we see that the effects reported here are substantially smaller. This is precisely because the identity preservation requirement introduces much stronger restrictions on intermediate input choice for livestock producers and food processors. In our previous analysis, intermediate users had a free choice between GM and non-GM varieties and could therefore benefit fully from the lower GM prices. In this model, however, intermediate users are required to use only GM or non-GM inputs.

References

James, Clive. 1997. "Global Status of Transgenic Crops in 1997." ISAAA Briefs 5. International Service for the Acquisition of Agri-Biotech Applications, Ithaca, N.Y.

———. 1998. "Global Review of Commercialized Transgenic Crops: 1998." ISAAA Briefs 8. International Service for the Acquisition of Agri-Biotech Applications, Ithaca, N.Y.

———. 1999. "Global Status of Commercialized Transgenic Crops: 1999." ISAAA Briefs 12: Preview. International Service for the Acquisition of Agri-Biotech Applications, Ithaca, N.Y.

James, Clive, and Anatole Krattiger. 1999. "The Role of the Private Sector." In Gabrielle J. Persley, ed., *Biotechnology for Developing/Country Agriculture: Problems and Opportunities: Focus 2: A 2020 Vision for Food, Agriculture, and the Environment*. Washington, D.C.: International Food Policy Research Institute.

Lewis, Jeffrey D., Sherman Robinson, and Karen Thierfelder. 1999. "After the Negotiations: Assessing the Impact of Free Trade Agreements in Southern Africa." TMD Discussion Paper 46. International Food Policy Research Institute, Washington, D.C.

McDougall, Robert A., Aziz Elbehri, and Truong P. Truong, eds. 1998. *Global Trade, Assistance, and Protection: The GTAP 4 Data Base*. West Lafayette. Ind.: Center for Global Trade Analysis, Purdue University.

Nelson, Gerald C., Timothy Josling, David Bullock, Laurian Unnevehr, Mark Rosegrant, and Lowell Hill. 1999. "The Economics and Politics of Genetically Modified Organisms: Implications for WTO 2000." Bulletin 809. College of Agricultural, Consumer and Environmental Sciences, University of Illinois at Urbana-Champaign.

Nielsen, Chantal Pohl, and Kym Anderson. 2000. "GMOs, Trade Policy, and Welfare in Rich and Poor Countries." Paper prepared for a World Bank Workshop on Standards, Regulation and Trade, Washington, D.C., April 27.

Nielsen, Chantal Pohl, Sherman Robinson, and Karen Thierfelder. 2001. "Genetic Engineering and Trade: Panacea or Dilemma for Developing Countries." *World Development* 29(8):1307–24.

Nielsen, Chantal Pohl, Karen Thierfelder, and Sherman Robinson. 2001. "Consumer Attitudes Towards Genetically Modified Foods, the Modelling of

Preference Changes." SJFI Working Paper 1/2001. Danish Institute of Agricultural and Fisheries Economics, Copenhagen.

OECD (Organisation for Economic Co-operation and Development). 1999. *Modern Biotechnology and Agricultural Markets: A Discussion of Selected Issues and the Impact on Supply and Markets.* AGR/CA/APM/CFS/MD(2000)2. Paris.

Pray, Carl E., Danmeng Ma, Jikun Huang, and Fangbin Qiao. 2000. "Impact of Bt Cotton in China." Paper presented at a seminar at the International Food Policy Research Institute, May 9.

U.S. Department of Agriculture. 2000a. *Biotech Corn and Soybeans: Changing Markets and the Government's Role.* Washington, D.C. http://ers.usda.gov/whatsnew/issues/biotechmarkets/.

————. 2000b. *Biotechnology: U.S. Grain Handlers Look Ahead.* Agricultural Outlook. Washington, D.C.: Economic Research Service.

15

Trade Liberalization, the World Trade Organization, and Food Security

Eugenio Díaz-Bonilla and Marcelle Thomas

The links between trade liberalization and food security continue to be hotly debated. Some argue that trade causes hunger (Madeley 2000), and others believe a complete liberalization of world agricultural trade is the best possible approach (Griswold 1999). In the context of the Word Trade Organization (WTO) and more specifically the Uruguay Round (UR) Agreement on Agriculture (AoA), the debate centers on whether important policy objectives such as elimination of poverty and hunger (as cause and consequence of food insecurity) may have been helped or hindered by the current agreement, and whether further negotiations may improve upon the existing text or will further compromise the attainment of those objectives in poor countries.

Here we will try to contribute to that discussion. First, aggregate trends of food security indicators are presented as evidence of developing countries' performance and heterogeneity over the past four decades. Second, using a classification of countries based on various dimensions of food security, we argue that if food security concerns are to be part of the current WTO agricultural negotiations, then a more precise definition of food-insecure countries may be needed. Finally, we discuss some policy issues from the perspective of developing countries.

Food Security and Agricultural Performance of Developing Countries

Food security can be analyzed at the global, national, regional, household, and individual levels (figure 15.1). Since the World Food Conference of 1974, food security has been analyzed not only at the global and national levels but also at the household and individual levels, where issues of food security emerge in a more concrete way (Maxwell 1996). In addition to food supply, poverty, and lack of income opportunities (Sen 1981), variability around the trend of both food supply and access, and their sustainability

Figure 15.1. Conceptual Framework for Food Security

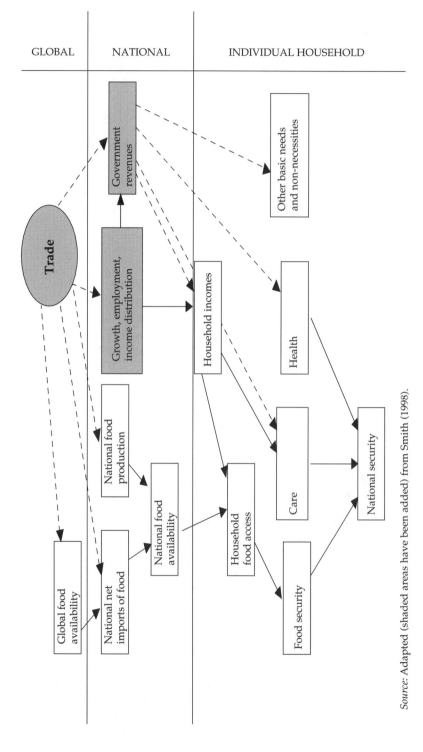

GLOBAL NATIONAL INDIVIDUAL HOUSEHOLD

Government revenues

Growth, employment, income distribution

Other basic needs and non-necessities

Household incomes

National food production

Health

National food availability

Care

Global food availability

Household food access

National net imports of food

National security

Food security

Trade

Source: Adapted (shaded areas have been added) from Smith (1998).

over time, were becoming the main obstacles to food access (Maxwell 1990). Food is required to provide more than what is needed for survival. Food also has to support an active and healthy life (Maxwell and Frankenberger 1992). The 1996 World Food Summit included this when it asserted that "food security exists when all people, at all times, have physical and economic access to sufficient, safe, and nutritious food to meet their dietary needs and food preferences for an active and healthy life" (FAO 1996).

But availability and access are only preconditions for adequate utilization of food. They do not determine the substantive issue of malnutrition or nutrition insecurity at the individual level (Smith 1998; Smith and Haddad 2000). The Food and Agriculture Organization's (FAO) recent report on the state of food insecurity in the world distinguishes between malnourishment linked to food intake and malnutrition, a physiological condition also related to food intake but affected by other determinants as well. In the report, malnourishment in 99 developing countries is measured using an indicator of food availability at the national level, doubly corrected by the gender and age structure of the population, and by the consumption or income distribution profile of the country (FAO 1999).

However, national indicators of malnutrition, although showing an almost perfect and highly significant correlation with national food availability measured by national consumption of calories per capita, are far more weakly correlated with "deeper" measures of malnutrition, such as the percentage of child malnutrition based on anthropometrical measures (Smith 1998). Analyzing nutrition insecurity at the individual level (utilizing child malnutrition as the indicator) requires the consideration of household and individual food access, as well as other determinants such as the health environment, women's education, and women's relative status in the society (Smith and Haddad 2000).

Though it is important to acknowledge the relevance of nutrition indicators for analyzing food insecurity at the household and individual levels, that is not the whole picture, and we would be remiss if we did not take into account the national perspective—that is, the level at which the negotiating categories are defined. We will focus mainly on food availability issues, utilizing consumption, production, and trade measures (figure 15.1).

Food security has improved over the past four decades. Total food availability in developing countries, measured in daily calories and grams of protein per capita, was 27 percent higher at the end of the 1990s than in the 1960s, even though the world population almost doubled during that time (figures 15.2 and 15.3). The number of malnourished children under five (a better indicator of food problems than average food availability) declined between the 1970s and the mid-1990s by about 37 million, and the incidence of malnutrition dropped from 47 percent to 31 percent (Smith and Haddad 2000).

Figure 15.2. Consumption Measured by Calories per Capita per Day

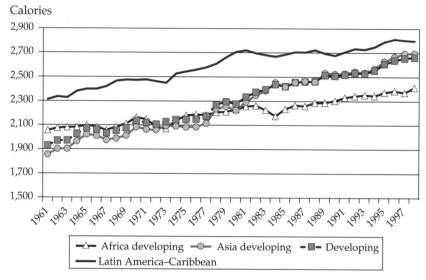

Source: Author calculations based on FAOSTAT (FAO Statistical) 2000 database.

Figure 15.3. Consumption Measured by Protein per Capita per Day

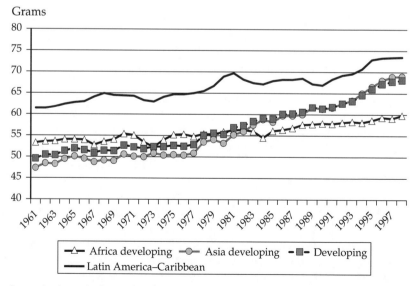

Source: Author calculations based on FAOSTAT 2000 database.

Plus, food availability in developing countries comes mostly from domestic production: imports were about 15 percent of total food production in the 1990s (up from 10 percent in the 1960s and 1970s). Food trade, along with stocks, contributed to reduce the variability of food consumption in developing countries to about one-third to one-fifth of that of food production. The burden of the total food bill (measured by food imports as a percentage of total exports) declined on average for developing countries from almost 20 percent in the 1960s to about 6 percent currently (figure 15.4). This was caused by the expansion of total trade, which has grown faster than food imports, along with a decline in real food prices. Finally, volatility of agricultural prices in world markets in the last half of the 1990s—since the implementation of the WTO agricultural agreements—does not seem to be higher than for the whole period since the 1960s (table 15.1). It is less clear what has happened to the volatility of agricultural prices within developing countries, which also depends on domestic policies.

However, although food security has improved in general, some regions and countries are at risk, and some have become more food insecure: (a) Average food availability is still low for regions such as Sub-Saharan Africa. And for more than one-fourth of all developing countries, per capita indicators have decreased since the 1960s. In most cases, those declines appear to be associated with war. (b) The number of malnour-

Figure 15.4. Ratio of Food Imports to Total Exports

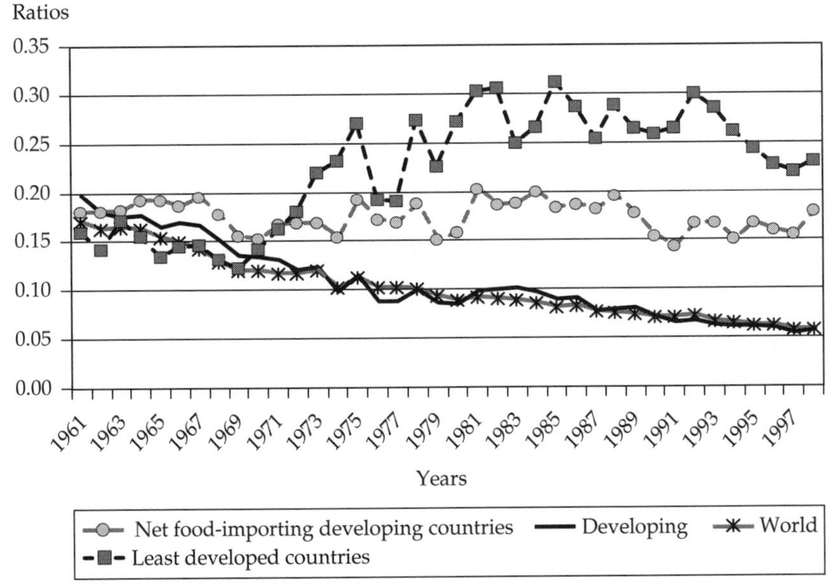

Table 15.1. Coefficient of Price Variability in Agriculture: Constant Value

Product	1960–99	1990s	1995–99
Cocoa (¢/kg)	0.54	0.14	0.13
Coffee, mild (¢/kg)	0.40	0.29	0.21
Coffee, robusta (¢/kg)	0.55	0.26	0.14
Tea (¢/kg)	0.20	0.19	0.21
Sugar (¢/kg)	0.81	0.16	0.17
Orange ($/mt)	0.11	0.08	0.01
Banana ($/mt)	0.11	0.12	0.11
Beef (¢/kg)	0.21	0.13	0.06
Wheat ($/mt)	0.22	0.14	0.16
Rice ($/mt)	0.34	0.13	0.07
Maize ($/mt)	0.21	0.16	0.17
Sorghum ($/mt)	0.21	0.13	0.15
Coconut oil ($/mt)	0.36	0.29	0.15
Soybean oil ($/mt)	0.30	0.18	0.13
Groundnut oil ($/mt)	0.28	0.15	0.08
Palm oil ($/mt)	0.30	0.29	0.19
Soybean ($/mt)	0.22	0.11	0.12
Soybean meal ($/mt)	0.27	0.16	0.21
Cotton (¢/kg)	0.19	0.14	0.12

Source: Author calculations based on FAOSTAT 2000 database.

ished children under the age of five has actually increased in Sub-Saharan Africa, and the incidence of malnutrition is still very high there and in South Asia. (c) For the 49 least developed countries, the total food bill has remained high at 20 percent, and several developing countries with large external debts face additional constraints in financing their food imports (figure 15.4). (d) Trends of production per capita of food and agriculture also differ among developing countries by regions and economic groups. The best performers are the Latin American and the Caribbean countries; Asian developing countries are steadily improving, but Africa's situation is at best stagnant. The net food-importing developing countries and the low-income developing countries are also improving their production of food and agriculture, but are still performing below developing country levels. However, the least developed countries and Sub-Saharan African countries continue to experience declining trends in food and agricultural production (figure 15.5).

While aggregate trends of food security indicators seem positive, the situation may be deteriorating in specific cases and would require a more disaggregated analysis of individual country situations.

Figure 15.5. Agriculture Production, 1961–98

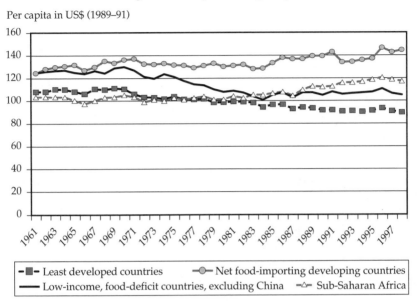

Agriculture net production per capita

Per capita in US$ (1989–91)

- **-■-** Least developed countries   **-●-** Net food-importing developing countries
- — Low-income, food-deficit countries, excluding China   **-△-** Sub-Saharan Africa

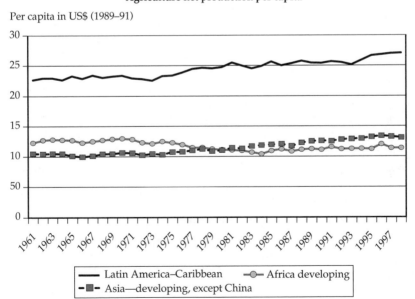

Agriculture net production per capita

Per capita in US$ (1989–91)

- — Latin America–Caribbean   **-●-** Africa developing
- **-■-** Asia—developing, except China

Source: Author calculations based on FAOSTAT 2000 database.

Variety of Food Security Situations and Implications for World Trade Organization Negotiations

Two issues need to be addressed for the coming negotiations to consider food security concerns in greater detail under WTO rules: first, the relevance of the current classification of countries with respect to their food security status and, second, whether the current legal texts, which define WTO commitments on the basis of those categories of countries, really address the issue of food security through that differential treatment. Both matters are related: If the categories are badly defined to capture food security concerns, then it is unlikely that the different treatment under WTO rules will deal with those concerns in a meaningful way. But even if these categories capture the variety in the situations of food (in)security, then current and future WTO rules and commitments may still be inadequate to treat it.

In addition to the obvious distinction between industrialized and developing countries, which are both self-identified groups, the WTO recognizes two other groups within developing countries: "least developed countries," a United Nations classification, and net food-importing developing countries, which are selected through the Committee on Agriculture of the WTO. Least developed countries have several legal implications under the WTO framework, and both types of countries were considered in the special ministerial decision approved at the end of the UR (Díaz-Bonilla, Piñeiro, and Thomas 1999). The United Nations, under the Food and Agriculture Organization (FAO), also defines low-income developing countries, but they are not subject to any special treatment or legal consideration under the WTO.

The question is how well those categories capture the heterogeneity of developing countries. A study by Valdes and McCalla (1999) identifies, among 148 developing countries, 105 countries that are net food importers and 43 that are net food exporters (15 are from the low-income group). In total agriculture, 85 are identified as net importers and 63 as net exporters (33 are from the low-income group). Among the most vulnerable economic groups, more than one-third of least developed countries are net agricultural exporters, more than half of the low-income developing countries are net agricultural exporters, 19 percent are net food exporters, and 22 net food importers are net agricultural exporters. These findings are consistent with the results emerging from the classification of the top 20 traders in food and agriculture in table 15.2. There are 7 developing countries among the top 20 food exporters, and half of the top 20 net food exporters are developing countries.

Table 15.2. Top 20 Food Products Exporters, Importers, and Net Exporters Average in Value, 1995–99

Exporters	Exports (US$ billion)	Share (%)	Importers	Imports (US$ billion)	Share (%)	Net exporters	Net exports (US$ billion)
United States	41.39	13.82	Germany	28.34	9.10	United States	18.41
France	26.94	9.00	Japan	25.91	8.32	France	8.99
Netherlands	21.90	7.32	United States	22.98	7.38	Australia	8.57
Germany	17.16	5.73	United Kingdom	18.37	5.90	Netherlands	7.80
Belgium-Luxembourg	14.77	4.93	France	17.95	5.76	Argentina	7.32
Spain	11.85	3.96	China	15.56	4.99	Denmark	5.09
Canada	11.57	3.86	Italy	15.52	4.98	Canada	4.45
China	11.44	3.82	Netherlands	14.10	4.53	Thailand	4.20
Italy	11.29	3.77	Belgium-Luxembourg	12.21	3.92	New Zealand	4.07
Australia	10.33	3.45	Russian Federation	8.01	2.57	Spain	3.85
Argentina	8.32	2.78	Spain	7.99	2.57	Ireland	3.67
United Kingdom	8.14	2.72	Canada	7.12	2.29	Brazil	3.44
Brazil	7.90	2.64	Mexico	5.92	1.90	Malaysia	2.90
Denmark	7.64	2.55	Korea, Republic of	4.95	1.59	Belgium-Luxembourg	2.56
Malaysia	5.81	1.94	Brazil	4.46	1.43	Turkey	1.86
Ireland	5.73	1.91	Saudi Arabia	3.95	1.27	Hungary	1.72
Thailand	5.36	1.79	Indonesia	3.17	1.02	Côte d'Ivoire	1.60
New Zealand	4.85	1.62	Austria	3.03	0.97	Ukraine	1.18
Mexico	4.27	1.42	Switzerland	3.02	0.97	Chile	1.08
Turkey	3.66	1.22	Singapore	2.98	0.96	Ecuador	1.00
Total	**80.26**		**Total**		**72.40**		

Source: Author calculations based on FAOSTAT 2000 database.

Cluster Analysis Classification

Focusing more specifically on food security, Díaz-Bonilla et al. (2000) employ various methods of cluster analysis and data for 167 countries to identify groups of countries categorized according to five measures of food security: food production per capita, the ratio of total exports to food imports, calories per capita, protein per capita, and the share of the non-agricultural population.[1] The results identify 12 clusters of countries according to their similarities in their food security profiles (measured by the variables listed above) from very food-insecure, cluster 1, to very food-secure, cluster 12 (table 15.3). In the context of the WTO negotiations on agriculture, this classification exercise is relevant to evaluate the usefulness of the categories currently utilized in the WTO to address food security concerns.

The conclusion is that some of the categories utilized by the WTO appear inadequate to capture food security concerns. The most obvious case is the category of "developing countries." These countries, which are self-identified, are subject to Special and Differential (S&D) Treatment first in the GATT and now in the WTO. In this analysis, developing countries appear scattered across all levels of food (in)security, except cluster 12, the very high food-secure group (tables 15.3 and 15.4).

In the category of net food-importing developing countries, 11 out of the 19 countries are in food-insecure groups (clusters 1–4), and the remaining 8 are in food-neutral groups (clusters 5 and 7), which have intermediate levels of food security. Being a net food importer appears to be only a weak indicator of food vulnerability. Some countries may be net food exporters but still have a larger percentage of their total exports allocated to buy food, and vice versa (for example, Mali is a net food exporter but its food bill is about 15 percent of total exports, while Venezuela, a net food-importing developing country, spends about 5 percent of total exports on imported food). Additionally, some countries may be net food importers just because of a dominant tourist industry (like Barbados, which also has the highest income per capita of the net food-importing developing countries, about US$7,000). Other net food-importing developing countries have important levels of oil exports (such as the case of Venezuela and Trinidad and Tobago) and therefore imports of food only reflect the comparative advantages of their production structure. With the exception of Egypt, food imports of the net food-importing developing countries in the food-neutral group represent about 9 percent of total exports, and for the food-insecure net food-importing developing countries (including Egypt), the average is about 16 percent.

(*Text continues on page 241.*)

Table 15.3. Classification of Countries in 12 Clusters: Mean Values of the Food Security Variables

Cluster	Calories per capita (calories)	Protein per capita (grams)	Production per capita (US$)	Export to food import ratio	Food import to export (percent)	Non-agricultural population to total population ratio
1	1,982.9	48.6	81.8	4.9	20.4	0.23
2	2,229.2	58.8	117.6	5.3	19.0	0.71
3	2,244.6	52.6	120.3	14.1	7.1	0.41
4	2,581.5	70.8	157.2	4.8	20.8	0.39
5	2,602.3	66.5	210.4	11.3	8.8	0.75
6	2,672.9	72.8	124.1	19.8	5.0	0.41
7	2,976.1	82.7	135.1	9.1	11.0	0.82
8	2,827.7	78.4	233.3	25.6	3.9	0.83
9	3,231.3	100.1	254.2	18.6	5.4	0.88
10	3,271.8	97.7	304.2	35.9	2.8	0.93
11	3,303.7	103.3	520.6	17.7	5.7	0.93
12	3,374.1	107.5	923.9	32.7	3.1	0.93

Source: Diaz-Bonilla et al. (2000).

Table 15.4. Country Profile Summary

Cluster	Category	Least developed countries	Net food-importing developing countries	Others
1. Food-insecure	WTO members	Angola, Bangladesh, Burkina Faso, Burundi, Central African Republic, Chad, Republic of Congo, The Gambia, Guinea, Guinea-Bissau, Haiti, Madagascar, Malawi, Mali, Mozambique, Niger, Rwanda, Sierra Leone, Tanzania, Uganda	Kenya	
	WTO observers	Cambodia,[a] Ethiopia, Nepal,[a] Yemen		
	Others	Afghanistan, Comoros, Eritrea, Liberia, Somalia		
2. Food-insecure	WTO members	Djibouti, Lesotho	Botswana, Cuba, Dominican Republic, Honduras, Peru	El Salvador, Georgia, Mongolia, Nicaragua
	WTO observers			Armenia, Azerbaijan
	Others			Tajikistan

3. Food-insecure	WTO members	Solomon Islands, Togo, Zambia	Côte d'Ivoire, Sri Lanka	Bolivia, Cameroon, Republic of Congo, Ghana, Guatemala, India, Namibia, Papua New Guinea, Philippines, Zimbabwe
	WTO observers	Laos[a]		
	Others			Vietnam
4. Food-insecure	WTO members	Benin, Mauritania	Pakistan, St. Lucia, Senegal	Albania, Grenada, St. Kitts and Nevis, St. Vincent
	WTO observers	Sudan,[a] Vanuatu[a]		
	Others	Kiribati		Seychelles
5. Food-neutral	WTO members		Jamaica, Trinidad and Tobago, Venezuela	Belize, Brazil, Colombia, Costa Rica, Croatia, Ecuador, Fiji Islands, Guyana, Kyrgyz Republic, Nigeria, Paraguay, Suriname, Swaziland
	WTO observers			Former Yugoslav Republic of Macedonia, Uzbekistan
	Others			

(Table continues on the following page.)

237

Table 15.4. (continued)

Cluster	Category	Least developed countries	Net food-importing developing countries	Others
6. Food-neutral	WTO members	Myanmar		Antigua and Barbuda, Gabon, Indonesia
	WTO observers			China
	Others			
7. Food-neutral	WTO members	Maldives	Barbados, Arab Republic of Egypt, Mauritius, Morocco, Tunisia	Brunei Darussalam, Dominica, Estonia, Jordan, Kuwait, Macau, Mexico
	WTO observers	Cape Verde		Algeria, Lebanon, Russian Federation, Saudi Arabia
	Others			Bahamas, Islamic Republic of Iran, Socialist People's Libyan Arab Jamahiriya, Syrian Arab Republic
8. Food-neutral	WTO members			Bulgaria, Chile, Republic of Korea, Latvia, Malaysia, Panama, Slovakia, South Africa
	WTO observers			Moldova
	Others			

9. Food-secure	WTO members	Czech Republic, Germany, Iceland, Israel, Japan, Malta, Poland, Portugal, Romania, Slovenia, Turkey, United Arab Emirates, United Kingdom
	WTO observers	
	Others	Belarus, Kazakhstan, Lithuania
10. Food-secure	WTO members	Austria, Hong Kong (China), Syrian Arab Republic, Finland, Hungary, Norway, Sweden, Switzerland, United States
	WTO observers	Ukraine
	Others	
11. Food-secure	WTO members	Argentina, Belgium, Luxembourg, Canada, France, Greece, Italy, Netherlands, Spain, Uruguay
	WTO observers	
	Others	

(Table continues on the following page.)

Table 15.4. (continued)

Cluster	Category	Least developed countries	Net food-importing developing countries	Others
12. Food-secure	WTO members			Australia, Denmark, Ireland
	WTO observers			
	Others			
Outliers	WTO members			New Zealand, Thailand

Notes: WTO members not included because of data unavailability: Bahrain, Cyprus, Liechtenstein, Oman, Qatar, and Singapore. WTO observers not included because of data unavailability: Andorra, Bahamas, Bhutan, Bosnia and Herzegovina, Samoa, Chinese Taipei, and Tonga. Other least developed countries not included because of data unavailability: Equatorial Guinea, São Tomé and Príncipe, and Tuvalu.

a. Countries in the process of accession to the WTO.

Source: Díaz-Bonilla et al. (2000).

The category of least developed countries, however, does correspond broadly to countries suffering from food insecurity, even though food security criteria were not explicit in their definition. Only 3 out of the 43 least developed countries covered in this study are not among the first four clusters (most vulnerable countries).[2] At the same time, some countries, like Kenya, have a food security profile similar to the more vulnerable least developed countries but are not included in this category. Others, which have somewhat better profiles but are still in the food insecure categories, are neither least developed countries nor net food-importing developing countries, such as El Salvador, Georgia, Mongolia, and Nicaragua (all WTO members).

It is also relevant to ask about the food security situation of the industrialized countries. Several industrialized countries have raised the issue of food security in the debate on the "multifunctionality" of agriculture, or, more generally, in the nontrade concerns. The cluster analysis classification, however, shows that industrialized countries are unanimously concentrated in the food-secure groups (clusters 9–12).

In terms of the WTO negotiations, this analysis suggests that to define specific rights and obligations in the WTO using the category of least developed countries appears an appropriate starting point, even though this group is not defined by food security criteria. Yet some countries, which are neither least developed countries nor net food-importing developing countries and are therefore excluded from WTO special treatment, are food insecure. One approach would be to give countries classified as food insecure by some objective criteria the same special rights and obligations in domestic support and market access as the ones received by least developed countries. In addition, they could be considered for the food aid, financial support, and technical assistance envisaged in the ministerial decision on possible negative effects of the agricultural reform program on least developed countries and net food-importing developing countries. The issue of special access to other countries' markets for least developed countries, and the additional benefits conferred upon least developed countries because of reasons other than food security, would still be limited only to the countries specified by the United Nations.

The current category of net food-importing developing countries, a classification negotiated during the UR, has some implications as defined in the ministerial decision, and constitutes an acquired right. The implementation of that ministerial decision, as discussed in the meetings of the Committee on Agriculture of the WTO, appears to have been limited mostly to exchanges of information among multilateral organizations and bilateral donors about programs already under execution. In particular, no special action was taken during the 1995–96 increase in agricultural prices, because the aid agencies considered that the rise was not related to the implementation of the AoA. For that reason, many least developed nations and net food-importing developing countries have been calling for objective criteria to "operationalize" the ministerial decision (UNCTAD 2000).

Defining more precisely the group of countries that appear vulnerable to food security problems would help accomplish such operationalization. It can be argued that the perception that the category of net food-importing developing countries is not adequate (because it leaves vulnerable countries out while including countries that are relatively better off) may have contributed to the lack of implementation of the ministerial decision. In any case, the current category of net food-importing developing countries has been defined for reasons beyond food security, and this analysis does not suggest that it be changed because it is less useful in addressing food security issues. Rather, the operationalization of the ministerial decision of food security concerns should also include other countries not currently considered within the net food-importing developing countries. Any quantitative measure of food security would provide a cutoff point, which would help differentiate developing countries that may need special treatment in terms of food security from those that do not.

Finally, the term "food security" has a different meaning in industrialized than in developing countries. In terms of policy implications and the agricultural negotiations, maintaining the same label for two altogether different situations only obscures the issues being negotiated. The discussion of food security should be limited to the vulnerability of developing countries, using a different terminology for industrialized countries.

Trade Liberalization and World Trade Organization Negotiations

Industrialized Countries

The combination of domestic support, market protection, and export subsidies in industrialized countries has reduced agricultural market opportunities for developing countries, including their own domestic markets. This is especially important for poor developing countries, where two-thirds of the population lives in rural areas, agriculture generates over one-third of the gross domestic product (GDP), and a substantial percentage of exports depend on agriculture. A key concern for developing countries, therefore, is the elimination of subsidies and protectionism in industrialized countries.

Against this general proposition, three concerns have been raised: (a) Will the food bill of net importing countries be increased by the liberalization of agricultural policies in industrialized countries? (b) For those developing countries that have preferential access to the protected markets of rich countries, will the liberalization of trade in those markets lead to the erosion of trade preferences? (c) Will export expansion have harmful effects on poverty and food security?

In the first two cases, a welfare-enhancing approach would be to proceed with the liberalization of markets in rich countries, along with cash grants or other financial schemes to compensate poor countries for higher prices and lost preferences. The third question is linked to earlier criticisms of the Green Revolution, later extended to commercialization and international trade: first, the limited resources of small farmers could prevent the farmers from participating in expanding markets and lead to worsening income distribution, and, second, and more worrisome, if relative prices shift against the poor, or if the power of already dominant actors (large landowners, big commercial enterprises) is reinforced to allow the dominant actors to extract income from the poor or to appropriate their assets, the poor could become worse off in absolute terms. It has also been argued that food security could decrease if cash or export production displaces staple crops, and if these changes will result in women having less decisionmaking power and fewer resources.

Yet several studies have shown that the Green Revolution—and domestic and international commercialization—can yield benefits for the poor because of its effect on production, employment, and food prices, although any uniform attainment of benefits is by no means guaranteed. Trade expansion that creates income opportunities for women may also give women greater control over expenditures, with positive impact on child nutrition and development, as well as greater incentives to invest in girls. But there may be a tradeoff between income-generating activities and the time allocated for childcare. Generally, complementary policies are needed to increase the physical and human capital owned by the poor and by women, to build general infrastructures and services, to ensure that markets operate competitively, and to eliminate institutional, political, and social biases that discriminate against these groups.

Developing Countries

During the current WTO agricultural negotiations, which began in March 2000, several developing countries indicated concerns that further trade liberalization could create problems for their large agricultural populations where poverty is concentrated. Poor countries have argued for a slower pace in reducing tariffs (or maintaining their current levels) on the premise that industrialized countries should first eliminate their higher levels of protection and subsidization. The aim is also to avoid any sudden negative impact on poor producers, whose vulnerable livelihoods may be irreparably damaged by drastic shocks (for instance, by forcing poor families to sell productive assets or to take children from school).

This policy debate reflects a permanent tension between maintaining high prices for producers versus ensuring low prices for consumers. While industrialized countries have used transfers from consumers and taxpayers to maintain high prices for producers, developing countries have enforced low agricultural prices to further the process of industrialization. Several studies have shown that poverty alleviation in developing countries was impaired by policies that protected capital-intensive industrialization and discriminated against agriculture. Post-1980s policy reforms in developing countries appear to have reduced or eliminated general policy biases against agriculture, but in some cases may have contributed to the decline of the infrastructure and institutions needed for agricultural production and commercialization. Further correction of market distortions may still be needed in some countries, but now the emphasis should be on policies for investing in the rural economy, and focusing on the poor.

Some have argued out of concern for small farmers that developing countries should move even further toward protection of the agricultural sector. However, considering that poor households may spend as much as 50 percent of their income on food, these recommendations could have a negative impact on the poverty and food security of not only the increasing number of poor urban households and landless rural workers but also poor small farmers, who tend to be net buyers of food. Trade protection for food products is equivalent to a very regressive implicit tax on food consumption, mostly captured by large agricultural producers, with a greater impact on poor consumers. Also, trade protection for any sector usually implies negative employment and production effects in other sectors, and the general effect of widespread trade protection is a reduction in exports.

Rather than increasing protection, the best approach for developing countries is to eliminate biases against the agricultural sector in the general policy framework, and to increase investments in human capital, property rights, management of land and water, technology, infrastructure, nonagricultural rural enterprises, organizations of small farmers, and other forms of expansion of social capital and political participation for the poor and vulnerable. At the same time, developing countries may legitimately insist that industrialized countries reduce their higher levels of subsidization and protection, and ask for policy instruments to protect the livelihoods of the rural poor from import shocks that could cause irreparable damage.

Conclusion

The AoA does not constrain good policies that genuinely address issues of poverty and food security (such as stocks for food security and domestic food aid for populations in need). Poor producers can also be helped by controls on subsidized exports. Yet some clarification of the language of the AoA may be required, along with a better definition of groups of countries based on objective indicators of food insecurity. The categories used by the WTO ("developed," "developing," "least developed," and "net food-importing developing countries") mask important heterogeneity (particularly the first two) and may leave out some food-insecure countries.

Overall, changes in food security have been positive but uneven, and populations in several countries and regions remain seriously at risk. But food security cannot be increased without changes in agricultural subsidies in developed countries, in addition to international funding to support rural development, food security, and rural poverty alleviation programs. The problems facing developing countries in ensuring food security are not legal constraints under the WTO but, rather, a lack of financial, human, and institutional resources. This should be recognized by linking agricultural trade negotiations to increased funding by international and bilateral organizations for agricultural and rural development, food security, and rural poverty alleviation.

Notes

1. This chapter is largely based on findings from two previous papers: Díaz-Bonilla and Thomas (2001) and Díaz-Bonilla et al. (2000). The indicators utilized in the study are considered proxies for three elements of food security at the national level: food availability, access, and utilization.

2. Cape Verde, Maldives, and Myanmar are in clusters 6 and 7.

References

Díaz-Bonilla, E., V. Piñeiro, and M. Thomas. 1999. *Getting Ready for the Millennium: Round Trade Negotiations: Least-Developed Countries' Perspective*. Washington, D.C.: International Food Policy Research Institute.

Díaz-Bonilla, E., and M. Thomas. 2001. "Trade and Food Security." In E. Díaz-Bonilla and S. Robinson, eds., *Shaping Globalization for Poverty Alleviation and Food Security*, Washington, D.C.: International Food Policy Research Institute.

Díaz-Bonilla, E., M. Thomas, A. Cattaneo, and S. Robinson. 2000. "Food Security and Trade Negotiations in the World Trade Organization: A Cluster Analysis of Country Groups." Trade and Macroeconomics Discussion Paper 59. International Food Policy Research Institute, Washington, D.C.

FAO (Food and Agriculture Organization). 1996. "Rome Declaration on World Food Security and World Food Summit Plan of Action." Paper prepared for the World Food Summit.

————. 1999. "Food Insecurity: When People Must Live with Hunger and Fear
    Starvation. In *The State of the Food Insecurity in the World*.
Griswold, D. T. 1999. *Bringing Economic Sanity to Agricultural Trade*. Washington,
    D.C.: CATO Institute. <http://www.freetrade.org/pubs/articles/dg-12-02-
    99.html>.
Madeley, J. 2000. "Trade and Hunger: An Overview of Case Studies on the Impact
    of Trade Liberalization on Food Security." *Globala Studier* 4:6–7.
Maxwell, S. 1990. "Food Security in Developing Countries: Issues and Options for
    the 1990s." *Institute of Development Studies Bulletin* 21(3):2–13.
————. 1996. "Food Security: A Post-Modern Perspective." *Food Policy* 21(6):
    155–70.
Maxwell, S., and T. R. Frankenberger. 1992. *Household Food Security: Concepts, Indi-
    cators, Measurements: A Technical Overview*. New York: UNICEF/FAO.
Sen, A. 1981. *Poverty and Famines: An Essay on Entitlement and Deprivation*. Oxford:
    Clarendon.
Smith, L. C. 1998. "Can FAO's Measure of Chronic Undernourishment be Strength-
    ened?" *Food Policy* 23(5):425–45.
Smith, L.C., and L. Haddad. 2000. "Explaining Child Malnutrition in Developing
    Countries: A Cross-Country Analysis." Research Report 111. International
    Food Policy Research Institute, Washington, D.C.
UNCTAD (United Nations Conference on Trade and Development). 2000. "Impact
    of the Reform Process in Agriculture on LDCs and Net Food-Importing De-
    veloping Countries and Ways to Address Their Concerns in Multilateral
    Trade Negotiations." Background Note TD/B/COM.1/EM.11/2.Geneva.
Valdes, A., and A. F. McCalla. 1999. "Issues, Interests and Options of Developing
    Countries." Paper presented at the Conference on Agriculture and the New
    Trade Agenda in the WTO 2000 Negotiations, Geneva.

Index

Absorption results, GM foods, 217–20
Access. *See* Market access
Accession, 85–107; acceding countries'
    perspectives, 102; costs and benefits,
    104–5; diplomacy, 97–98;
    diplomat/trade lawyer's approach,
    102–4; economist/reformer's
    approach, 104–6; focus, 93; GATT,
    90–92, 93; negotiations, 91; process, 98;
    Quad countries' perspectives, 99–102;
    rules, 100
Adjustment capacity, small economies,
    115–17
African Growth and Opportunity Act
    (AGOA), 125–26, 127
Agreement on Agriculture (AoA), 1, 7,
    21, 67, 244–45; before and after, 24–25;
    complexity, 23–24; domestic support,
    139, 141; implementation, 47; pillars,
    135; small economies, 117;
    weaknesses, 47; *see also* Uruguay
    Round
Agreement on Safeguards, 160, 161
Agriculture: food security and, 225–31;
    production, 231; support, TSE, 26, 29
Aid, 14
Alignment to WTO rules, accessions, 100
Amber box, 61
AMS. *See* Support, aggregate
    measurement of
Annecy Round, 90
Antidumping, 150, 157, 158, 162–63;
    controversies, 158–61; dumping,
    definition, 159–60; laws, 79, 160
Articles: VI, 155, 159; XI, 156; XII, 87,
    155; XIII, 101; XVI, 155, 156; XVIII,

155, 156; XIX, 156, 159, 160, 161, 162;
    XX, 3–4, 23, 70, 156; XXI, 156; XXV,
    156; XXVIII, 156; XXXIII, 87, 92; XXXV,
    101
Association of Southeast Asian Nations
    (ASEAN), 129; integration initiatives,
    130
Australia, integration initiatives, 131

Benchmarks, 24
Bernal, Richard L., 108–22
Biotechnology. *See* Genetically modified
    (GM) foods; Genetic engineering
Blair House Accord, 22
Blue box policies and programs, 43, 61
Boisvert, Richard N., 165–92
Burfisher, Mary E., 135–44

Cairns Group, 10–11, 60–61, 67–68,
    69–71; Farm Leaders Meeting, 62;
    membership, 71; perspective, 60–64;
    proposal, 5; WTO Round, 73, 74
Cereal grains, 196, 199, 215
China, integration initiatives, 131
Closed economy, environmental policies,
    169–73, 185–86
Cold War, end, 95–96
Colonialism, collapse, 123–24
Commitments, circumvention, 8
Committee on Agriculture, 3, 5, 7
Commodity Credit Corporation, 146
Common agricultural policy (CAP), 66;
    reform, 70
Competition, 6; laws, 78–79, 160
Competitiveness, small economies,
    114–15

Confrontation (pending), key players,
69–71
Consensus-building process, 72
Consultative Group on International
Agricultural Research (CGIAR), 16
Consumer nominal protection
coefficients (CNPC), 25, 29, 30–31, 36
Consumer preferences and attitudes:
CGE model, 203–5, 212, 216, 217–19;
GM foods, 193–94, 220–21
Corbet, Hugh, 65–82
Corporate accountability, 14
Costs, food production, 15
Counterfactual, 32
Country classification: food products
exporters, importers, net importers,
233; food security, 232, 234–42
Country profile summary, food security,
236–40
Credibility, 3
Cross-section analysis, 29, 32–36

Decisionmaking: process, 77; prospects,
78
de Gorter, Harry, 165–92
de minimis provision, 22, 45
Developing countries, 6, 9; agriculture
and, 2; attitudes, 5; interests, options,
and objectives, 9–10; as major players,
4; negotiation process, 10; trade
liberalization and WTO negotiations,
243–44
Development Round, 13, 71, 132
Diakosavvas, Dimitris, 21–59
Diaz-Bonilla, Eugenio, 225–46
Differentiated treatment. *See* Special and
differential (S&D) treatment
Diplomats, accessions, 102–4
Disincentives, 17
Disputes, small economies, and access to
mediation, 120–21
Doha meeting, 12; declaration, 3–4, 5–6;
labor standards, 75, 79–80
Domestic markets, insulating, 146
Domestic support, 22, 41–47, 48;
composition, 44; constraints, 43;
options for reforming, 139, 141–43;
reductions, 41
Due restraint, 22

Dumping, definition, 159–60; *see also*
Antidumping

Economies in transition (EIT), 96
Economies of scale, small economies,
114
Economists, accessions, 104–6
Emergency safeguard actions, 161–63
Enabling box, 132
Enabling clause, 129; small economies,
119
Environmental policies, 79, 165–92;
closed economy, 169–73, 185–86; equilibrium framework, 167; interdependence, 167, 181, 183; model economy,
167–69; models vs. domestic policies,
181, 183–84; open economies, 173–76,
186–89; policy implications, 184–85;
relationships among, 181; simulation
model, 176–81, 182; trade distortion
and, 167; U.S. agriculture and, 176
Equilibrium framework, environmental
policies, 167
Escape clauses, 79, 155–64; coordination,
156–57
European Community, 66
European Union, 70; accessions, 100;
Mauritius and, 124–25; WTO Round,
73
Exemptions, small economies, 119–20
Exports, developing country: focus, 68;
market, 196; patterns, 200–1; small
economies, 111
Export subsidies, 8, 9–10, 46–47, 48, 61;
countries that offer, 57; limits, 22–23;
reform, 143
Externalities. *See* Environmental policies

Fairness, 13
Farm Act (1996), 146
Farm lobby, 68
Federal Agriculture Improvement and
Reform Act (FAIR) of 1996, 146–48
Firms, small economies, 111, 114
Flexibility, small economies, 120
Food: availability and access, 227, 229;
consumption, 228; GM vs. non-GM,
193, 221–22; household spending and,
244; safety, 70

Food security, 2, 6–7, 225–46;
agricultural performance and, 225–31;
cluster analysis classification, 234–42;
country classification, 232, 234–42;
definition, 242; trade liberalization
and, 242–44; WTO negotiations and,
232–33, 242–44
Freedom to Farm, 146–47
Futures contracts, 149

Gardner, Bruce L., 145–52
Gene transfer, 194
General Agreement on Tariffs and Trade
(GATT), 1, 21, 85; accessions, 90–92,
93; agriculture and, 65, 66; developing
countries, 73; differentiated treatment,
117–18; exceptions to GATT
obligations, 155; membership, 89,
90–91; *see also* Trade policy
Generalized System of Preferences
(GSP), 125, 130
Genetically modified (GM) foods,
193–224; benefits, 193, 194, 195, 203;
consumer preferences and attitudes,
193–94, 216, 220–21; consumption
patterns, 210–12; cultivation of
transgenic crops, 194–95; potential
crops, trade and, 196; producers, 195
Genetic engineering, in agriculture,
194–99; absorption results, 217–20;
global computable general
equilibrium model and scenarios,
199–214; production results, 215;
usage, 195
Genoa Economic Summit, 77
Global computable general equilibrium
(CGE) model, GM foods, 199–214;
consumer preferences, 203–5, 212; GM
and non-GM production technologies,
202–3; price and trade results, 205–14;
segregated food markets, 199, 202
Globalization, 5–6, 17; social
dimensions, 75
Government procurement, 79
Green box policies and programs, 43, 45,
61
Green Revolution, trade liberalization
and WTO negotiations, 3
Growth, lack of, 62

Haberler Report, 66
Harmonization, 139
Horlick, Gary, 155–64

Imperfect markets, small economies, 111
Implementation: neglect, 76–77; WTO
Round, 73
Import penetration: model, 34–35; ratios,
25
Incidence-based measures, 24–25
Income, agricultural export, 62–63
Income transfers, contingent, 151
Industrial tariffs, accessions, 100
Industrialized countries, trade
liberalization and WTO negotiations,
242–43
Information, 151–52
Ingco, Merlinda D., 1–11
Institutional reforms, 77
Integration of global market, 129–32;
regional initiatives, 131–32
Interdependence, environmental
policies, 167, 181, 183
Interests, 9–10, 69
International commerce, post–World
War II, 66
International community, 14, 15
International Labour Organisation
(ILO), 75
International trade agreements, small
economies and, 116–17
Investments, 17; regulations, 78, 79

Jackson-Vanik law, 101–2
Japan, integration initiatives, 131
Jeetah, Usha, 123–28
Johnson, Ian, 12–18

Kennedy Round, 66, 90

Labor force, agriculture and, 2
Labor standards, 75, 79–80; WTO
system, 74–76
Least developed countries, attitudes, 4–5
Legislation. *See* Regulations
Like-Minded Group, 76; WTO Round, 73

Maize, 195, 196, 202
Malnutrition, 227, 229–30

Market: access, 2, 13, 21, 36–41; distortion, 1–2, 13–14; export concentration, small economies, 111
Mauritius, 124; European Union and, 124–25
Mediation, small economies, 120–21
Mega-tariffs, 138
Merchandise exports, 25–26
Michalopoulos, Constantine, 126–27
Model economy, environmental policies, 167–69, 181, 183–84
Multifunctionality, 5, 8, 70, 165–92, 241

Negotiating authority, Geneva, 72
Negotiation process, developing countries, 10
Net food importing countries, 71, 241
Net food producers, 63
Net trade performance, 25
New Zealand, integration initiatives, 131
Newly independent countries, 123
Nielsen, Chantal Pohl, 193–224
Nonmarket economies, GATT and, 92
Nontariff barriers, 21
Nontrade concerns (NTC), 8, 48, 64, 70

Objectives, 9–10
Obligations, small economies, 119
Oilseeds, 196, 199, 215–16
Open economies, environmental policies, 173–76, 186–89
Openness: measures, 24, 25; small economies, 111, 115
Options, 10, 17–18
Organization for Economic Cooperation and Development (OECD), 1, 75
Outcome-based measures, 25

Payments, 43
Peace clause, 22
Per capita income, small economies, 110
Percentage consumer support estimate (%CSE), 25
Percentage producer support estimates (%PSE), 25
Peterson, Jeffrey M., 165–92
Piampongsant, Krisda, 129–32
Policy: coordination, 14; distortions, 136, 144; domestic agriculture, 22; environ-

mental policies and, 184–85; price risk, 145–52; production limiting, 22
Policymaking, global coherence, 76–77
Policy reform, 2–3, 15, 16–17; global, 143–44; options, 135–44
Politics: accessions, 106; storage, 151
Population, small economies, 110
Poverty alleviation, 71
Predatory behavior, 159
Presidential power, 103
Price and trade results, CGE model, 205–14
Price risk: management, 148–49; policies for, 145–52
Prices: consumer preferences and, 204–5; GM crops, 205–10; international pressures, and domestic policies, 149–52; liberalization and, 145–48; variability, 230
Price supports, 45, 166
Price-takers, small economies, 114
Producer nominal protection coefficients (PNPC), 25, 29, 30–31
Producer subsidy equivalents (PSE): composition, 49–53; 1986–98, 56
Production results, GM foods, 215
Proposals: small economies, 118, 122; submitted, 7; under discussion, 5
Protected sectors, 17
Protection: effect of, 61–62; rates, 29
Public good, 15
Public sector, small economies, 115

Quadrilateral Group: leadership, 69; perspectives on accession, 99–102
Quarantine, 13

Reform: accessions, 104–6; process, 6
Regulations: antidumping laws, 79, 160; competition, 78–79, 160; environment, 79; investments, 78, 79
Request-and-offer, tariffs, 138
Resource use, small economies, 113
Restrictions, 2
Robinson, Sherman, 193–224
Rules-based discipline, 1
Rural infrastructure, investment, 17

Safeguards, 150, 155–56; emergency actions, 161–63; requirements, 162
Sanctions, 75
Science and technology, benefits, 15
Seattle meeting, 4, 5, 75, 76, 77; failure, 69; WTO system since then, 72
Segregated food markets, CGE model, 199, 202
Self-selection, small economies, 110
Services, accessions, 100
Shifting crops and production, 17–18
Short-term loss, 17, 18
Simulation model, environmental policies, 176–81, 182
Size, implications of, 112–16
Small economies, 108–22, 126; access to mediation, 120–21; characteristics, 110–12, 121; definition, 110; differentiated treatment, 117–18; exemptions, 119–20; flexibility, 120; implications of size, 112–16; international trade agreements and, 116–17; obligations, 119; proposed provisions for, 118, 122; technical assistance and training, 121; timetables, 119
Social clause, 74
Soybeans, 195, 196, 202
Special and differential (S&D) treatment, 8, 124–26, 129; agriculture for developing countries, 130; Mauritius, 118, 127; principle, 94–95; small economies, 117–18
Stability, liberalization and, 146
Stabilization policy, small economies, 115–16
Stockpiling, 150–51
Stocks, storage, 150–51
Subsidies, 70, 166; countervailing actions, 157–58, 162–63; effects, 62; exemptions, 43; export, 143; optimal, 184; tax and, 183
Supply response, 3
Support: 1986–98, 56; aggregate measurement of, 45–46, 48; commodity-specific, 142; levels, 42; market-distorting, 1–2; reduction, 41, 43

Swiss formula, 139

Tariffication, 36–37, 61
Tariff-rate quotas (TRQs), 8, 21–22, 37–39, 48, 64; countries that have, 54–55; elimination, 136–37
Tariffs, 8, 13–14, 21–22, 38, 47–48; dispersion, 137–38; elimination, 136–37; formula, 138; GATT and, 89–90; negotiations, 91; protection, 37; quotas, 39–41; rates, 37, 137–38; reduction, 93, 137–39, 140; UR and, 61
Tax: optimal, 172, 184; subsidies and, 183
Technical assistance and training, 14; small economies, 121
Thierfelder, Karen, 193–224
Thomas, Marcelle, 225–46
Time-series analysis, 29, 32–36
Timetables, small economies, 119
Tokyo Round, goals, 66–67
Trade, 198; agreements, 13–14, 88; agriculture and, 2; barriers, 15, 21, 24, 47, 63; benefit, 13–14; capacity, 14; conditions and restrictions, 8; dependencies, 196–97; facilitation, 79; GM-potential crops, 196; issues, 12–13; leveraging, 129–32; model, construction, 32; negotiation, 3–6; openness, 25–26; priorities, 87–88; taxes, small economies, 111; unfair practices, 159, 160
Trade distortions, 8, 22, 47; environmental policies and, 167, 183
Trade lawyer's, accessions and, 102–4
Trade liberalization, 23, 61; benefits to date, 123–28; developing countries, 243–44; as development tool, 62–63; industrialized countries, 242–43; prices and, 145–48; resistance, 70; WTO negotiations, 242–44
Trade performance indicators, 24, 26–29, 30–31; calculation, 32–36
Trade policy focus, 88–89, 93, 96; 1949–79, 89–92; current, 96–98; mid-1980s, 92–96
Trade restrictions, 159; effects, 62
Trade restrictiveness indicator (TRI), 25

Trading systems: fair and market-oriented, 70; rules-based multilateral, 109–10
Training, 18
Transgenic crops, 194–96; see also Genetically engineered food
Transportation costs, small economies, 114–15
TRQs. See Tariff-rate quotas
Tucker, Simon, 60–64

United States, 68, 70; accessions, 99–102; attitude, 72; consensus-building process, 72; environmental policies, 176; GM crops, 195; labor standards, 75–76; laws and policies, 101–2; WTO and, 72; WTO Round, 73–74
Uruguay Round (UR) of 1986–94, 1, 9, 21–59, 67–68; before and after, 24–25, 29, 32–36; escape clauses, 155–64; gains, 61; lessons, 6, 63–64; weaknesses, 36–41; see also Agreement on Agriculture; Cairns Group

VanGrasstek, Craig, 85–107

Volatility, small economies, 112
Voluntary export restraints (VERs), 156–57, 161, 162
Vulnerability: definitions, 126–27; small economies, 112–13

Wealthy countries, 64
World Trade Organization (WTO): agricultural negotiations, 1; escape clauses, 79; integration initiatives, 131–32; launch, 65; membership, 86– 87, 96–97, 103; negotiations, situations and implications for 232–33; priorities, 87–88; regime, 88; see also Accession
World Trade Organization Round: attitudes, 71–72; content, 80; impediments, 74–76; issues, 76, 77; players, 73–74; preparations, 71–72; problems, 73
World Trade Organization system: changes, 72–73; developing countries membership, 72–73, 103; extending, 78–79; post–Seattle meeting, 72

Yeutter, Clayton, 67–68